10.95

Rothman Foundation Series
JEP

מנוחה
ושמחה

A GUIDE TO BASIC LAWS AND THEMES
OF SHABBOS AND YOM TOV AND THEIR
APPLICATIONS IN THEORY AND IN PRACTICE

Rabbi Mordechai Katz

© Copyright 1982 by
JEP PUBLICATIONS

JEWISH EDUCATION PROGRAM

425 East 9th Street
Brooklyn, New York 11218
212-941-2600

First printing January 1982
First Israel Printing 1988

Sole Trade Distributors
PHILIPP FELDHEIM INC.
200 Airport Executive Park
Spring Valley, NY 10977

FELDHEIM PUBLISHERS Ltd.

Jerusalem, Israel

ISBN 0-87306-977-3

Printed in Israel

Jewish Education Program

The Joseph & Faye Tanenbaum Jewish Education Program of Zeirei Agudath Israel was organized in September 1972, and since its inception has become a well-known, active force in the field of Jewish education. Its guiding principle, "Jewish power and Jewish pride through Jewish education," was formulated in response to what has become a Jewish tragedy of massive proportions, namely assimilation and its tragic by-products.

Under the guidelines of prominent Roshei Yeshivos and leaders in the field of Jewish education, and staffed entirely by B'nei Torah and Yeshiva graduates, JEP relies almost entirely on the talents and efforts voluntarily contributed by capable young Torah students.

Some of JEP's programs include: Shabbatones, in which hundreds of children from various communities in the United States and Canada experience the beauty of Shabbos in a Torah true environment; Release Hour classes for spiritually-starved public school children; programs for needy Russian immigrants; Ruach and Seminar sessions for day school students; Chavruso Big Brother Programs; High School Encounter Groups; Holiday Rallies; Yeshiva and Camp Placement; and the publication of educational material for thousands of young people. Through these and other various programs, JEP hopes to ignite the spark of Yiddishkeit deep within the hearts of these individuals, and turn it into a blazing, warmth-emanating fire. It hopes to instill within these youngsters a love of Hashem and His Torah and an understanding of Torah-true Judaism.

RABBI MOSES FEINSTEIN
455 F. D. R. DRIVE
New York, N. Y. 10002

ORegon 7-1222

משה פיינשטיין

ר"מ תפארת ירושלים

בנוא יארק

בע"ה

הנני בזה להודיע לבני הישיבות ולאחינו בני ישראל בכל אתר ואתר על
העבודה הפוריה של העוסקים במלאכת הקודש "החכנית לחנוך היהודי"
הנודע בשם "דזשעפ", וליישר כוחם וחילם לאורייתא שמקרבים לבבות
הרחוקים לאביהם שבשמים. והנה כבר הוחזקו גברא בשני ספרים הראשונים
שהוציאו לאור שנקבו בשם "ללמוד וללמד" על התורה ו"להבין ולהשכל" על
עניני השקפה. ועכשיו הם מדפיסים שני ספרים על הלכות יום יומיים,
מיוסד על אר"ח (על פי רוב לפי פסק המשנה ברורה) ויר"ד, אחד בשם
"לשמור ולעשות" ואחד בשם "מנוחה ושמחה" על עניני שבת ויו"ט. והנה
לא ראיתי את הספר, לפי שאיני מכיר את השפה האנגלית, וכבר העידו כמה
ראשי ישיבות שעיינו בה והוטב בעיניהם, שיש תועלת גדולה בזה להבאים
לחסות בצל התורה ואינם בקיאים בהלכות **שלא** למדו , וחזקה על חבר שלא
יצא מתחת ידו דבר שאינו מחוקן ובפרט שכבר הוחזקו גברא .

והריני מברכם שי**צליחם** השי"ת בעבוד**תם** הקדושה, וברכה מיוחדת להרב
המחבר, מוהר"ר מרדכי קאטז שליט"א, שיזכה להוציא עוד ספרים להגדיל
תורה ולהאדירה.

ועל זה באתי על החתום לכבוד התורה ביום י"ב לחודש כסלו תשמ"ב.

משה פיינשטיין

משה פיינשטיין

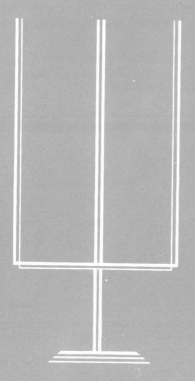

*Other volumes in the Jewish Education Program
Rothman Foundation Series . . .*

Lilmod Ul'amade
from the teachings of our Sages . . .
a compendium of insights, homilies, and interpretations of the
weekly Sedra.
by: Rabbi Mordechai Katz

L'hovin Ul'haskil
a guide to Torah Hashkofoh . . .
Questions and answers on Judaism.
by: Rabbi Eliezer Gevirtz

Lishmor V'Laasos
a guide to basic principles of Jewish law and their applications
in theory and in practice . . .
by: Rabbi Mordechai Katz

ACKNOWLEDGEMENTS

At this juncture, I would like to express my deepest feelings of gratitude to those who have graciously given of themselves and their time to help me in this holy endeavor.

I would first of all wish to express thanks to, my parents, Mr. and Mrs. Moshe Katz, and my in-laws, Mr. and Mrs. Yitzchok Berger, and all the members of my family for their encouragement and support. May *Hashem* grant them long life and *nachas* from their offspring.

An undertaking such as this must be guided by *Gedolei Torah*. I would, therefore, like to thank: Horav Yisroel Belsky, *Shlita*, Rosh Yeshiva, Yeshiva Torah Vodaath; Horav Reuven Feinstein, *Shlita*, Rosh Yeshiva, Mesifta Tiferes Yerusholayim; Horav Shlomo Frankel, *Shlita*, Horav Elazar Kahana, *Shlita*, Rosh Yeshiva, Yeshiva Torah Vodaath; and Horav Leibel Katz, *Shlita*, Rav of Khal Zichron Yosef. I would like to thank these people for reading the material, reviewing the *Halachos*, and offering comments and suggestions which have been incorporated into the text. I am humbly grateful for their efforts.

I would like to thank the following *chaverim* who assisted in the writing and editing of the work, and without whose tireless efforts this volume never would have become reality: Rabbi Eliezer Gevirtz, talented writer of the *Sefer, Lehovin Ulehaskil*; Bezalel Lerner and Dovid Zwiebel.

Special thanks and deepest appreciation to Rabbi Yosef Chaim Golding, who put in countless hours and exceptional effort in reviewing this work and seeing to it that it was properly produced and made available to the public.

I would like to thank Mrs. Malky Bodenstein and Mrs. Chavy Aranoff who assisted in the writing and typing of the manuscript.

I would like to thank Malya Karmel for proofreading, typing and technical advice.

We are greatly indebted to the members of the Henry, Bertha, and Edward Rothman Foundation for sponsoring this publication. May *Hashem* grant them continued success in all of their worthy endeavors and may they continue to spread Jewish education to those who so desperately need it.

Special thanks to . . .

Nutty Goldbrenner and Shiya Markowitz of the Goldmark Group, for their invaluable technical assistance.

Mr. Max Septimus for allowing us to utilize his priceless library collection for the front covers of JEP's educational series.

Mr. Samuel Shpelfogel for his technical assistance.

Mrs. Judy Dick, Feigy Gurkov, Moshe Friedman, Yaakov Rosen, Dr. Phil Abramowitz and Yitzchok Feldheim for their proofreading and suggestions.

I would like to express my deepest gratitude to, and reverence for, my *Rebbeim* and *Roshei HaYeshiva,* for their guidance and encouragement throughout the years.

These people's interest and inspiration are what made this publication possible. May they continue to devote their supreme abilities to the furtherance of *Yiddishkeit* and may *Hashem* grant them the spiritual well-being that they so richly deserve.

My deepest gratitude and appreciation goes to my wife, Pessi, for her support, self-sacrifice, and dedication. Without her this work never would have been completed. May her sincere and untiring efforts be rewarded in the blessing most precious to her—that our children merit to sit in the House of *Hashem.*

I humbly thank the *Ribono Shel Olam* for permitting me to accomplish this task.

Rabbi M. Katz
Kislev, 5742

PREFACE

"ותתן לנו ה' אלקינו באהבה שבתות **למנוחה** ומועדים **לשמחה**"
(מוסף שבת-שלש רגלים)

"And G-d . . . gave us with love Sabbath days for rest and Festivals for joy." (Sabbath Festival Mussaf Prayer)

Shabbos and *Yom Tov*, we proudly proclaim, are ours alone; G-d in His love for His people bestowed these holy days upon the Children of Israel. Yet "Sabbath" and "holiday" appear in the non-Jew's dictionary as well. Wherein lies the uniquely Jewish character of *Shabbos* and *Yom Tov?*

The Jewish Education Program offers this volume, *MENUCHA V'SIMCHA*, in response. The laws, stories, parables and homilies that appear on these pages show that *Shabbosos* and *Yomim Tovim* are not merely "days off". To the contrary, they are "days on", days in which the Jew spends his every minute in the harmonious company of his family, his friends, his G-d. What passes in the non-Jewish world as a time for physical relaxation and self-indulgent hedonism is, to the believing Jew, a time for spiritual rejuvenation and selfless devotion.

Shabbos reminds us that Hashem created Heaven and Earth and sustains all of Creation. Is it any wonder that the Jew who has assimilated this weekly lesson of faith is secure in the knowledge that his Creator will sustain him as well? *Shabbos* reminds us also that Hashem redeemed a nation of slaves and transformed them into a Kingdom of holy people; can the Jew who has digested that lesson ever despair of attaining salvation? *Shabbos* thus rewards the Jew who has invested *menuchas ha'guf*—abstention from physical labor—with *menuchas ha'nefesh*—spiritual contentment, tranquility and security.

Yom Tov transports the Jew to, and makes him a participant in, the formative events in his nation's history. Thus did our ancestors, through the generations, heroically celebrate the *Yomim Tovim* even in the shadow of death; for how could death intrude upon our escape from Egypt, our acceptance of the Torah, our sheltered and privileged forty year tenancy under the Clouds of Glory? *Yom Tov* is thus celebrated with *simcha*—unbridled joy in being a part of G-d's chosen people.

Menucha Ve'simcha are the reasons that *Shabbos* and *Yom Tov* are a uniquely Jewish treasure. We hope this volume will promote knowledge among our people of just how special that treasure is.

TABLE OF CONTENTS

מנורה
ושמחה

שבת

Shabbos

SHABBOS—INTRODUCTION

"Remember the Sabbath day to keep it holy. Six days shall you labor, and do all your work; but the seventh day is a Sabbath unto the L-rd your G-d. On it you shall do no manner of work, neither you nor your son, nor your daughter, nor your man-servant, nor your maid-servant, nor your cattle nor your stranger who is within your gates, for in six days the L-rd made heaven and earth, the sea and all that is in them, and rested on the seventh day; wherefore the L-rd blessed the Sabbath day and hallowed it." (Shemos 20:8-11)

"Speak also unto the children of Israel, saying: Verily you shall keep My Sabbaths, for it is a sign between Me and you throughout your generations, that you may know that I am the L-rd who sanctifies you. You shall keep the Sabbath therefore, for it is holy unto you; whoever profanes it shall surely be put to death; for whoever does any work therein, that soul shall be cut off from among his people." (Shemos 31:13-14)

"Happy is the man who does this, and the son of man who holds fast

SHABBOS

Just as every man must review his deeds on the Eve of *Yom Kippur*, which is the end of the year, so too should he take stock of himself on Friday which is the end of the six days of the week. It is therefore fitting that a man should confess his sins and repent of them on Friday, and assume holiness and purity. In this way, he will enter the Holy *Shabbos* in purity and with the fear of heaven and will never, not even for a moment, forget the holiness of the *Shabbos*. (Toldos Aaron, Kee Seesah)

THE UNIQUE ROLE

The unique role of the *Shabbos* in Jewish life transcended the tragedies of the Nazi era.

At the very outset of his book, *"The Shabbos,"* Dayan Grunfeld cites an eyewitness account of a remarkable incident which took place in a packed cattle car transporting Jewish victims from their homes to a Nazi concentration camp.

"The train dragged on with its human freight. Pressed together like cattle in the crowded trucks, the unfortunate occupants were unable even to move. The atmosphere was stifling. As the Friday afternoon wore on, the Jews in the Nazi transport sank deeper and deeper into their misery.

16

by it; who keeps the Sabbath from profaning it, and keeps his hand from doing any evil." (Yeshaya 56:2)

The Hebrew word "Shabbos" means to "cease from work." But the Shabbos is not only a day of rest. It is also a unique day of holiness when man should cast aside the cares and material pursuits and devote himself to reviving his religious spirit.

In reference to the Shabbos, the Torah says, "Kodesh Hee Lochem" (the Shabbos is holy unto you). We are Mekadesh (sanctify) the Shabbos with kovod (respect) by making it a day of physical rest and spiritual elevation.

Our Chazal (Sages) tell us that whoever enjoys the Shabbos in the proper manner: (a) will be saved from Sheebud Malchus (domination by a foreign government), (b) will enjoy material wealth and (c) will receive his reward in Olam Haboh (the World-to-Come).

PREPARATION FOR THE SHABBOS

1. "Remember (Zachor) the Shabbos day to keep it holy," includes remembering it during the entire week. The great Torah leader, Shammai, was known to save special foods for Shabbos, starting from the beginning of the week. Anytime he saw something appropriate, he set it aside "L'Kovod Shabbos" (in honor of the Shabbos). Thereafter, if he found a finer food, he would use the first one during the week and save the better one for Shabbos.

2. One should do the housecleaning and Shabbos preparations on Erev Shabbos (Friday), making it obvious that they are being done in

"Suddenly an old Jewish woman managed with a great effort to move and open her bundle. Laboriously, she drew out—two candlesticks and two Challahs. She had just prepared them for Shabbos when she was dragged from her home that morning. They were the only things she had thought worthwhile taking with her. Soon the Shabbos candles lit up the faces of the tortured Jews and the song of 'Lechah Dodi' transformed the scene. Shabbos, with its atmosphere of peace, had descended upon them all."

"The Shabbos candles are a sign of pleasure and peace. They are also a sign of blessing, both for the day and for the person observing the Mitzvah."

"Rav Huna used to say, "He who lights the Shabbos candles will be blessed with scholarly sons." (Shabbos 23b)

"Two ministering angels accompany each person on the eve of Shabbos from the Shul to his home. One is a good angel and the other, an evil one. When he arrives home and finds the table set for Shabbos, the good angel exclaims, "May it be this way on another Shabbos, too." The evil angel unwillingly responds, "Omein." If everything is in disorder and gloomy, then the evil

17

honor of the *Shabbos*. However, when the Fridays are very short, some of these *Shabbos* preparations should be done earlier.

3. Even if one has servants who make the preparations for *Shabbos,* it is proper that he do some physical work himself *"L'Kovod Shabbos."* We find in the *Talmud* that Rav Chisda used to cut vegetables, Rav Nachman cleaned the house, and Rav Zeira helped prepare the fire—all for *Shabbos*. One should not feel that it is beneath his dignity to do such work. This is part of displaying kovod for the *Shabbos*.

4. It is not proper to eat a complete meal on Friday afternoon, although a snack or drink of water or juice is permissible. After three-quarters of the day passed, one should refrain from eating a complete meal.

5. Special celebrations that are not normal, every-day occurrences, such as banquets, birthday parties, etc. should not be held on *Erev Shabbos*. The reason for this is to have *tai'avon* (an appetite) for the *Shabbos Seuda.*

6. Although it is permissible to perform a marriage ceremony on *Erev Shabbos*, the *Seuda* should be postponed until after candle-lighting and davening. In certain localities, it was allowed to make a Friday afternoon wedding meal, ending early and keeping it short.

7. A *Seudas Bris Milah, Seudas Purim,* or any other *Seudas Mitzvah* that occurs on Friday should be held as early in the day as possible.

8. Drinking alcoholic beverages which cause one to lose one's appetite is not advisable on *Erev Shabbos*.

9. The only time one should fast on *Erev Shabbos* is on *Assara B'Teves* or when certain urgent conditions necessitate a *taanis*.

---

angel exclaims, "May it be this way on another Shabbos," *and the good angel unwillingly responds,* "Omein." *(Shabbos 119b)*

THE DISAPPEARING SIGN

Every storekeeper or shopowner places a sign on top of his store entrance that describes his business. Even if he leaves for a few weeks, the sign indicates that he is still in business. But if the sign is removed, it is certain evidence that the store is closed.

So it is with the *Shabbos*. The *Shabbos* is a sign between the Creator and the Jews that He created heaven and earth in six days and rested on the seventh. The *Shabbos* is also a sign for every individual Jew testifying to his Jewishness and the Covenant between G-d and His people. Even if it should happen that a Jew violates some commandment, he still hasn't lost his Jewishness. The temporary absence of the storekeeper doesn't mean that the sign is taken down. As long as he observes the *Shabbos*, he is still "in business." But if a Jew desecrates the *Shabbos*, he takes down the sign atop his entrance and announces that his Jewish soul is no longer fully there, just like the storekeeper who has abandoned his store.

10. A person should spend extra money to honor the *Shabbos*. If one does not have enough money to prepare for the *Shabbos,* he should borrow it and G-d will give him the means to repay the loan.

11. Enough food should be prepared for three meals. It is appropriate that each meal include fish.

12. Before the *Shabbos* candles are lit, the table should be set in preparation for the *Shabbos*. Even if there are no guests, the house should be neat, and the *bnai bayis* (members of the household) should be dressed for the occasion.

13. One should be especially careful not to have any quarrels before or during *Shabbos*.

14. One must make sure to wash himself, cut his nails, and if need be, cut his hair.

15. One should not travel distances on *Erev Shabbos* that may cause problems for *Shabbos*.

16. If one cooks food and wishes it to be hot for *Shabbos,* he should place a *Blech* (tin sheet) covering on the fire before *Shabbos*.

HILCHOS CANDLE LIGHTING

1. The ritual of lighting the *Shabbos* candles is considered the duty of the woman of the house. Even if the husband wants to light the candles, it is the wife who takes precedence to do so. If, for some reason the woman of the house is not home, then the husband or another individual is required to light the candles.

This is what our Sages meant when they said, "One who desecrates the Shabbos is considered as if he denies the entire Torah."

In our Shabbos Zemiros, we sing of those "who sanctify the seventh day as befits it and of those who observe the Shabbos so as not to violate it." The first group consists of those Jews who sanctify the Shabbos with their deeds, their words and their thoughts; the other group is limited to those who simply avoid violating the Shabbos. Each one gets rewarded, but "his reward is plentiful according to his deed"—each Shabbos observer is rewarded according to the quality of his sanctification. (Beis Yisroel).

The Chofetz Chaim once gave the following sermon on Shabbos Shuva to the inhabitants of his town Radin: "Some of you, while standing before the court of judgement on high, might attempt to defend your lack of repentance by saying that Yisroel Meir lived in your town and said nothing to you. Therefore, be you all forewarned that the desecration of the Shabbos is deserving of fire, and a violation of family purity brings on *kores* (shortening of one's life); and the education of children is the foundation of Judaism. I am now publicly declaring that when I stand before the Honorable Throne, I shall claim that I am not guilty, for I have constantly warned you." (Chofetz Chayim, His Life and Work)

2. At least two candles are lit in honor of the *Shabbos* to symbolize the two-fold command of *Shabbos* observance: "Remember *(Zachor)* the *Shabbos* day to keep it holy" and "Observe *(Shamor)* the Shabbos to keep it holy."

3. The *Shabbos* candles are a sign of peace and harmony in the house. They are also a sign of blessing. That is why women often add a special prayer for their children when lighting and saying the blessing over the *Shabbos* candles. They pray that their children should grow up to follow in the ways of *Hashem.*

4. In some households, it is customary to light 7 candles, or even 10. Others light a candle for each member of the household.

5. If, for some reason, there is only one candle available for *Shabbos,* one is still *yotzai* (fulfills the *Mitzvah*) by lighting it.

6. One should use fine quality candles or pure olive oil for *Shabbos.*

7. After the *Shabbos* candles are lit, they are not to be used for any other purpose, such as lighting the oven.

8. The candles should be lit *b'makom acheeloh* (in the place where the family will be eating the *Shabbos Seuda*).

9. The candles are lit approximately 20 minutes before sunset. Once the sun has set, the candles can no longer be lit.

10. *Shabbos* candles must be lit in every household, even if only one person is living there.

11. If one does not have enough money for candles, he should borrow some. However, if he has only one candle, he need not borrow funds to purchase a second candle.

THE INTERRUPTED SHABBOS

It was a typically serene *Shabbos* afternoon in the household of Rabbi Shmuel Hanagid. As the family sat at the dining room table, about to eat the *Shabbos* meal, Rabbi Shmuel Hanagid could only smile at his good fortune. Though he was living in Spain, far from the Holy Land, he had been blessed with a fine family, a prosperous carpet business, and the freedom to study Torah as he pleased. G-d was certainly most kind to him.

Then abruptly, he heard a forceful knock at the door. Who could be calling now during the *Shabbos* meal? This was most unusual! Rabbi Shmuel's son went to the door, talked to someone for a moment, and then rushed back to the dining room in a tizzy. "Father, there is a minister of the Prince waiting to see you—and he says it's urgent!"

Rabbi Shmuel was shocked. He had thought that his relations with the Prince were good. Yet, who really knew? After all, this was *Golus*, and the Jews were in exile. Who could fully trust the gentiles to treat the Jews kindly? What in the world did the Prince want from him?

To find out, Rabbi Shmuel rushed to invite the minister inside. The minister quickly got to the point. "The Prince is

12. If for some reason the parents do not light the candles, then any one of the children should do so with a *Brocho*.

13. If someone is away on vacation, he must light the candles where he is staying for *Shabbos*.

14. If a person finds himself in a situation where he has no candles, but someone else is lighting the *Shabbos* candles (for example, in a hotel where everyone eats in the same dining room) then he may give that person some money before *Shabbos* and ask that he be a partner in the *Mitzvah* of lighting the *Shabbos* candles.

In hotels or other places where people are grouped together, each family should light candles separately. It is best that they do so on the table where they are eating. However, because of fire regulations this is not always possible.

15. A woman who is in a hospital which prohibits lighting candles may light an electric candelabra or any other bulb instead. Consult a *Rav* whether or not to make a *Brocho*. In any case, the husband lights at home with a *Brocho*.

16. One should not light candles before *Plag Ha'Mincha*.

17. A blind woman may make the *Brocho* upon lighting the *Shabbos* candles even though she cannot see the flame. However, if her husband is there, she should light the candles and he should make the *Brocho*, since he is the one who derives benefits from seeing the light of the candles. If the blind woman is with a group of other women who are lighting the candles, it is best that she be *yotzai* with their *Brocho*.

18. If it is impossible for one to light the candles where he is eating, then he may do so in the room where he is sleeping.

---

sorry to disturb you on this holy day of yours, but a very important matter has come up, and I have been asked to escort you to the palace immediately."

"Have I done anything to offend His Majesty?"

"No. The Prince is entertaining some very important guest today, and he wants to impress them with his wealth. The Prince knows that you can help him greatly if you prepare and sell him one of your excellent carpets. He, therefore, wants you to come to the palace immediately to deliver the goods and conclude the deal."

So that was it! Rabbi Shmuel considered the situation carefully. The Prince was certainly important, and could not easily be refused. Nevertheless, Rabbi Shmuel didn't consider his request for even a moment. It was, after all, the holy *Shabbos*, and the sanctity of the Shabbos could not be traded in for a mere business deal. Rabbi Shmuel wasted no time in politely telling this to the minister.

"I will report your reply to the Prince, but I don't know if His Majesty will be happy with it." With that, the minister left.

19. Procedure for lighting the *Shabbos* candles: (a) The woman lights the candles. (b) She extinguishes the match and discards it (her husband may do so afterwards). (c) She then covers her eyes, and (d) recites the following *Brocho*: *"Boruch Ata Hashem Elokeinu Melech Ha'olam Asher Kid'shanu B'Mitzvosov V'Tzeevanu L'Hadlik Ner Shel Shabbos."*

20. In the above *Brocho*, the singular form, *"Ner"*, is used even though several candles are lit.

21. After finishing the *Brocho*, the woman uncovers her eyes. Since the *Brocho* must be made before one gets any benefit, no enjoyment may be derived from the lights until the blessing has been recited.

The reason the *Brocho* is recited after, and not before, the lighting of the candles is that if the blessing were to be recited first, it would seem that the woman had already accepted the *Shabbos*. In that case, she could no longer light the candles, since the kindling of lights is forbidden on the *Shabbos*.

22. Once the woman has lit the candles and made the *Brocho*, she has been *"Mekabel Shabbos,"* (accepted the restrictions of *Shabbos)* and is no longer allowed to move the candles or matches. The husband, however, is still allowed to do *Melochoh* (work that is normally forbidden on *Shabbos)* as long as it is not yet the exact time for accepting the *Shabbos*, or until he is *Mekabel Shabbos* (says the *Tefillos* of *"Kabbolas Shabbos."*—*"Lecho Dodi"* or *"Mizmor Shir L'yom HaShabbos."*)

23. It is best to place the *Challahs* on the table before lighting the *Shabbos* candles. Since the candlesticks become *Muktzeh* (forbidden to be moved on the *Shabbos),* the table would, therefore, become a base to

"Was that really wise of you, father?" asked one of Rabbi Shmuel's sons. "The Prince might get angry at you."

"Princes come and go," said Rabbi Shmuel, "but our holy traditions remain constant throughout the ages. Now let us take our minds off the Prince and honor the *Shabbos* with some *Zemiros* songs."

But the challenge was not yet over. Soon after *Birchas Hamazon* had been said, there was a second knock at the door. This time, an even higher ranking representative of the Prince appeared. "I have here a written state-ment from the Prince," he said. "He again asks that you come with me to his palace. If you do, he will reward you generously."

"And if not?" asked Rabbi Shmuel.

"Then the Prince may decide to cancel all his dealings with you and may urge others to do the same."

Rabbi Shmuel's response came in one second flat. "Please tell the Prince that I will be honored to come to the palace—after the *Shabbos*. But until the *Shabbos* is over, I cannot. I regret it if I am causing the Prince any difficulties, but that is G-d's will."

The representative left.

something that is *Muktzeh,* and consequently, could not be moved. Therefore, by putting the *Challahs* on the table before *Shabbos,* the table becomes additionally a base for something that one is allowed to move on *Shabbos,* and as a result it can be moved. (The candlesticks and the tray underneath them, however, are in all cases *Muktzeh.*)

24. It is preferable to light the candles in a place from which they will not have to be moved.

If one cannot leave them in their place (such as in the *Succah),* then it is best to light the candles in the house rather than to make the *Brocho* in the *Succah* and transfer them afterwards.

25. Someone who was already *"Mekabel Shabbos"* (accepted the restrictions of *Shabbos)* by lighting the candles may tell another person who has not yet been *"Mekabel Shabbos"* to do that which would ordinarily be prohibited on *Shabbos* (e.g., to shut a light that remained open).

Similarly on *Motzai Shabbos,* even though one has not yet davened *Ma'ariv* or said *"Baruch Hamavdil . . . ,"* he may still tell someone who has said *"Baruch Hamavdil"* to do *Melochoh* for him.

26. If a *Yom Tov* occurs on *Shabbos,* then the *Brocho* for lighting the candles is *"L'hadlik Ner Shel Shabbos V'Shel Yom Tov."*

27. Normally, as soon as a woman lights the candles with the *Brocho,* she has been *"Mekabel Shabbos."* If extraordinary circumstances warrant her doing *Melochoh* right afterwards, she should make a special *T'nai* (condition) when she lights the candles. This condition specifies that she had not yet accepted the *Shabbos* when she lit the candles and

---

"Do you think that the Prince will really carry out his threat?" asked Rabbi Shmuel's wife.

"Probably," said Rabbi Shmuel. "But all the riches the Prince could give me would mean nothing if I'd have to desecrate the Shabbos to get them. Don't worry about how we'll live if the Prince stops dealing with me. We'll survive. Just let us trust in G-d; He will protect us."

Night had already fallen when the third knock was heard at the door. This time, a band of four soldiers came in, bearing orders to bring the Rabbi directly to the palace. Rabbi Shmuel

was ready for them. "The *Shabbos* is over. I am now ready to go wherever you say." He calmed his worried family, and left with the soldiers.

They led Rabbi Shmuel to the Prince's chambers and departed, leaving the two men alone. Rabbi Shmuel wondered what type of punishment was in store for him now. But then, he took a closer look at the Prince. What was this? He couldn't be sure, but it seemed to him that the Prince was actually smiling, and was happy to see him.

"I must really apologize to you," said the Prince. "I did not want to

recited the *Brocho*. However, a *Rav* should be consulted first about this procedure.

HILCHOS LECHEM MISHNA

1. One must have two complete *Challahs* or *Matzos* for *Lechem Mishna*. This is to remind us of the double portion of *mohn* which fell on Fridays in the desert.

2. If there is *Lechem Mishna* for one person who is *motzee* all the others at the table, they should intend to be *yotzai* with his *Brocho*, and not make a *"Hamotzee"* on their individual pieces of *Challah*.

3. It is best to hold the *Lechem Mishna* with all ten fingers. In many homes, it is customary for each member of the household to put his hands on the *Challahs* after the *"Hamotzee."*

4. The others should not eat their pieces of *Challah* until the one who was *motzee* has eaten his.

5. Some have the custom for the one making the *Hamotzee* to make a very slight cut with a knife on top of the *Challah* that he is going to use. The cut should not be too deep, so the *Lechem Mishna* will still be left whole. It is done only to make a mark where to cut the *Challah*, so that there shouldn't be an interruption looking for the spot to cut.

6. The person making the *"Hamotzee"* holds one *Challah* on top of the other. On Friday night, the bottom one is cut; otherwise the top one is cut.

7. The larger *Challah* should be used for the *Shabbos* meal during the day.

bother you during your holy day, but I wanted to prove a point.

"You see, a neighboring Prince came to visit me today. He claimed that the Jews were a greedy people who would do anything for money. I bet him that he was wrong, and told him of my friend Rabbi Shmuel Hanagid, who valued his religious beliefs above wealth. We agreed to test you by ordering you to sell me carpets on the *Shabbos*. Was my guest amazed when you refused me not once, but twice, even though it meant a loss of great riches!

"You more than proved my point, and for that I am grateful. As a result,

not only will I continue to deal with you, but I will find you many new customers. You are indeed a loyal Jew, and I wish you much success in the future."

Rabbi Shmuel's refusal to desecrate the Shabbos had paid off. He became very wealthy but more importantly, he gained enormous respect for proving that Jews are loyal to their G-d.

A Jew will be asked: Why did you open your shop on the *Shabbos*? Aren't you aware of the severity of the prohibition of desecrating the *Shabbos*? Every defiler of the *Shabbos* is considered to have denied the entire

8. Salt should be on the table, and the piece of *Challah* cut for the *Brocho* should be dipped in it three times.

9. One must have *Challah* or *Matzoh* (even if he does not have complete *Lechem Mishna*), for both the Friday night and the *Shabbos* meal.

10. It is best to have the *Shabbos Seuda* before *Chatzos* (mid-day) so as not to fast on the *Shabbos*.

11. One should finish davening *Mussaf* before eating a full *Seuda*.

HILCHOS ONEG SHABBOS (Enjoyment of Shabbos)

1. On the Shabbos day, one should eat fruits and cake (that require the recitation of additional *Brochos*), which adds to the enjoyment of *Shabbos*.

(It is an obligation to recite 100 *Brochos* daily. Since the *Shabbos Shmoneh Esrei* contains only 7 *Brochos* rather than the 19 of the week-day *Shmoneh Esrei*, we try to make up the difference by making *Brochos* on additional foods, eaten "*L'Kovod Shabbos.*")

2. We also make up the additional *Brochos* when reading the Torah in *Shul*, since there are additional *Aliyos* with additional *Brochos*.

3. One should be *Ma'aver Sedra* (read the *Parsha* twice) before *kiddush*. If one did not, one can do so during the remainder of *Shabbos*.

HILCHOS SHALOSH SEUDOS (Seuda Shlishis)

1. The word *Yom* (day) is written three times in one *posuk* of the Torah in reference to *Shabbos*. We learn from here that there should be three meals in honor of the *Shabbos*.

Torah itself. Is it worth it to defile the valuable vessel given to Israel for a few additional pennies of profit? The man will certainly reply: What can I do? The needs of a man are many and his sustenance is meager. He feels that he is obligated to keep his trade open. Would it be possible for him to keep his business shut two straight days in the week?

To whom can he be compared? To the same fool who thought that he could produce more cups of water out of a jug by adding another tap. It didn't even occur to him that the new tap not only couldn't add any more water, but would even empty the water faster.

The L-rd of our universe nourishes and sustains the entire world. He prepares our weekly food according to how we have pleased Him; for some in abundance; for others, not. Our weekly income comes to us from six "faucets." Only a fool will think that he will receive more sustenance by opening additional taps. Therefore, how does the Jew, who has desecrated the *Shabbos*, benefit? *(Parables of the Chofetz Chayim)*

CHOOSY BEGGAR

There was once a man who had to leave his country on a business venture and go to a far-off land from where it was impossible for him to

2. It is best not to overeat at the mid-day *Seuda* so one can have an appetite for the *Seuda Shlishis* (the third meal).

3. The reason this meal is called *Shalosh Seudos* (three meals) is because this one is really the hardest to eat in the winter. Before the two previous meals, one is hungry and eager to eat. By late *Shabbos* afternoon, the person's appetite has been satisfied. He eats this *Seuda* because of *Hashem's* mitzvah to eat *Shalosh Seudos*.

4. *Shalosh Seudos* may be eaten anytime after approximately 12:30 (standard time) in the afternoon. It is best to do so after *Tefillas Mincha*. If one cannot, then he may eat it before *Mincha*.

5. It is appropriate to have fish as part of the *Shalosh Seudos*.

6. If one cannot have *Challah* for this meal, he may have "*Mezonos*" (pastry). If there is no "*Mezonos*" available, one can be *yotzai* the mitzvah of *Shalosh Seudos* with fruit.

Some eat the second *Seuda* early and then have *Shalosh Seudos*. (This is especially pertinent on *Shabbos Erev Pesach* when one cannot have *Challahs* for *Shalosh Seudos* at the usual time.)

7. If *Shalosh Seudos* extends into the night after *Shabbos* has already ended, one should still say "*R'tzai*" in the "*Birchas Hamozon*," since he started his meal during *Shabbos,* and it is still *Shabbos* to him.

8. It is customary to prolong the *Shabbos* somewhat, past the official time (*Tzais Ha'Kochavim*) for ending it.

9. Following *Shalosh Seudos,* we *daven Tefillas Ma'ariv*. In the middle of the "*Shmoneh Esrei*" we say "*Atoh Chonatonu.*"

10. If one has already said the *Brocho* of "*Atoh Chonain*" and forgot to

contact his family. Whenever a stranger came to the island, this man would ask him if by any chance he had any news to tell him of his dear ones at home.

After months of searching, he finally found a beggar whom he had known in his old home town. He asked the beggar many questions, but the beggar told him that he had no time for such things, since he had to beg all day long in order to get enough money to survive.

"Tell me," asked the anxious father and husband, "how much money do you make each day?"

"Around $25," replied the beggar.

Finally, the man agreed to pay the beggar $25 on the condition that the beggar stay with him all day long and tell him everything he knew about the man's family.

The next day, the beggar had hardly begun to talk when he suddenly fell asleep. When he finally awoke, he told his employer that he felt too weak to answer his questions and that he needed a good meal before he could continue. The man granted his request, and let the beggar eat to his heart's content.

say *"Atoh Chonantonu"*, he does not have to repeat the *Shmoneh Esrei,* since he will be making *Havdalah* on the cup of wine.

(a) This applies only in a case where the person did not eat between the *Birchas Hamazon* of *Shalosh Seudos* and *Havdalah.* If he did, then he must say *Shmoneh Esrei* again.

(b) If he skipped *"Atoh Chonantonu"* completely and for some reason it's impossible for him to recite *Havdalah* that night, then he must repeat the *Shmoneh Esrei.*

11. *"Vi'hee Noam"* and *"Atoh Kadosh"* is said at the end of *Tefillas Ma'ariv* on *Motzai Shabbos,* except when *Yom Tov* occurs during that week.

HILCHOS TEFILLAH ON SHABBOS

1. Whoever says *"Vayechulu Ha'shomayim"* with the proper *kavono* (devotion and concentration) is considered a partner with *Hashem* in *"Ma-aseh Beraishis"* (creation of the world). (*Shabbos* 119b)

2. If, by mistake, one has started saying the week-day *Shmoneh Esrei* on *Shabbos,* he should finish the *Brocho* that he is in the middle of, and then start the *Shmoneh Esrei* for *Shabbos* with the paragraph immediately following *"Ho'Kail Ha'kodosh."*

3. This rule applies to all the *Tefillos* except *Mussaf.* If one made this mistake during *Mussaf,* he should stop in the middle as soon as he realizes his error and continue with the *Shmoneh Esrei* for *Mussaf,* also from the point immediately following *"Ho'Kail Ha'kodosh,"* because there is no *Mussaf* at all during the week.

4. If one has said *"Atoh . . ."* in the *Shmoneh Esrei,* intending to say *"Atoh Chonain"* (as in the week-day *Shmoneh Esrei)* instead of *"Atoh*

After the beggar had finished eating, instead of continuing the conversation, he said that he needed a brief nap before he could answer any more questions.

Now the man got impatient and screamed, "Look, I have paid you at least as much as you would have earned begging during all this time. All I asked was that you reserve this whole day for me. Instead, you've done nothing but eat, drink and sleep until you've practically wasted the entire day, which you should have devoted to me. You seem to forget

that for this day I am your master and I have a right to your attention."

So it is with the *Shabbos.* All week long, we are busy with our worldly pursuits, but on *Shabbos* we are expected to devote all our efforts and energies to *Hashem,* as it is written, "Six days a week shall work be done, but on the seventh day there shall be to you a holy day, a *Shabbos* of solemn rest unto the L-rd."

THE COW THAT WOULDN'T MOVE

"Get up and work, you fat old cow," the gentile farmer yelled as he gave the

27

Keedashtah" (in *Ma'ariv)* or *"Atoh Echad"* (in *Mincha)* he may continue with the *Shabbos* version of the *Shmoneh Esrei.* If, however, this occurs in the *Shmoneh Esrei* of *Shacharis,* one has to finish off the *Brocho* of *"Atoh Chonain,"* because the word *"Atoh"* does not start that paragraph of the *"Shacharis L'Shabbos."* (It starts with *"Yismach Moshe.")* One must finish that *Brocho* and then start the *"Shmoneh Esrei L'Shacharis"* which begins with *"Yismach Moshe."* This applies only if he forgot it was *Shabbos.*

5. If the person knew that it was *Shabbos,* but accidentally uttered *"Atoh,"* then, even in *Shacharis,* he does not have to finish that *Brocho,* and he can go immediately into *Shmoneh Esrei* of *Shabbos.*

6. Once one has said the word *"Chonain,"* he must finish that *Brocho,* no matter what *Tefillah* he is saying, even if he did remember that it was *Shabbos.*

7. If one said the week day *Shmoneh Esrei* instead of the one for *Shabbos,* he must repeat the one for *Shabbos.* However, if he remembered before the last *"Yihiyu L'Ratzon,"* he may go back to the beginning of the *Tefillah* for *Shabbos* and not start from the beginning of the *Shmoneh Esrei.* *The same law applies to Mussaf.* If one remembers before the conclusion of the week-day *"Shmoneh Esrei"* and inserts the following *posuk: "V'Na'aseh L'fonechoh Es Korbonos Chovosainu T'midim K'Sidrom V'Es Mussaf . . ."* then he was *yotzai* and need not repeat the entire *Shmoneh Esrei.* However, for the other *Tefillos* of *Shabbos* this would not be acceptable.

animal a swift kick. The cow would not budge.

John, the farmer, had bought this cow from his Jewish neighbor, Shmelke. Shmelke's business was bad and he needed money quickly, so he had sold his cow to John. The cow was a hard worker during the week, and John was pleased. But now it was Saturday, and all of a sudden the cow lay down and refused to budge.

John decided to try a new method. He got down on his hands and knees. "Pleeease," he begged. "My dear cow, all week long you worked so wonderfully. Why spoil it today? I'll let you eat some extra pieces of grass if you will be good." The farmer tried to pull the

cow to a standing position. But the animal would not be disturbed.

"Well, if that's the way you want it," said John as he angrily walked away, "I'll go and return you to your old boss, Shmelke, and I'll take back my money." And off he went.

"What is it?" Shmelke said as he opened the door. Shmelke was in the middle of his *Shabbos* meal. He was wearing his long silk coat and his special *Shabbos* yarmulke.

"Neighbor John, what could be the purpose of your visit on this holy day? You know that I can do no business with you on the *Shabbos.*"

"My dear neighbor Shmelke. It upsets me to disburb a pious man like

8. If one said the wrong *"Shmoneh Esrei,"* such as by saying the one for *"Shacharis Shel Shabbos"* instead of the one for *Mincha,* he is still *yotzai.*

This pertains to any of the three different *Shmoneh Esrei's* that are recited on *Shabbos.* If at any time one says the wrong one, he is still *yotzai.* However, one cannot interchange it for *Mussaf.* If he did, he was not *yotzai.* However, this error can still be corrected before the last *"Yihiyu L'Ratzon."*

9. If one said *Mussaf* instead of *Shacharis,* he still has to say the *Shmoneh Esrei* of *Shacharis.* However, he does not have to repeat the *Shmoneh Esrei* for *Mussaf* since one can say *Mussaf* at any time during the day.

10. On Friday night the *Ashkenazim* say *"B'meh Modlakim . . .",* unless *Shabbos* falls out on *Yom Tov.* On Friday night if one said the weekday *"Shomer Amo Yisroel L'ad"* after the *Shema* instead of *"Haporesh Succas . . ."* he is *yotzai* and need not repeat the *Brocho.*

11. On Friday night, after conclusion of the *Shmoneh Esrei,* we repeat *"Vayechulu Ha'Shomayim"* while standing. This is said together by the entire *tzeebur* (congregation).

If one could not say *"Vayechulu"* with the *tzeebur* (e.g., if he didn't finish *Shmoneh Esrei* yet), then he should have someone else say it with him, word for word. One is not allowed to talk in the middle of *"Vayechulu."* The *Tur* relates the dire consequences that befell those who did so.

yourself on your *Shabbos* day. But I would not have come if I didn't have to. It is about the cow I bought from you. You see, all week long it worked fine, but . . ."

Shmelke interrupted him. "Say no more. I know just what your trouble is. Lead me to the cow, and in but a few minutes she will again be pulling your heavy plow. But first you must permit me to finish my meal and say *Birchas Hamazon."*

And so, Shmelke returned to his table, sang the *Shabbos Zemiros* (songs) finished his meal, and recited *Birchas Hamazon.* Afterwards, John and Shmelke proceeded together to the wheat field in which the rebellious cow lay.

"A Gutten Shabbos," Shmelke called out as he approached the cow. "How are you, my dear cow? Now listen to me . . ." Shmelke whispered into the cow's ear. Almost instantly the cow stood up, her eyes opened wide and she began pulling the plow up and down the rows of the field.

"You are certainly a magician," John said. "Please tell me the magical phrase which you told the cow. I would like to know it so that if the cow decides to be lazy again, I will tell it to her myself."

"I didn't say magical words" answered Shmelke, "You see, as long as the cow was mine, it did not work on the *Shabbos,* for we Jews may not

12. The *Brocho* immediately following *"Vayechulu,"* which is called *"May'ain Sheva"* (a summary of the repetition of *Shmoneh Esrei*), is recited by the *Chazan* only when he is *davening* with a *Minyan* that has a *Sefer Torah*. If it is a steady *Minyan* without a *Sefer Torah*, consult a *Rav*. However, a person davening alone does not say this *Brocho*.

13. If, through an error, a person has to repeat the *Shmoneh Esrei*, he should do so before the *Brocho* of *"May'ain Sheva"*, because if he heard the *Chazan* recite that *Brocho*, it is questionable if he should repeat it.

The *Brocho* *"May'ain Sheva"* is said only after the *Shmoneh Esrei* on Friday night, not on *Yom Tov*. If *Yom Tov* occurs on *Shabbos*, the *Brocho* is recited just as is, with no additions made in reference to the *Yom Tov*. The exception to this rule is when the first night of *Pesach* occurs on Friday night, in which case we don't say the *"May'ain Sheva."*

14. In many *Shuls*, it is customary to make *Kiddush* in *Shul* after the davening. This custom started many years ago when travelers, guests, or poor people eating in the local *Shuls* had to have *Kiddush* recited for them. The *Kiddush* is said while one is standing.

The wine of *Kiddush* made in *Shul* should be given to a koton (child under 13) to drink, because no one is really *yotzai* with this *kiddush* since no one eats the *Seuda* there. It is done merely to follow an old custom.

15. If there is no *koton* to drink that wine, then the person making the *Kiddush* should drink a full *reviyis* (most of the cup of wine containing the proper amount) and make a *"Brocho Ach'ronah."* He is still allowed to make *Kiddush* again at home for his household.

even let our animals work on the *Shabbos*. The day is devoted totally to the service of the L-rd. And so my cow did not want to work today because she knew it was the *Shabbos*. I whispered into her ear and told her that she was no longer owned by a Jew, and that she must, therefore, work on *Shabbos*."

John was so filled with emotion that for a long time he could not speak. Finally he said with awe in his voice, "I have decided. I also want to be a Jew. If your Torah is so great—if your belief and devotion is so great that even a cow knows to rest on the *Shabbos*, then it must be the most wonderful, complete and only way of life for a human being. Please teach me. I, too, will be a *Shabbos* observer. I too will be a Jew."

And so it was, John the gentile became Yochanan ben Avrohom. He was happy and his family was happy.

(This is an adaptation of a true story. The gentile-turned-Jew became a great scholar and is mentioned in the Talmud under the name Yochanan ben Torso.)

CARAVAN AND THE LION

Walking down the ancient streets of Yerushalayim one day, a kindhearted man was deeply moved by the sight he

16. During the reading of the Torah in *Shacharis*, seven men plus one for *"Maftir"* are called up. (Additional *aliyos* may also be given out.) The *"Haftorah,"* a portion of the *"Novi"* (Prophets) is read.

17. *Av Harachamim* is said before *Mussaf*, except when they don't say *Tachanun* and on *Shabbos Mevorchim*.

18. At *Mincha*, we add *"Uvoh L'Tzion"* to the regular *"Ashrei"* prayer. Three *aliyos* are given out during the reading of the Torah. *"Tzidko-schoh Tzedek"* is said after the *Shmoneh Esrei*. It is not said on those days when *"Tachanun"* would not be said (e.g., *Yom Tov*).

HILCHOS KIDDUSH

1. Upon returning from Shul on Friday night, one sings *"Sholom Aleichem"* and recites the *Kiddush* as soon as possible. There should be no unnecessary delays, especially if one has guests.

2. The Torah tells us to remember the *Shabbos* to keep it holy. *"Zachor Es Yom HaShabbos L'Kadsho."* By reciting the *Kiddush*, one fulfills this commandment to remember the *Shabbos*.

3. Women are obligated to fulfill the Mitzvah of *Kiddush* even though it is a *"Mitzvas Assai She'Hazman Gromma"* (a positive precept fixed by time from which women are normally exempt), because of the biblical teaching *"Shamor, V'Zachor."* *"Shamor"* refers to not violating the negative commandments of *Shabbos*, and *"Zachor"* refers to observing the positive ones. Just as a woman is required to observe the negative precepts, she must also keep the positive ones.

4. If one does not have wine, one may make *Kiddush* on *Challah*.

saw. The sound of little children playing happily was music to his ears, but their tattered clothing and obvious poverty brought tears to his eyes. He decided he must do something to remedy the situation.

Nowadays, it is common practice for emissaries from all over the world to come to American Jewish communities to raise money. In those days (about 1500 years ago), people traveled to the wealthy Jewish communities that existed in the ancient city of Baghdad in Iraq. The man decided that despite the dangers and difficulties involved in such a long trip, he would travel to Baghdad to raise mo-

ney for the poor Yerushalmi families and their children.

The journey meant a long bumpy trip on top of a camel's hump. Travelers considered themselves lucky, indeed, if they were able to join up with a caravan going in their desired direction. This kindhearted man was very happy when he found a caravan going to Baghdad. He had to make one condition clear, though, before joining it. He paid the caravan leader a considerable sum of money in return for a favor. The caravan must not travel on *Shabbos*.

The caravan started out at the beginning of the week and traveled

5. If *Shabbos* and *Yom Tov* follow one another, and one has sufficient wine for only one of the days, it should be used for *Kiddush* on *Shabbos*.

If there is sufficient wine to make *Kiddush* only once, it should be used for the Friday night *Kiddush*, even though the primary *Seuda* is served during the day.

6. A *koton* (male child under the age of 13 years) cannot be *"motzee"* (fulfill the obligation on behalf of) anyone else with *Kiddush*, although he may fulfill his own obligation.

7. If two groups of people eating together will both make *Kiddush*, the leader should not recite it out loud simultaneously, because those who want to fulfill their obligation with the *Kiddush* will not be able to hear both at the same time.

8. After davening, one is not allowed to eat or drink anything before *Kiddush*, but one is permitted to rinse his mouth.

9. If one decides on Friday afternoon that he wants to be "Mekabel Shabbos" (accept the restrictions of *Shabbos)* earlier than the official appointed time, he must stop eating at the time that he is *"Mekabel Shabbos"* even though the *"Zeman Shabbos"* (time for *Shabbos)* has not yet arrived.

10. If after reciting the *"HaMotzee,"* a person remembers that he had accidentally omitted *Kiddush*, he recites the *Kiddush* on the *Challah* and eats a bit of the *Challah*. We do not consider the *Kiddush* an interruption between the *"Hamotzee"* and the eating of the *Challah*. However, the paragraph of *"Vayechulu"* should be said after the *Challah* has been eaten.

through deserts, oases, plains and valleys. Erev Shabbos arrived, and the man approached the leader to remind him of his promise. The latter laughed in his face.

"Do you really expect me to halt a caravan of 85 camels and their riders for a mere Jew who wants to laze around for the day? You can't be serious!"

The man was stunned. He had not expected this. What should he do? It might be dangerous to remain by himself in this uncivilized wilderness.

Realizing the sacredness of his own mission on behalf of so many needy people, the man felt confident in his heart that *Hashem* would guard him from danger. He took his belongings off the camel while his fellow passengers looked on in amazement. Some felt a sense of respect for this principled man. Others ridiculed his devotion to his beliefs.

The caravan continued on while the man unpacked his satchel. He placed a white cloth on the ground, took out his two loaves of *Challah*, a flask of wine and his wine-cup. He was prepared to daven *"Kabbolas Shabbos,"* when he suddenly sensed that he was not alone.

He turned around and almost fainted from fright. Facing him was a huge

11. If one remembered right after "Netilas Yodayim" (washing of the hands) that he did not say the *Kiddush,* he should recite the *Kiddush* on the wine then, and not wash again for the bread.

12. If one ate the entire meal and then realized that he forgot to make *Kiddush,* he should make *Kiddush* after the meal.

13. If for some reason a person couldn't make *Kiddush* at night (e.g., he was stranded somewhere) then he should make the Friday night *Kiddush* (without *"Vayechulu"*) in the daytime. Once the evening is over, one cannot say *"Vayechulu."*

If there was a delay until twilight, which is after sunset of the next day, then the *Kiddush* is recited without *Hashem's* name.

14. If one begins *Shabbos* earlier than the appointed time, he may make *Kiddush* before *"tzais hakochavim"* (appearance of the stars). Some eat some *Challah* or cake after *"tzais hakochavim."*

15. When one makes *Kiddush,* the *Kos* (wine cup) should be completely filled with wine. Spoiled wine, wine that was left uncovered for a long period of time and *Yayin Pagum* (wine from which people already drank) should not be used. However, *Yayin Pagum* may be used if other wine is added to it, or if no other wine is available.

16. The wine cup should be completely clean. One should not use a cup that cannot stand by itself. It is best not to use a disposable cup.

17. *Kiddush* may be recited while one is either standing or sitting, depending on one's *minhag* (custom).

18. When one begins the Friday night *Kiddush,* one is supposed to look towards the candles while holding the cup of wine.

lion with an enormous mane. The man stood petrified. After a few moments, he realized that the lion was not moving from its spot. It just stared at him with the look of a gentle kitten.

The man started *davening.* The lion did not stir. The man made *Kiddush,* washed his hands for *Netilas Yodayim,* and recited the *Ha-Motzee* on the *Challahs.* All this while, the lion did not budge. It seemed as if it were standing guard-duty over the Jew.

The man sang beautiful *Shabbos zemiros* and his voice echoed in the night. His "guest" seemed to enjoy the entertainment and it must have found

it soothing, for its eyes began to droop. The lion fell asleep and the man felt it was safe for him to do likewise.

He awoke in the morning to see his *shomer* (guard), the lion, still standing in the same spot. The man washed up, put on his *Tallis,* and *davened* the *Tefillos* for *Shabbos.* Afterwards, he made *Kiddush* and *HaMotzee* for the second *Shabbos* meal. After reciting the *Birchas HaMazon* (Grace After Meals), he reviewed the *Parsha* of the week and then took a *Shabbos* rest.

In the evening after *Mincha,* he ate the *Seuda Shelishis* (the third *Shabbos* meal) and *davened Ma'ariv.* He

19. The wine cup must be large enough to contain a *reviyis* (4.42 ounces) of wine, but one does not have to drink the entire amount. It is sufficient to drink most of the cup *(rov kos)*, and one should not take more than a half minute to drink it.

20. If a person cannot drink the wine, it may be given to someone else to drink. Although it is customary to distribute some of the wine to the rest of the family, this should be done only after someone has already drunk most of the cup.

21. One is not allowed to talk between the *Kiddush* and the beginning of the drinking of the *rov kos* unless the conversation involves the *Kiddush.* If one talked after the *Kiddush,* before drinking the wine, he has to say *"Borai Pri HaGofen"* again but does not repeat the entire *Kiddush.*

22. If one said *"Borai Pri HaGofen"* intending to drink the wine, but all of the wine spilled before he could do so, he must pour himself another cup and make the *Brocho* again.

23. If one intended to drink more wine during the meal on *Shabbos* or *Yom Tov* he need not repeat the *Brocho.*

24. Other people at the table who are being *yotzai* with his *Kiddush* are not allowed to eat or drink until he starts to drink the wine.

25. Although it is best to make *Kiddush* on red wine, one may also use white wine, raisin wine, cooked wine or grape juice. There is no need to recite a *"Brocho Ach'ronah"* (blessing after eating food) since the *"Birchas Hamazon"* (Grace after meals) covers wine used for *Kiddush.*

26. The procedure for making *Kiddush* on challah is as follows:

---

made *Havdalah,* and the *Shabbos* was officially over.

Then the lion did something strange. It lowered its head and body, as if inviting the man to mount its back. The man took his few belongings, and climbed onto the lion, which took off like a streak of lightning. The man held tightly to the lion's mane as they raced through the night.

At daybreak, he found that they had caught up to the caravan. He dismounted from the lion and bade it good-bye. He had no doubt that *Hashem* had provided him with a special "guardian-angel" because of his special mission.

As the man walked back to his camel, his fellow passengers stared at him in awe. He was obviously a holy man who had merited divine intervention.

Thereafter, he was given the name "Ariel", which means "Lion of G-d." When Ariel arrived in Baghdad, he was treated with great respect especially when they heard about his faith in *Shabbos.* Therefore he was able to raise huge sums of money, which people were more than eager to give him.

"Shemiras Shabbos" (Keeping the *Shabbos*) helped save Ariel's life, while

(a) Wash and recite the *Brocho "Al Netilas Yodayim."*

(b) Put your hands on the cloth covering the *Challahs.*

(c) Recite the part of the *Kiddush* which precedes the *Brocho "Hamotzee."*

(d) Uncover the *Challahs* when reaching the Brocho, *"Hamotzee,"* and raise the *Challahs* when saying *"Hashem"* in that *Brocho.*

(e) On Friday night, after the *Brocho,* cover the *Challahs* until the conclusion of the *Kiddush,* when you are ready to cut the *Challah.*

27. When making *Kiddush* on wine, one should cover the *Challahs* for three reasons:

(a) To remember the *"mohn"* in the *"midbar"* (desert) that was covered by a layer of dew both beneath and above.

(b) Bread is really the most important of foods, and a *Brocho* should first be made on the bread. However, since the Challahs are covered, it is as if they are not on the table and we are, therefore, able to make the *Brocho* on the wine first.

(c) The *Shabbos* table should really be brought into the room after the *Kiddush.* Since tables are large and cannot be shunted from room to room, the *Challahs* are covered during *Kiddush* and first "presented" afterwards.

28. If there is no wine available for the *Kiddush* during the day, one may use *chamar hamedina* (common beverage of the country) such as whiskey or beer. The *Brocho,* in this case, would be *She'Hakol.*

It is questionable whether other beverages may be classified as *chamar hamedina.* There is a question whether or not soft drinks should be used because they are comprised mainly of water.

---

he, in turn, was instrumental in improving the lives of countless numbers of poor families in Yerushalayim, long, long ago.

REB YISROEL YITZCHOK

A certain shopkeeper complained to Reb Yisroel Yitzchok of Alexandria, the author of *Yismach Yisroel,* that his shop did not provide him with a livelihood. The *tzaddik* gathered that the shop was open seven days a week and made a proposal: "If you agree to accept me as a partner in your business to the extent of fifteen percent, though without any investment on my part, then I will promise you a proper income."

The shopkeeper agreed at once, and they drew up a legal partnership contract. But the rebbe still had something to add. "Since I now own one seventh of the business," he said, "the share I am choosing as mine is *Shabbos.* The profits of that day are to be mine, while the profits of the other six days are to be yours. You will therefore close the shop on *Shabbos,* for that is my day. And now, my good man, go along and prosper."

KIDDUSH B'MAKOM SEUDA

1. One must make Kiddush *"B'Makom Seuda"*—in the place where one eats.

2. *"Makom Seuda"* does not necessarily mean one must afterwards eat a full meal with bread. It also refers to eating a *shiur* (required amount) of *mezonos* (cake), which should be eaten after *Kiddush*.

3. The *"seuda"* should be eaten in the same room where the *Kiddush* was made.

4. If one wishes to hear *Kiddush* in one part of a large hall and eat in another part, he may do so.

5. If one wishes to make *Kiddush* in one room and eat in another, he must have intended to do so at the time he made *Kiddush*. Both must be in one building. However, if he did not intend to do so and he cannot see from one room to the other, then he was not *yotzai*.

6. If one makes *Kiddush* indoors and wishes to eat the *Seuda* outside or in another house (as when *Kiddush* is made in the *Succah* and the wife eats in the house), he may do so, provided that the second site can be seen from where the *Kiddush* was made. It is best to have in mind that one intends to eat there.

7. On *Succos,* if one made *Kiddush* in the house because of rain, and then it suddenly stopped raining, (even if he already made *Hamotzee*), one may go out and eat the meal in the *Succah* if the *Succah* can be seen from the room where *Kiddush* was made. This is especially true in the case where one had in mind that if it stops raining, he will go out to eat in the *Succah*.

The new policy of the shop's new joint management quickly showed tangible results for the business boomed.

Reb Shimon Bar Yochai said, "Shabbos said before G-d, 'Everyone has a partner and I do not.' G-d said to it, 'The Jews are your partner.' When the Jews stood on Mount Sinai, G-d said to them, 'Remember what I said to the Shabbos—the Jews are its partner." (Medrash Rabah, Beraishis 11:8)

Keeping the Shabbos is equal to keeping the whole Torah. (Yerushalmi Brochos)

"Were Israel to observe two Shabbosos properly, they would be redeemed at once." (Shabbos 118b)

Elsewhere the *Chazal* (Sages) observe: "Ain Yisroel Nig'alin Eloh B'Zchus Shabbos. *Israel's redemption will be achieved only in the merit of the* Shabbos." (Vayikra Rabba 3:1)

"An extra soul is given by G-d on every Shabbos; Motzei Shabbos, He takes it away." (Betza 16a)

Today, the *Shabbos* still performs its age-long function:

If, however, the *Succah* cannot be seen from the house, then it is best to drink an extra *reviyis* (4.42 oz.) of wine in the house in order to be *yotzai* the *Kiddush.*

8. It is best to be *"kovea seuda"* (eat the meal) right after *Kiddush* without any interruptions.

9. If one intended to be *"kovea seuda"* immediately after *Kiddush* but there was an interruption and he left the room for some reason (e.g., to go to the bathroom or to investigate a noise outside), he may start the *Seuda* when he returns without having to repeat the *Kiddush.*

10. If one left the place of *Kiddush* with the intention of eating elsewhere, and then came back to eat, he was not *yotzai*. For example: A person heard *Kiddush* at someone's house but decided that he was going to eat at home. When he went outside, it started raining and he came back inside to eat there. In such a case, he was not *yotzai* with the original *Kiddush* and would have to make *Kiddush* again.

11. One can be *"motzee"* others (include them in the *Mitzvah*) with *Kiddush* even though he is not going to eat with them. He is *"motzee"* them even with the *Brocho* of *"Borai Pri HaGofen,'* and those who hear it do not have to recite it later by themselves.

12. It is best that *Kiddush* be made by someone who will be *"kovea seuda"* at that place.

13. One can be *"kovea seuda"* either by eating *mezonos* (cake) after the wine or by drinking an additional *reviyis* of the wine. This law also applies to the daytime *Kiddush.*

1) It enables us to devote one full day each week to our task of becoming a "kingdom of priests and a holy nation" (*Shemos* 19:6) and thus beautifies our lives.

2) It prevents our becoming enslaved to secular activities. This way we show that we are free men as we were when we were freed from the bondage of *Mitzrayim*. The *Shabbos* is a memorial to this freedom; in fact, the *Kiddush* mentions, "... *Zecher L'Yetzias Mitzrayim"* (a remembrance of the redemption from Egypt).

3) It proves our trust in the Almighty that He will provide for us even without the possible material gain of working on *Shabbos.*

UNDERSTANDING THE CUSTOMS OF SHABBOS

The reason we put two covers on the *Shabbos* table, one above the *Challah* and another underneath it, is because: a) The *Challah* which symbolizes the *Shabbos* meal is kept covered until the feast has been properly "introduced" by the *Kiddush.* b) In the *Kiddush*, the blessing over the wine precedes the blessing made over the bread. Once the wine has been blessed, the bread may be uncovered. (*Tur*, Ch. 271) c) It recalls the *manna* of the wilderness which did not fall on

HILCHOS HAVDALAH

1. The Rambam states that *Havdalah* is *mid'oraysah* (commanded in the Torah). It is part of *"Zachor"*: just as we remember *Shabbos* on its entrance so must we remember it on its departure. Others say it is *D'Rabbonon* (Rabbinical).

2. In *Shul*, someone usually makes *Havdalah* right after *davening* in order to be *"motzee"* those who would not otherwise be able to make *Havdalah*.

3. One who heard *Havdalah* in *Shul* may recite it again at home for the benefit of his *"bnai bayis"* (household) but it is better that he shouldn't have in mind to be *yotzai* in *shul* to begin with.

4. Women are also supposed to hear *Havdalah*. It is best that a man make it for them, but if the person who could make *Havdalah* for them already did so elsewhere, then the women should make it by themselves.

However, if for some reason they cannot make it themselves, then that first person should be *"motzee"* them even though he already made *Havdalah*.

5. One may not eat before *Havdalah*.

6. Unlike *Kiddush*, *Havdalah* cannot be made on bread.

7. If one doesn't have wine, he may use *"chamar hamedina"* (beverage commonly used in the country, such as beer).

If it is absolutely impossible to obtain wine or *"chamar hamedina,"* then *"b'dee'eved"* (as a last resort) one may eat if he cannot fast any longer before *Havdalah* (even though this is not usually allowed). The maximum one waits to eat before making *Havdalah* is until mid-day Sunday.

Shabbos and Festivals and which would be found between two protective layers of dew, one below and one above. Therefore we enclose the *Challah*. *(Tosofos Pesachim* 100b).

Even though women are not obliged to perform *Mitzvos* that depend on a fixed time, they are duty bound to hear the *Kiddush* recited because this is a precept which contains both positive and negative aspects. "Remembering" the *Shabbos* by hearing the *Kiddush* recited is an essential component of *Shabbos* observance. *(Brochos* 20b). Women are involved in all positive *Mitzvahs* relating to Shabbos.

The reason we must have two loaves of bread at every *Shabbos* meal is because it is written concerning the *Manna* in the wilderness: *"Laktu Lechem Mishna"* *(Shemos* 16:22) "And it came to pass that on the sixth day they gathered twice as much bread."

The *Shabbos Tefillah* contains only seven *Brochos* instead of 19 because the congregation should not be burdened with an overly-long service. Also the *Shabbos* service was meant for joyful communion with G-d. It is only right therefore, that all those

8. Before the *Havdalah* is recited, the cup is completely filled with wine so that it overflows. This is a *siman Brocho* (sign of blessing). It is customary to look into the *"kos"* (wine cup) when making *Havdalah*.

9. Whether one stands or sits while making *Havdalah* is *"tolui b'Minhag"* (depends on one's custom). However, the drinking of the cup should be done while sitting.

10. While making *Havdalah* one should:

(a) hold the wine cup in his right hand.

(b) transfer the cup to his left hand when reciting the *Brochos* on the *"besomim"* (spices) and on the *"ner"* (candle); and then

(c) transfer the cup back to his right hand for the *Brocho* of *Havdalah*.

11. If the *besomim* aren't readily available, one does not have to look for them.

One should make sure that the *besomim* are fresh and pleasant smelling for this *Mitzvah*.

Some people use the leaves of the *Hadas* (myrtle) on the *Lulav* for *besomim*, provided of course, that they are still sweet smelling.

12. One cannot be *"motzee"* other people with the *Brocho* on the *besomim* unless he himself smells the *besomim* as well.

13. When making the *Brocho*, *"Borai Me'Oray Ha-aish"* on the *"ner,"* one is supposed to look at one's nails and palm at the same time. That is why we bend our fingers onto our palm when reciting that *Brocho*.

One is supposed to hold the fingers in such a position so that they cover the thumb. Afterwards, we turn the hand the other way and again look at our nails.

blessings in the 19 that refer to guilt, want, tribulation or sorrow should be omitted on the *Shabbos* so as not to mar the worshipper's joy and serenity on the Day of Rest. *(Halochos Ketanos)*.

In the days of Rav, founder of the Talmudical Academy of Sura, King Yuzdegar of Persia issued a decree prohibiting the reading of the Shema in the Synagogues. He sent out spies to make sure that the *Shema* was not read during *Shacharis*. The sages of that generation therefore decided to insert the first and last line of the *Shema* in the *Kedusha* on *Shabbos* and *Yom Tov* where they would not be conspicuous, but would still keep the *Shema* from being forgotten by the young. In response to our fervent prayers, the King's law was annulled by a Higher Power for King Yuzdegar was killed by a snake which had made its way into his regal bedchamber. The sages then decided that this short form of the *Shema* should be retained in the *Kedusha* as an everlasting memorial of the miraculous turn of events which enabled the Jews of Persia to recite the *Shema* once again openly and unafraid. *(Bais Yosef*, Ch. 423 in the name of the *Gaonim)*.

14. The only time one can make this *Brocho* is when he is close enough to see and recognize a coin from the light of the fire.

15. Those who are *yotzai* with another person's *Havdalah* should also be *yotzai* with his *Brochos* on the *besomim* and the candle. (In other words, they should not say the *Brochos* by themselves.)

16. If one cannot find the *Havdalah* candle, one can still make Havdalah without it. One should either use a candle made like a torch (with at least two wicks) or else two candles held together, forming one flame. (It is best to close the lights so as to get the best use from the flame.)

17. If there is only one candle available, one can be *yotzai* with that.

18. If one had neither the *besomim* nor the *ner* at the time he made *Havdalah,* but found them later that night, he may make the *Brocho* at that time. Once the night is over, he can no longer make these *Brochos.*

The reason for the use of the *besomim* at the close of the *Shabbos* is that we no longer have the *"neshoma yesaira"* (additional soul) that we had on *Shabbos.* The smelling of the *besomim* is intended to dispel the sadness resulting from this loss.

19. A blind person does not make the *Brocho "Borei Me'Oray Haaish"* and cannot be *"motzee"* other people with this *Brocho.* However, he can be *"motzee"* others with the rest of *Havdalah.*

20. A lantern that is completely covered by glass cannot be used for *Havdalah.* If the flame can be seen clearly through an opening at the top, then it may be used.

21. If one has absolutely no candles for *Havdalah,* he may use an electric light, preferably a non-frosted one. A *Rav* should be consulted as

---

The *Levush* (291) maintains that the eating of three meals on *Shabbos* is not merely a Rabbinical precept, but a Scriptural command, for it is written in the Talmud: "The word 'today' occurs three times in the biblical verse (*Shemos* 16:25) regarding the partaking of food on the *Shabbos*, viz, "And Moshe said: 'Eat this (the manna) *today;* for *today* is a *Shabbos* unto the L-rd; *today* you shall not find it in the field' (*Shabbos* 117b). This message is taken to imply that at least three meals must be eaten on the *Shabbos.*

Rabbi Yehuda Hanasi once invited the Roman emperor Antonius to a meal on *Shabbos.* Food was served and the emperor thought it delicious. Another time, they dined together on a weekday. "How is it," asked Antonius, "that the other meal I ate with you tasted so much better than this, even though that was cold and this is hot?"

"This one lacks spice!" explained Rabbi Yehuda.

Astonished, the emperor inquired, "Is there any condiment that the emperor's kitchen cannot supply?"

"Yes" replied Rabbi Yehuda, "Its name is *Shabbos.*" (*Shabbos* 119a)

to whether a *Brocho* is permitted in this case.

22. After the person making *Havdalah* drinks from the cup, he spills off some wine with which he extinguishes the flame of the *Havdalah* candle.

23. One should drink a *reviyis* of the wine so that there is no doubt about the need for saying a *"Brocho Ach'ronah."*

24. If, by mistake, one ate before making *Havdalah*, he may still make *Havdalah* afterwards.

If he is in the middle of a meal, he should stop eating in order to recite the *Havdalah*. He may then resume the meal without having to wash again.

25. If one is in the middle of *Shalosh Seudos*, he need not stop to make *Havdalah*. He may continue the meal, say *"Birchas Ha'mazon"* with *"R'tzai,"* *daven Ma'ariv*, and then make *Havdalah*. If, however, he was in the midst of drinking or eating a snack and it was close to nightfall, he must stop eating.

26. A woman who forgot to say *"Atoh Chonantanu,"* in the *Shmoneh Esrei* of *Ma'ariv*, or did not daven, should say *"Baruch Hamavdil Bain Kodesh L'Chol"* before she does any *"melochoh"* (work). If *Yom Tov* follows *Shabbos*, and a woman wishes to cook for *Yom Tov*, she should say *"Baruch Hamavdil Bain Kodesh L'Kodesh."*

Women should be cautioned not to eat before *Havdalah*. This also applies to the *Havdalah* in the *Yom Tov Kiddush*.

27. If one cannot make *Havdalah* on *Motzai Shabbos*, he has time to do so up to three days later (ending Tuesday at sundown); he should, of

---

Reb Nechemia Alter recollected: "I once travelled to Piltz on a Thursday evening to spend *Shabbos* there at the home of Reb Pintchi. After we had eaten supper together, the *Tzaddik* favored me with a wealth of expositions and insights on passages in the Torah, and it was clear that he was in a most joyful frame of mind. When I later went to bed, I overheard my host walking up and down in the next room, praying: 'Master of the Universe. The kugel that my wife is now cooking in honor of the holy day— please make it come out tasty, for I have a very special guest for *Shabbos*.

And when the holy day comes in, grant me that its sanctity should permeate my body, and my house and the food prepared in its honor. And please give the food the flavor of the sanctity of *Shabbos*.'" This then was the prayer of Reb Pintchi of Piltz on a Thursday night.

"Remember the Shabbos day to make it holy." (Shemos 20:8)

Chazal—"Remember the Shabbos day to make it holy"—Remember the Shabbos on Sunday by saying, "This thing I will leave for Shabbos." (Mechilta)

course, make it as soon as possible. However, besomim and Ner are used only on Motzai Shabbos.

Following Yom Tov, he has only one day to make Havdalah.

28. If one is going to eat a Seuda following Havdalah:

(a) He should not put out the Challah (or bread) before making Havdalah.

(b) If he did put it out, it should be covered till after Havdalah.

(c) If he will drink wine in this meal, he does not have to make a Brocho Ach'ronah following the Havdalah, and does not have to make a "Borai Pri Hagofen" if he drinks wine during the meal.

(d) If one does not intend to have wine during the meal, then he must be sure to say a Brocho Ach'ronah following the wine of Havdalah. If he started the Seuda, however, without saying the Brocho Ach'ronah, he will be yotzai with the Birchas Hamazon.

(e) One should be certain to make a Brocho Ach'ronah if there is a long interruption between the Havdalah and the Seuda of the "Melave Malka."

29. Following Havdalah, the table furnishings should be set in preparation for the "Melave Malka," the meal after Shabbos marking the symbolic departure of the "Shabbos queen."

During this meal, which is considered "Seudas Dovid HaMelech," we also sing songs about Eliyahu HaNavi. Since he was not able to come on Shabbos, we hope that he will come on Motzai Shabbos and bring us news of the coming of the Moshiach.

Rav Chiya bar Abba related, "I was once invited to a wealthy man's home in Ludkya. A table was carried in by 32 people who supported it with 16 poles. Heaped upon it were all imaginable types of delicacies. A child, who had been employed by the master of the house specifically for this purpose, sat in the center of the table and proclaimed, "Hashem's is the earth and its fullness." (Tehillim 24:1).

The master of the house used this means to remind himself that his wealth was not his own, but Hashem's, so that he should not become conceited."

Rav Chiya continued to relate, "I then said to him, 'My son, how do you deserve such riches?' He replied, 'I used to be a butcher. Whenever I saw a particularly nice animal, I set it aside for Shabbos.' I said to him, 'It is not without a reason that you have become so rich. Your merit is great.'" (Shabbos 119a)

"It was said of Shamai that all his days he ate for the honor of the Shabbos. If he found a nice animal he would say during the week, "This is for Shabbos." (Betza 16a)

"The Shabbos day has been compared to a precious pearl which was stored by Hashem in

MELACHOS

(THE 39 FORBIDDEN CATEGORIES OF WORK (MELACHA) ON SHABBOS)

(Gezeros (special rabbinic prohibitions) are included in some categories.)

NOTE: Since the following Melachos are so complicated and involved, we have given only a brief overview of them. One should learn all the Halachos of Shabbos in depth to ensure their proper observance.

1. "Ploughing"—Any activity which improves or prepares the soil for plant growth. Examples: ploughing, digging, fertilizing or cultivating the soil, clearing stones from the soil.

2. "Sowing"—Any activity causing or promoting a plant to grow. Examples: placing seeds in the soil, pruning or grafting plants; watering the lawn or plants, weeding. This includes washing one's hands over growing plants or grass.

3. "Reaping"—Any activity severing a plant from its normal place of growth. Examples: plucking flowers from the ground, picking fruit or berries from trees or bushes; plucking twigs or leaves from shrubs.

Gezeros include: climbing a tree.

4. "Sheaf-making"—Any activity by which natural products that grow from the ground are gathered together in the place where they grow. Examples: piling fruit into a heap for storage; bundling sheaves of wheat together, stringing or pressing fruit together.

5. "Threshing"—Any activity by which a natural, organic product

His treasures until He revealed it to His children, the Bnai Yisroel.

The glow of this precious pearl illuminates both man and the grey days of the rest of the week. The whole week is nothing more than an anticipation of the Shabbos." (Sefer Kuzari)

One who continues his weekday activities well into Shabbos eve, content with the fact that he is observing the Shabbos day, is like a fellow who believes that there is a difference between taking poison all day long and drinking it down in a few minutes. Just as it takes only a little poison to kill a

man, it takes only a moment of Shabbos violation to cut his soul off from the land of eternal life. (Nidchei Yisroel, Chofetz Chayim)

THE FARMER WHO COULDN'T RESIST

A farmer used to bring his grain to a certain Jewish dealer. They made an arrangement for recording the number of sacks sold. Each time a sack was weighed, the dealer would make a line on the wall. At the end, they would count up the lines and would know how many sacks the farmer had brought.

(solid or liquid) is separated from its natural enclosure. Examples: shelling nuts (except for immediate consumption); squeezing or pressing fruits for juice; milking a cow.

6-8. "Winnowing," "Selecting," "Sifting"—Those activities by which a mixture is improved by removing its less desirable parts. Examples: sifting flour, straining liquids to remove dirt or waste; sorting out good fruit from a heap containing both good and rotten fruit (except if sorting is done by hand for immediate consumption).

9. "Grinding"—Any activity by which a natural solid is divided into small pieces in order to make better use of it. Examples: milling corn; crushing substances in a mortar; grating or dicing vegetables (except for immediate consumption).

Gezeros include: taking medicine (except in cases of acute pain or actual illness).

10. "Kneading"—Activities by which small particles are combined by means of a liquid to form a dough or paste. Examples: kneading; mixing cement.

11. "Baking"—Any activity by which a substance is improved for consumption by a change of its state through the application of heat. Examples: cooking; baking; roasting; stirring while on a flame, boiling food.

Note: The prohibition of cooking does not limit us to eat only cold food on *Shabbos*. We may use the stove when it is prepared before *Shabbos* in such a way that the actual burners are covered (usually by means of a tin sheet) to make it recognizable that one is not allowed to regulate the

After a while, the farmer decided that this system was dangerous, since the dealer could erase one of the lines and cheat him out of a sack. He, therefore, suggested a different arrangement. For every sack weighed, the dealer would put a coin of small value in a plate. At the conclusion, they would count the coins to determine how many sacks must be paid for.

They started using this new system. But as the farmer saw the pile of coins growing, he could not resist temptation. When he saw that the dealer wasn't looking, he sneaked a coin from the plate and quickly put it into his pocket.

Naturally, the dealer later paid him according to the number of the coins in the plate. By sneaking a few coins from the plate, the farmer had cheated himself out of a lot of money.

So it is with anyone who tries to cheat the *Shabbos*. He is following the example of that "smart" farmer. We depend on the kindness of *Hashem* to send us His blessing and He has commanded us in his Torah, "Six days shall you labor and do all of your work and the seventh day you shall rest." Our sages have explained that the blessings for the entire week flow from

heat on *Shabbos*. Hot cooked food and an urn of hot water can then be placed on the stove before *Shabbos* begins, and can be kept warm during *Shabbos* until needed.

12. "Shearing"—Any activity that severs what grows on the outer covering of a human or animal. Examples: shearing wool; cutting hair or fingernails; plucking feathers.

Gezeros include: combing hair with a hard brush (highly probable that hair would be removed.)

13. "Bleaching"—Any activity by which a garment or cloth is freed from dirt or stains. Examples: bleaching or soaking clothes; removing stains from clothes by water or other means.

14. "Combing Raw Materials"—Any activity by which a compact raw material is beat into separate fibers. Examples: combing raw wool; beating flax stalks into fibers.

15. "Dyeing"—Any activity which changes an object's existing color. Examples: painting; dyeing clothes; dissolving colors in water.

16. "Spinning"—Any activity by which thread is formed from fibers. Examples: spinning thread; making felt; making rope.

17-19. "Weaving Operations"—Those activities involved in the whole range of weaving technique from start to finish. Examples: knitting; weaving; embroidering; braiding; basket-weaving.

20. "Separating into threads"—Any activity by which interwoven threads or strands are separated. Examples: unraveling any part of a knitted garment.

21. "Tying a knot"—Any activity by which a permanent type of knot or

the *Shabbos*. If he cheats the *Shabbos* and takes off hours from its beginning and its end, he is only cheating himself for he is only cutting down the influence of the *Shabbos* on his entire week.

"*Jerusalem was destroyed only because of the profanation of the* Shabbos." (Shabbos 119b)

"*G-d said to the Jews, 'My sons, borrow for me and make holy the holiness of the day and trust in me and I will pay you back!'* (Betza 15b)

"*The* Shabbos *is Hashem's most precious gift to His beloved people.*

A Jew who violates it is like a bride who returns her wedding ring and announces that the shidduch *(match) no longer exists.*" (Hundred Mesholim of the Chofetz Chayim)

A man was riding his coach down a long winding road one day when he passed a man trudging along. The man was old, and he grunted under the load of an obviously heavy package. "Would you like a lift?" asked the rider. The old man readily agreed and entered the coach. He took a seat, yet he did not remove the heavy package

lasting connection between two objects is brought into being. Examples: tying a permanent knot; making twine.

22. "Untying a knot"—Any activity by which a permanent type of knot is untied. Examples: untying a permanent knot; removing strands of twine. (It is, however, permissible to tie and untie a bow, since a bow is intended merely as a temporary connection.)

23. "Sewing"—Any activity that permanently joins together the surfaces of two materials by means of a third substance. Examples: sewing fabrics together; pasting.

24. "Tearing"—Any activity that tears joined materials apart to facilitate re-joining. Examples: tearing or removing stitches for purposes of repairing.

25. "Trapping"—Any activity that so restricts the movement of a non-domesticated creature that it comes under the control of a human. Examples: fishing; hunting; catching a bird or insect in a net.

26. "Slaughtering"—Any activity which causes loss of life or blood to a living creature. Examples: killing an animal, bird, insect, or fish, taking a blood specimen.

27. "Skinning"—Any activity by which the skin of a dead animal is separated from its flesh. Examples: skinning an animal, peeling layers of animal hide for parchment.

28. "Tanning"—Any activity by which rawhide is made more usable or durable. Examples: all parts of the tanning process.

29. "Scraping"—Any activity that smoothes roughness from the surface of a material by means of grinding, polishing, etc. Examples: sanding, plastering, using solid soap.

from his back. After observing the old man for a while, the rider's curiosity got the better of him. He turned to the old man and asked, "Why don't you remove the package from your back and put it down?"

The old man shook his head. "You were nice enough to give me a lift. How can I have the nerve to impede your trip by placing such a heavy burden in your coach?"

"Don't worry" responded the rider. "The horse will be bearing the weight of the burden whether you place it on your back or the horse's. You may as well make matters easier for yourself and place it directly on the horse."

Likewise, we should have enough faith in the power of *Hashem* to trust His ability to bear the burden of our troubles during the *Shabbos*. After all, it is He who carries us through every other day of the week. Therefore, there is no need to fret that if one observes the *Shabbos* he will suffer great losses. In the long run, the *Shomer Shabbos* has only to gain from his *Emunas Hashem*.

(*Rosh Hashono* 26b)

30. "Marking out"—Any activity that marks lines on a surface in preparation for cutting or writing. Examples: marking a line to guide a saw; marking a line to guide a margin in writing *mezuzos*.

31. "Cutting to Shape"—Any activity by which the size or shape of an object is altered to one more suitable for human use. Examples: cutting or tearing any material to a definite shape or pattern; sawing lumber; sharpening a pencil; cutting out a newspaper paragraph.

32. "Writing"—Any activity that makes lasting and meaningful figures on a surface. Examples: writing; drawing, painting, typing, embroidering letters on a cloth.

Gezeros include: Drawing with a finger on a moist windowpane; tracing patterns in the sand; doing anything that is usually accompanied by writing or which might lead to writing.

33. "Erasing"—Any activity whose effect is the production of a clean surface for writing. Examples: Any erasing of writing whereby space is gained for new writing.

34. "Building"—Those activities connected with constructing, repairing, or erecting a usable structure or shelter. Examples: All building operations (hanging a door, installing a window pane, nailing wall panelling together, leveling the ground for building, pitching a tent, etc.).

Gezeros include: opening an umbrella.

35. "Demolishing"—Those activities that prepare space for building operations by demolishing an existing building or structure. Examples: tearing down a dwelling to make room for a new one; removing a window pane to prepare for its replacement.

The *Gaon* **Rabbi Hillel**, the son-in-law of Rav Chaim of Volozhen, was seen on *Shabbos* evening carrying a lamp through the town of Horodna. The people of the town were shocked. The *Gaon* was violating the *Shabbos* by carrying a burning lamp in the street! Soon a crowd gathered and they followed the *Gaon* until he came to a house belonging to a poor family. The *Gaon* entered the house and later exited without the lamp.

"Master!" the people exclaimed. "Why were you carrying a lamp on *Shabbos?*"

The *Gaon* replied: "In this house lives a person who is dangerously ill. The candle inside the house had burned up and the entire house was shrouded in darkness. As a result, those inside could not take proper care of the ill person. The family sent a messenger to me to ask what could be done. To emphasize the *Halacha*, I took a lamp and brought it to their house on *Shabbos*. For it is a *Mitzvah* to violate the laws of the *Shabbos* to help save the life of a dangerously ill person."

"Keeping the Shabbos is tantamount to keeping the whole Torah." (Pesikta)

36. "Kindling a Fire"—Any activity which initiates or prolongs a flame or hot glow (or similar light and heat-producing processes). Examples: lighting a fire, regulating a flame by turning it up, smoking a cigarette, switching on an electrical appliance; driving a car.

37. "Extinguishing a fire"—Any activity which terminates or diminishes a flame or hot glow, if for some productive purpose. Example: putting out a candle to improve the wick.

38. "The final hammer-blow"—Any activity that puts the final touches upon, or improves or repairs, an article. Examples: removing hanging threads from a new suit, repairing a clock or other appliance.

39. "Carrying"—Any activity by which an object is transferred from an enclosed "private domain" *(r'shus hayachid)* to a "public domain" *(r'shus harabim)* or vice versa. Also moving any object a distance of four cubits (about seven feet) within a "public domain." "Private domain" means, for this purpose, any enclosed space not less than four handbreadths (about fifteen inches) square, bounded by walls not less than ten handbreadths (about three feet) high. The usual form of this "domain" is a house, enclosed garden, etc. "Public domain" means a street, road or square frequented by the public, unroofed, open at both ends, and having a width of at least sixteen cubits (about twenty-eight feet). Examples: carrying objects from one "domain" to the other, or from point to point within the "public domain." (One may, however, carry as much as one wants within a "private domain.")

THE ANGUISH OF SHABBOS

It is Shabbos, *when one may not cry out; healing will come soon* (Shabbos 12a).

Reb Hillel of Paritsh used to spend a substantial part of every year traveling through the towns of the southern parts of Russia in order to give instruction in the applied ethics of *Chassidus,* and to arouse people to repentance wherever the need arose.

He once arrived in a town where the Jewish tavern keepers kept their businesses open on *Shabbos.* Reb Hillel was shocked to hear this, and invited them all to meet him. When he had explained to them what a serious matter this was they all undertook to cooperate, though on one condition: that he persuade a certain wealthy tavern keeper, whose tavern was the biggest in town, to do likewise; for otherwise they would not be able to survive competition with him. The *tzaddik* thereupon sent for that man— once, twice, three times—but he ignored the invitation. Reb Hillel stayed on in the town for the Shabbos. In the morning the wealthy tavern keeper suddenly suffered increasingly severe stomach pains, and his wife, fearing that they were brought on by the disrespect her husband had shown the *tzaddik,* hastened to seek him out so that he should intercede on his behalf. While Reb Hillel was at the *Shabbos*

OTHER LAWS OF "CARRYING":

A Karmelis is neither a public nor a private domain and it is at least four *tefachim* by four *tefachim*. It is rabbinically prohibited to either carry in it, or from this domain into another, or from another domain into it.

One cannot carry from one private domain to another. In the case of adjoining private domains an *Eruv Chatzeros* may be made. This *eruv* is made by taking some food (preferably a complete *Matzoh*) before the *Shabbos*, "transferring" it to the possession of all "partners" in the common courtyard and then putting it in one of the private places. This place is thus given a symbolic status of "mixed ownership."

Note: All of the above *Melachos* cannot be done through a gentile, except in special circumstances, when a *Rav* should be consulted.

midday meal surrounded by a large company of *Chassidim*, she burst into the room, and with tears in her eyes implored the rebbe to give her husband his blessing for a speedy recovery.

The *tzaddik* remained silent.

His *chassidim* were dismayed: "Rebbe, at least give the blessing that is traditional in such cases on the holy day—'It is *Shabbos*, when one may not cry out; healing will come soon!'

But the *tzaddik* said not a word.

The woman left bitterly disappointed, and her husband's pains grew worse.

On *Motzai Shabbos*, when night fell and the holy day had passed, the *tzaddik* was discoursing with his *chassidim* at a table on which stood a samovar, in fulfillment of the Talmudic dictum: "Hot beverages at the close of *Shabbos* serve as a cure." In ran the same woman, weeping and wailing, begging the *tzaddik* to have pity on her husband and to pray for him.

Reb Hillel simply said: 'It is *Shabbos*, when one may not cry out; healing will come soon' ...

The *chassidim* were amazed. On *Shabbos* itself the *tzaddik* had said nothing—and now, when the holy day was over, he said these words?!

The *tzaddik* continued: "It is *Shabbos* when one may not cry out. If *Shabbos* itself will no longer have cause to cry out against him, then healing will come soon. Go ahead and tell him that if he gives a solemn pledge in the presence of three witnesses that he will close his business on *Shabbos*, then he will be cured."

Three *chassidim* hastened to his bedside to convey the rebbe's words—and he earnestly gave his word of honor.

His illness passed, and the sanctity of *Shabbos* was upheld in that town.

"To know I am G-d who made you holy." G-d said to Moshe, "I have a great present in the treasure house. Its name is Shabbos. *When you give it to the Jews, let them know who gave it to them."* (Shabbos 19)

"If someone keeps the Shabbos *the right way, all his sins will be forgiven."* (Shabbos 118b)

THE HAVDALAH

During the *Shabbos*, man is given an additional soul, the *Neshama Yesera*, which adds "spice" to his life throughout the *Shabbos* day. When the *Shabbos* ends and this 'additional soul' leaves us, we inhale the aroma of spices to make up for this loss. On *Shabbos* nights falling on a festival, the spices are omitted since the joy of the incoming festivals is at least the equivalent of the enjoyment we get from inhaling the aroma of the fragrant spices. (*Abudraham:* see *Tosfos Pesachim* 102b, sub voce, *Rav*)

The reason why we pronounce the *Brocho* over fire after the conclusion of *Shabbos,* is because it was at the end of the first *Shabbos* that man first learned how to kindle a fire. The Jerusalem Talmud records the following legend: "When Adam saw the sun go down for the first time, leaving all of creation in ever-deepening darkness, his heart was filled with terror. Thereupon, G-d took pity on him and gave him the intelligence to take two stones—the name of one was Darkness and the name of the other was Shadow of Death—and to rub them against each other. In this manner,

man first discovered fire. When he saw the flame he had produced, on *Motzei Shabbos* Adam exclaimed with gratitude: "Blessed be He, the Creator of Light!" *(Kol Bo)*

On *Shabbos* night at the *Melava Malka* meal, it is customary to chant, "This is the meal of David our King." In this way, we recall the feast King David would hold at the end of each *Shabbos* in gratitude for having been preserved in life. According to the Rabbis (*Shabbos* 30a), G-d had informed David he would die on a *Shabbos*. Hence he was grateful for having lived through the *Shabbos*.

The hymn of "*Eliyahu Hanavi*" is sung on *Shabbos* night at the *Melava Malka* because *Eliyahu* will not come on Friday, so as not to disturb Israel's preparations for the *Shabbos*. The hour when the *Shabbos* departs, on the other hand, is considered the proper time for saying a prayer that *Eliyahu Hanavi* should come to us and bring us good things. (*Tur*). Also the *Medrash* states that every *Shabbos* night, *Eliyahu* enters Paradise, sits down beneath the Tree of Life, and records the merits of the Jews who observed the *Shabbos*. (Rabbi Jacob Molin, the *MaHaril*.)

ראש חודש
Rosh Chodesh

ROSH CHODESH—INTRODUCTION

"Also in the day of your gladness and in your appointed seasons, and in your New Moons shall you blow the trumpets." (Bamidbar 10:10)

On the fourth day of Creation, Hashem created the two great luminous bodies, the sun and the moon. They enable us to establish day and night, and to count months and years.

The Jewish calendar (Luach) is a lunar calendar, based on the monthly revolutions of the moon around the earth. The day on which the New Moon appears (or occasionally the following day) is designated as Rosh Chodesh *(the beginning of the lunar month).*

This half-holiday is observed at the beginning of every Hebrew month, as commanded in the Torah. During the times of the Temple, it was celebrated as a full holiday. Today it is celebrated by having additional prayers and Torah readings.

THE CALENDAR

The basic difference between our Hebrew calendar and the civil calendar in everyday use is that the latter is based on the movements of

ROSH CHODESH

THE *MOLAD*

In old times, the *Molad* of *Rosh Chodesh* (appearance of the New Moon) would be announced by the *Beis Din* (Court) on the basis of testimony from two witnesses who said that they had seen the New Moon. In those days, *Rosh Chodesh* was a *Yom Tov* marked by special singing by the *Leviyim* for the additional *Korban* (sacrifice) brought by the *Kohanim* in the *Bais Hamikdosh.* Today, in place of the "additional offering" on *Rosh Chodesh*, we add *Tefillas Mussaf* for *Rosh Chodesh.*

Originally the new moon was calculated according to witnesses until the time of Hillel HaNasi II.

Hillel HaNasi saw the many difficulties involved in waiting for the appearance of witnesses in order to declare *Rosh Chodesh.* Judea was under frequent foreign rule by Greeks, Romans, and others, who tried to interfere with the declaration of *Rosh Chodesh.* In this manner, they would also prevent the Jews from celebrating their *Yomim Tovim.* Therefore, Hillel HaNasi II established thereafter a calendar which would be used by the Jews.

The significance of *Rosh Chodesh* lies in the fact that it is the foundation

51

the sun and is therefore called a solar calendar. Our Hebrew calendar, on the other hand, is based on the movements of the moon and is therefore a lunar calendar.

A solar year consists of 365 days because it takes the earth 365 days to revolve around the sun. But the moon makes its trip around the earth in 29½ days. In an entire year there are 12 trips equalling 354 days, eleven days less than the earth takes to travel around the sun.

This eleven-day difference, then, makes each day in our lunar calendar come out eleven days earlier than it did the year before.

In order to balance our Hebrew calendar against the civil year, a leap year occurs every two or three years, consisting of one additional month of thirty days.

The order in which a leap year occurs in a cycle of 19 years is as follows: 1 2 (3) 4 5 (6) 7 (8) 9 10 (11) 12 13 (14) 15 16 (17) 18 (19). The years in parentheses are leap years. The ordinary Jewish year (that is, when there is no leap year) contain 354 days. During a leap year there are 384 days because of the additional month, with the extra month of *Adar*.

We can tell when the next leap year will occur by determining what the present Jewish year is, and then dividing it by nineteen. Thus, the present year 5741 divided by 19 equals 302, plus a remainder of 3, which means that during the past 5741 years, there have been 302 full cycles of 19 years each, plus 3 remaining years.

This remainder of 3 shows us to be at the third year in the 19 year cycle. Referring again to the above listing of the cycle, we can see that this third year is a leap year. The next two years will be ordinary years

for all the festivals of Israel. The festivals, in turn, are what give a special *Kedusha* (sanctity) to *Bnai Yisroel*, setting them apart from the other nations of the world.

Our Sages have always likened the Jewish people to the moon. It is symbolic of the history of the Jews throughout the ages. Just as the moon is small and insignificant-looking, (at the beginning of the month) so the Jewish people as a nation are at present small, and their influence upon the world sometimes seems insignificant. But just as the moon, day after day, reveals more of itself to us, so that at the middle of the month we see it in its fullness and its beauty, so too, the Jewish religion from day to day reveals more of itself and becomes better understood by the other nations.

Just as the moon is sometimes eclipsed and cannot be seen, so the Jewish people sometimes seem isolated from the mainstream of history. But, just as the moon shines brightly the following night, so the Jewish people continuously reappear on the world scene, and they can never be destroyed.

In the days when the *Beis Din* waited for the appearance of the two

but the third year, (No. 6) will again be a leap year—in 5744.

Our Hebrew months are as follows:

Spring	Summer	Fall	Winter
Nisan	Tammuz	Tishrei	Teves
Iyar	Av	Cheshvan	Shvat
Sivan	Elul	Kislev	Adar

The Jewish day, as in the civil calendar, is twenty-four hours in length, but it begins at sundown instead of at midnight (as in the civil calendar). The days of the week (other than *Shabbos*, the seventh day) have no special names (as they do in the civil calendar) but are referred to by number. Thus, Sunday is the first day, Monday, the second day, and so forth. The reason is that all the days of the week revolve around *Shabbos*.

HILCHOS ROSH CHODESH AND ITS TEFILLAH:

(All these *Halachos* pertain to both days of *Rosh Chodesh* equally.)

1. In *Shmoneh Esrei* one adds *Yaale V'Yovo* before "*V'Sechezenoh.*"

2. During *Ma'ariv*, if one forgot *Yaale V'Yovo*, one does not repeat the *Shmoneh Esrei*. In fact, once one mentions "*Hashem*" in the *Brocho*, "*Ha'Machazir Sh'Cheenoso L'Tzeeyon*," one should continue, leaving out the *Yaale V'Yovo*. (This *Halacha* regarding *Yaale V'Yovo* at night does not apply to *Tefillas Maariv* on *Yom Tov* or *Chol Hamoed*. Then, the *Shmoneh Esrei* must be repeated if *Yaale V'Yovo* was omitted.)

3. Regarding *Tefillas Shacharis* or *Mincha*:

(a) If someone forgot to say *Yaale V'Yovo* and has already finished the *Shmoneh Esrei*, he must repeat the entire *Shmoneh Esrei*.

witnesses who had seen the New Moon, it happened, occasionally, that the witnesses arrived late. Then the "additional-offering" for *Rosh Chodesh* would no longer be brought on that day, but on the following one. In such a case, the *Beis Din* declared that there were two days of *Rosh Chodesh*—the last day of the previous month and the first day of the new month.

Nowadays, although the calendar is calculated accurately, and we know when *Rosh Chodesh* is, the Rabbis nevertheless declared that certain months would have two days *Rosh Chodesh* and others only one day.

The Hebrew months are either "full" or "incomplete." A "full" month (1) consists of thirty days, and (2) has one day *Rosh Chodesh* except for *Cheshvan* and *Kislev* which are variable months. An "incomplete" month (like *Teves, Iyar, Tamuz*) (1) consists of 29 days, and (2) has two days *Rosh Chodesh*.

The *Shabbos* preceding *Rosh Chodesh* is the time when we "bless" the new month. The reason we have *Shabbos* "*M'vorchin*" (the *Shabbos* on which we bless the month) is to inform the public about the coming of the new "*Chodesh.*" This is done every month except before *Tishrei*.

(b) If one remembered before saying the name of *"Hashem"* in the *Brocho* of *V'Sechezenoh*, then he may go back to the beginning of *Yaale V'Yovo* and continue from there.

(c) If one did say *"Baruch Ata Hashem"* and in that second remembered that he didn't say *Yaale V'Yovo*, he must then say *"Lamdeini Chukechoh."* He then says *Yaale V'Yovo* and continues from there. He thus avoids saying a *Brocha L'vatala* (an unnecessary *Brocho).*

(d) If he had already completed the *Brocho*, he just adds *Yaale V'Yovo* before he says the *Modim.*

(e) If he had already started *Modim*, he goes back to *R'tzay*, and then he says *Yaale V'Yovo.*

(f) As long as the person has not yet completed the *"Y'hiyu L'Ratzon"* which is said before *"Oseh Shalom,"* he can go back to *R'tzay* and say *Yaale V'Yovo.* Once he has completed the last *"Y'hiyu L'Ratzon,"* he must repeat the entire *Shmoneh Esrei.*

(g) If one completed davening and is not sure whether or not he recited *Yaale V'Yovo*, he must repeat *Shmoneh Esrei*, but he repeats it with a *T'nai* (condition) that if he really did say *Yaale V'Yovo*, then this additional *Shmoneh Esrei* is a *Tefillas N'dovoh* (a voluntary gift) to Hashem. However, one should avoid needing a *Tefillas N'dovoh* if possible, since it requires special concentration.

(h) If the person knew it was *Rosh Chodesh* before he prayed, but the doubt of whether or not he said *Yaale V'Yovo* came about after the completion of the *Tefillah*, then he does not have to repeat the *Shmoneh Esrei.*

THE "IMPOSSIBLE" MISSION

Dovid tried to speed up his horse. "I guess he doesn't realize how important my mission is," he said to himself. "Imagine! The whole *Tzefas* (Safed) and *Tveria* (Tiberias) area is waiting for the message I'm bringing."

Dovid was one of the many messengers sent out by the *Sanhedrin* in *Yerushalayim* to all the provinces in Judea. *Rosh Chodesh* was established through the testimony of witnesses before the *Sanhedrin* (chief judicial body) and not through a calendar, as is done today. After these witnesses reported seeing the new moon, word had to be passed on throughout the land so that Jews would know when to celebrate the *Yomim Tovim* (holidays).

Dovid rode quickly, scarcely feeling the horse's hoofs striking the ground. His assigned province was far from *Yerushalayim.* Faster and faster he rode. He must get there in time or the Jews of *Tveria* would miscalculate the days until the holiday of *Pesach* on the 14th day of *Nissan.*

Those were the days of "horse" power—not engine power. A trip that would take a few hours today by car or bus, took several days by horseback then. But the second day, Dovid's horse stumbled, and would not go any further.

(i) A *Sh'liach Tzeebur* (chazan) who forgot to say *Yaale V'Yovo* in his quiet *Shmoneh Esrei* need not repeat the *Shmoneh Esrei* since he will be repeating it anyway in the *Chazoras HaShatz* (Repetition of the Amidah).

If a chazan forgets to say *Yaale V'Yovo* during the *Chazoras HaShatz,* he does not have to repeat it since we do not want to cause an additional delay for the congregation. For him, the special mention of *Rosh Chodesh* in *Mussaf* suffices. A *yochid* (individual) who must repeat *Shmoneh Esrei* should do so before *Mussaf.*

HALLEL ON ROSH CHODESH:

1. *Hallel* (special psalms of praise and thanksgiving to *Hashem)* is recited while standing.

2. Ashkenazim say *Hallel* on *Rosh Chodesh* with a *Brocho.* Since there is a question of whether an individual makes the *Brocho,* it is best to say *Hallel* with the *Tzeebur* (congregation). Therefore, if one comes to *Shul* just in time for the start of *Hallel,* it is best for him to say *Hallel* with the *tzeebur* and then say the rest of the prayers. In fact, one may stop in the middle of *P'sukei D'Zimrah* after *Boruch She'amar* to say *Hallel* with the congregation. In this case, one does not say the *Brochos* before or after *Hallel,* since he is *yotzai* (has fulfilled the *Mitzvah)* with the *Brocho Rishona* (first *Brocho)* that he just recited of *Boruch She'a-mar* and the *Brocho Ach'ronah* (closing *Brocho)* of *Yishtabach.*

The above applies only on *Rosh Chodesh.* However, on *Yom Tov,* where the *Hallel* requires a *Brocho Rishona* and *Brocho Ach'ronah,* one

"What do I do? If I'm late with this news, the Jews of *Tzefas* may be late in celebrating *Pesach.*" By now Dovid felt that there was no chance in the world that he would arrive on time with his message. By riding hard he could make it by nightfall. On foot, he would arrive too late.

Dovid felt terrible at the thought of having let down his fellow Jews who were depending on him. But how was he to go on? With a heavy heart, he started walking back in the direction from which he had come.

Dovid continued walking along the lonely road. Not a person was in sight. Suddenly, he heard someone scream-

ing, "Help! Help! I can't swim!"

Dovid ran in the direction of the screams and came to a small lake. Floundering in the water was a Roman soldier. Apparently, his speeding chariot had overturned along the road and he had been thrown into the water. Dovid took a quick look around to see what he could use to help the drowning man. He saw a long tree branch and pushed it into the water. Wading out into the lake, Dovid was able to reach the Roman soldier with the tip of the tree branch. By now, the soldier was bobbing up and down in the water. Dovid waited another second until the soldier came up for

should not recite *Hallel* in the midst of *P'sukei D'Zimrah.*

3. If a person prays alone, he may still say the *Brochos* before and after *Hallel.* However, *Sephardim* say it without a *Brocho. L'chatcheeloh* (if at all possible), it is best to have at least two other people present so that he may say *"Hodu La'Hashem Kee Tov. . ."* and have them respond. (The *Tzeebur* responds *"Hodu La'Hashem Kee Tov . . ."* after the *Chazan* says each of the four lines in *"Hodu La'Hashem . . ."*) However, if this is not possible, he can still say *Hodu.*

4. One is not allowed to interrupt the saying of *Hallel,* but one is permitted to answer *Omein.* The *dinim* of *Hallel* on *Rosh Chodesh* are similar to *P'sukei D'Zimrah,* where it is permissible to answer *Omein.*

(See *Hilchos Tefillah* for more details on *Hallel* of *Yom Tov* and *Chanuka,* except for *Chol Hamoed* and last days of *Pesach.* The dinim of interrupting *Hallel* for *Yom Tov* and *Chanuka* are like those of *Birchos Krias Shema.*)

5. *Hallel* must be recited in its proper order, from beginning to end. If someone comes into *Shul* while the congregation is in the midst of *Hallel,* he cannot simply continue saying it with the congregation and then go back to the beginning afterwards. He must start from the beginning of *Hallel,* and say it entirely in order, from beginning to end.

6. After *Hallel,* the *Chazan* recites the entire *Kaddish* with *Tiskabel,* because one thus completes the entire *Shacharis* prayer (except on *Chanuka* when there is no *Mussaf* and half *Kaddish* is said).

SPECIAL TEFILLOS ON ROSH CHODESH:

1. On *Rosh Chodesh,* four people are called up to the Torah.

---

breath, and he gave a strong thrust with the branch. It worked! The soldier grabbed hold of it and Dovid tugged at the other end.

After his wearying two-day ride, Dovid didn't think he would have the strength to pull the man out of the water, but somehow, with G-d's help, he did. As soon as he saw that the Roman soldier felt better, Dovid set out to return to *Yerushalayim.* Just as he started walking, he heard the man calling, "Young man, please wait. You didn't even give me a chance to thank you properly for saving my life. How can I repay you? Just name it."

Dovid thought for a moment and suddenly saw the two beautiful horses standing next to the overturned Roman chariot. "I want no monetary reward for myself, but perhaps you would be good enough to lend me one of your horses. My own horse went lame. I am on a very urgent mission to the people of *Tveria,* and I don't think I could make it in time if I were to continue on foot."

The Roman soldier was both surprised and impressed by this request. Turning to Dovid, he said, "My friend,

2. On *Rosh Chodesh*, in some places, *Borchi Nofshi* is said at the end of the *Tefillah*.

3. The *Tefillin* must be taken off before the *Mussaf Tefillah* of *Rosh Chodesh*. Since the *Mussaf* of *Rosh Chodesh* is like an *Os* (a sign from *Hashem*, similar to *Shabbos* and *Yom Tov*), we do not need another *Os* (such as *Tefillin*) during the *Mussaf* of *Rosh Chodesh*.

4. *Yaale V'Yovo* is recited in the *Birchas Hamazon* on *Rosh Chodesh*.

(a) If one forgot to say it, he does not have to repeat the *Birchas Hamazon*.

(b) If one remembered *Yaale V'Yovo* before he got up to *"Hashem"* in the *Brocho* of *"HaTov V'Ha'mayteev,"* then he can insert a special *Brocho*, *"Boruch Atoh . . . She'Noson Roshei Chodoshim L'Amo Yisroel L'Zeekoron."*

(c) Following *Shalosh Seudos* on *Shabbos Rosh Chodesh* one adds *Yaale V'Yovo* in the *Birchas Hamazon* even if one completes eating after *Shabbos* is over since one goes according to the time that he started eating (which was still *Shabbos Rosh Chodesh*).

KIDDUSH LEVANA (Blessing of the New Moon)

The custom of standing while reciting the *Brocho* over the New Moon started in olden times. The *Rosh Chodesh* would be announced by the Rabbis on the basis of testimony from two witnesses who had seen the New Moon. The Rabbis would make the announcement standing up; therefore we *bentsch Rosh Chodesh* standing on the the *Shabbos* before *Rosh Chodesh*, except by the month of *Tishrei*. The *Moled* is announced at this *Rosh Chodesh bentsching*. (*Magen Avraham* 417:1)

choose whichever horse you wish, and he'll be yours to keep."

Dovid felt grateful for this sudden good fortune. He thanked the soldier for his kindheartedness, chose one of the two fine horses, and set out to complete his mission.

Hashem's help frequently comes in a most surprising manner, especially for those who are on an errand to perform a *Mitzvah*. As Dovid was riding along, he lifted his eyes to *shomayim* (heaven) and said, *"Ribono Shel Olam,* I thank You for Your assistance."

By nightfall, Dovid reached *Tveria* and headed straight for the *Bais Med-* rash where he met with the elders of the town. Dovid felt very proud of himself as he said, "The New Moon was sighted two days ago in *Yerushalayim*. We hope the New Month will be a happy and a healthy one for *Klal Yisroel."*

It is best to say *Kiddush Levana* on Saturday night. Since the *Bais HaMikdosh* was destroyed on *Motzai Shabbos* and the *"shechina"* (Divine Presence) went into exile, it is proper to proclaim a message of hope at a time that recalls tragedy. In *Kiddush Levana* it says: "For in days to come, they (Israel) are also to be renewed like her (the moon)." Thus, at the

1. Men are obligated to say *Kiddush Levana*. Many people perform a *"Rekida"* (dance) in celebration of the New Moon.

2. *Kiddush Levana* should be recited at night, after the appearance of the stars.

3. It is best to recite the *Brocho* when the moon is shining brightly. If it is cloudy and the moon is not at all visible, it is not recited.

4. If one had already started the *Brocho* and then it became cloudy, he can continue. If he didn't start yet, and he feels the clouds will block out the moon, then it is best not to even start the *Brocho*. Discretion should be used.

5. A blind person should also say *Kiddush Levana*, since people around him are able to see the moon. It is best, however, for him to say it with someone else who should be *motzee* (include) him with the *Brocho*.

6. It is best to say it on *Motzai Shabbos* while one is still dressed in his *Shabbos* clothes.

7. If *Motzai Shabbos* will fall out after the tenth of the Hebrew month, one shouldn't wait until then to say *Kiddush Levana*, for one might then miss the opportunity altogether. One has only until the middle of the month (14½ days after the *Moled*) to say it.

8. Some are of the opinion that *Kiddush Levana* should not be recited before seven days have elapsed in the new month. However, some say that it is permissible to say it after the third day of the new month.

9. In the winter, when it is cloudy more frequently, it might be best to say it already after the third day of the month, especially when this is *Motzai Shabbos*.

same time of the day that the *Bais HaMikdosh* was destroyed, we announce the good news that Israel will be renewed as in the days of old.

It is customary to say, *"Dovid Melech Yisroel Chai V'Kayom"* (David, King of Israel, lives and endures) when blessing the New Moon. This reminds us of the promise that the throne of Dovid will be "established forever." Even though the moon is occasionally eclipsed, it still renews itself and spreads its light over the world. Similarly, the kingdom of Dovid will be restored and will endure forever.

After making the *Brocho* over the New Moon, we say *"Shalom Alei-* *chem."* This is to contrast the misfortune on our foes that we mention in the *Tefillah*, by wishing peace upon our fellow *"Bnai Yisroel."*

We conclude *Kiddush Levana* with *"Oleinu."* This *Tefillah* proclaims the unity of *Hashem*, and includes the words, *"Va'anachnu Kor'im U'Mishtachavim U'Modim Lifnei Melech Malchei Hamlochim. . . ."* (We kneel and bow before the Supreme King of Kings . . .) Thus, we declare that, unlike other peoples, who worship the sun or the moon, the Jewish people bless the New Moon but worship only *Hakadosh Boruch Hu* (the Holy One, Blessed is He).

58

10. The only times when we definitely say it after the tenth of the month are following *Yom Kippur* (tenth of *Tishrei*) and *Tisha B'Av*. If someone is in the midst of the week of mourning *(Shiva)*, then he can wait until after the *Shiva* to say it, but only if the *Shiva* is over by the tenth of the month. Otherwise, he should say it right away.

11. A person should not be *"Mekadesh Levana"* under a roof or indoors but one should go outside to greet the New Moon. But, if one said it while sitting or while indoors, then he is nonetheless *yotzai* (fulfilled the *Mitzvah).*

ROSH CHODESH—SIMILAR TO A YOM TOV:

1. One is not permitted to fast on *Rosh Chodesh.*

2. Many people try to enhance the *Yom Tov* of *Rosh Chodesh* by preparing a special *Seuda* or adding something special to the meal.

On *Rosh Hashana*, Hashem assigns each person a certain income. This income, however, is not affected by the money he spends to glorify the *Shabbos, Yom Tov* and *Rosh Chodesh.* In other words, if a person is going to earn $10,000 a year and will spend $1,000 extra for these "*Seudos*" throughout the year, then he will actually earn $11,000.

3. Some women refrain from doing specialized work on *Rosh Chodesh*, such as sewing.

Hashem gave the women *Rosh Chodesh* as a festival to recall the merit of Israel's women in the *midbar* (desert). When the men asked their wives to give them their gold earrings and trinkets to make the Golden Calf, the women refused to do so, for they didn't want to have any part in the making of the idol. The men took it forcibly.

4. Rosh Chodesh is also a "day of forgiveness" when we are pardoned for all the sins we have committed throughout the entire month. In the Mussaf service it is referred to as *"Z'man Kapara L'chol Toldosom,"* (a time of forgiveness throughout their generations).

ראש השנה

Rosh Hashono

ROSH HASHONO — INTRODUCTION

"Speak unto the children of Israel, saying: In the seventh month, on the first day of the month shall be a solemn rest unto you, a memorial proclaimed with the blast of horns, a holy convocation." (Vayikra 23:24)

The festival of Rosh Hashono marks the beginning of the Jewish New Year and is observed on the first and second days of the month of Tishrei. On Rosh Hashono we pray that every person will be inscribed in the Book of Life for the coming year. Amidst much prayer, the Shofar (ram's horn) is sounded to herald the beginning of the Ten Days of Penitence and to proclaim Hashem as the Master of the World. It should inspire us to pray for forgiveness and dedicate ourselves to G-d.

The actual meaning of Rosh Hashono is "head of the year." According to the teachings of Judaism, it is the "nerve center" of the year. From

THE SHOFAR

Rabbeinu Saadya Gaon wrote that there are ten reasons why *Hashem* commanded us to blow the *Shofar* on *Rosh Hashono*. One reason is that *Rosh Hashono* commemorates the creation of the world. Just as kings have trumpets and horns blown on the anniversary of their coronation, so, too, we blow the *Shofar* on *Rosh Hashono* to commemorate and accept the kingship of the Creator.

The blowing of the ram's horn also announces the beginning of the ten days of *Teshuva*, which commence with *Rosh Hashono* and end with *Yom Kippur*. It reminds the people to repent during these most important ten days.

A third reason is to remind us of the time when the Jews accepted the Torah on Mt. Sinai. At that time, the

sound of the *Shofar* was heard. We blow the *Shofar* in order to show that we wait to accept the Torah, just as our forefathers did when they said, "We will obey and listen" (*Shemos* 27:4)

Because the purpose of the *Shofar* is to inspire us to adopt humility and repentance, it is not elaborately decorated. In fact, if decorations and ornaments pierce the sides of the horn completely, it becomes useless. Perhaps this can serve as a reminder to us of the importance of simplicity and humility.

"Ba'Chatzotzros V'Kol Shofar Hariyu Lifney Hamelech Hashem." "With trumpets and the sound of the horn, make a joyful noise before *Hashem*." (*Tehillim* 98:4)

A king once went hunting in the

it flow the decisions which mold our thoughts and determine our actions for the twelve months to come. Therefore, we ought not to let these two days pass without mustering all our spiritual resources for the lofty task of purifying and enobling our soul.

HILCHOS ROSH HASHONO

HILCHOS EREV ROSH HASHONO

1. We start blowing the *Shofar* (ram's horn) a month before *Rosh Hashono*, on the first day of the month of *Elul*.

2. We also start saying *"L'Dovid Hashem Ori V'Yishee"* following the *Shacharis* and *Ma'ariv* of that same day. (Some say it after *Mincha* instead of *Ma'ariv*.) It is part of the daily *Tefillah* (prayer service) until after *Shemini Atzeres*.

3. *Selichos* are special *Tefillos* that are recited before *Shacharis* during the week before *Rosh Hashono*, and during the *Aseres Yemei Teshuva* (the 10 days of repentance from *Rosh Hashono* to *Yom Kippur*). *Selichos*, according to *Ashkenazic* custom, are recited from early Sunday morning (beginning at midnight) before *Rosh Hashono* and should be said for at least 4 days. Therefore, if *Rosh Hashono* falls out on Monday or Tuesday, *Selichos* are started on Sunday of the week before.

woods. As he entered deep into the forest, he lost his way and could not find the road back to his palace. Meeting some farmers, he asked directions to the city, but they were unable to help him because they had never been there. Eventually, he met a well-informed person who knew the way and gave him detailed instructions. The man found favor in the eyes of the king, who invited him to the palace, befriended him, and eventually made him one of his ministers. The king ordered suitable clothing for him to wear, and the old clothing that he had worn at the time of their meeting was placed in a treasury room.

Many years passed, and then the minister did something that displeased the king, and was ordered to stand trial. The minister knew that he would surely be put to death for the crime he had committed, if he didn't act quickly.

He, therefore, asked for an audience with the king which was granted. When he found himself in the king's presence, the minister fell to his knees and pleaded to at least be permitted to wear the clothes he had worn when the king had first met him. This request was also granted him. When the king saw his minister dressed in the old clothing, he recalled the latter's great kindness to him in the past. The king forgave the minister and cancelled his death sentence.

So it is with the Jewish nation. When G-d wished to give the Torah to other nations, not one was anxious to accept. Only the Jews agreed to abide by its laws, even before they knew its contents. They accepted the yoke of the heavenly kingdom, made the L-rd their King, and observed all the com-

4. An individual may also say *Selichos* when praying alone, but he should omit the 13 *Midos* which are descriptions of the attributes of *Hashem.* (These may be said only with a *Minyan.*) One also omits anything written in Aramaic in this case.

5. It is best to recite the *Selichos* very early in the morning while it is still dark. However, since it is still too early to recite the *Brocho* on a Tallis at this time, the *Chazan,* who has to wear the *Tallis* when leading the *Selichos,* should preferably borrow someone else's *Tallis* and not recite a *Brocho.*

6. An *ovel* (mourner) may lead the *Selichos,* but he should preferably not be the *chazan* on *Rosh Hashono.*

7. There are several qualifications required for one to be a chazan *(shliach tzeebur)* on *Rosh Hashono* and for *Selichos:*

a) He should be a G-d-fearing person who learns Torah and adheres to its teachings.

b) Preferably, he should be a married man over the age of 30 with children.

c) He should also be a person who is well liked by the people.

d) He should have a pleasant voice.

mandments. Now, when they commit a sin against the L-rd, they appear before Him on *Rosh Hashono,* in white, as they did when they accepted the Torah. They blow the trumpets and horns as they did on that day, as it is written in the Torah (*Shemos* 19:19) 'And the voice of the horn went on, and grew louder and louder.' Then G-d will remember their acceptance of the Torah, and in that merit forgive them their transgressions, free them from the harsh verdict, and inscribe them in the book of long life.

"Rav Yitzchok Blazer used to say of his teacher, Rav Yisroel Salanter, that from the face of his Rebbe, he could tell how close it was to Rosh Hashono."

"On Rosh Hashono we pass before G-d like sheep being counted." (Rosh Hashono *16a*)

"There are 3 books opened Rosh Hashono; *one for the wicked ones, one for the righteous ones and one for the average ones. The righteous ones are immediately written down as deserving life; the wicked ones are immediately written down as deserving death; and the judgment for the average individuals is postponed from* Rosh Hashono *until* Yom Kippur. *If they merit, they will be written for life; if not, they will be written for death."* (Rosh Hashono *16a*)

The years 1933 to 1945 were among the darkest days in the history of the Jewish people. Never before had so many Jews been tortured and killed in such a short time. Six million sacrifices were offered to G-d as atonement for the sins of His people. All the prophecies of evil and destruction of which

8. Some of the customs of *Erev Rosh Hashono* include the following:
a) Some people fast half a day.
b) *"Tachanun"* isn't said because it is *Erev Yom Tov.*
c) The *Shofar* is not blown on that morning in order to confuse the *Soton* as to which day is *Rosh Hashono.* Thus he would not be able to appear as a prosecutor against the Jewish people. Another reason is to make an interruption between that which is commanded by the Torah and that which is not.
d) Men go to the *Mikveh* before *Yom Tov.*
e) One should give charity and reflect on the holiness of the day.

CUSTOMS OF ROSH HASHONO

1. On *Rosh Hashono* evening it is customary to dip a piece of an apple into honey and to recite the following: *"Yehee Rotzon . . . She'T'Chadesh Oleinu Shono Tova U'Mesooka."* ("It should be G-d's Will to renew upon us a good and sweet year.")

2. We eat pomegranates which have a lot of seeds, as a symbol of our hope that *Hashem* will multiply our *z'chuyos* (merits), and recite *"Yehee Rotzon . . . She-Yarbu Zechuyoseino."*

3. It is customary to eat sweet foods and avoid bitter ones as an

---

the Torah warned were fulfilled in the last generation. But out of the ashes and ruins of the concentration camps come stories of faith and heroism that shine as a light amidst all the desolation and waste.

One of the inmates of the dreaded Buchenwald concentration camp was an aged rabbi from Poland. He resigned himself to the hopeless situation by telling himself, "I am truly fortunate to follow in the footsteps of Rabbi Akiva, who died a martyr for his faith."

Like everyone else who came to the concentration camp, the old rabbi had left most of his possessions behind. He had but one little chest which he guarded with his life, for it contained his most valuable treasures—a small *Sefer Torah* and a *Shofar.*

Every *Shabbos,* the rabbi would read the *"Parsha"* of the week from the Torah before the prisoners left for their back-breaking 15-hour work shift. It somehow gave them courage and faith to stay alive.

Shortly before *Rosh Hashono,* the rabbi gathered a few people together and suggested to them that they make a *Minyan* (quorum of ten men needed to pray) on *Rosh Hashono.* Perhaps *Hashem* would listen to their sincere prayers, and ease their burdens.

"But what good is a *Minyan* if we don't blow the *Shofar?*" asked one of the prisoners.

"But we *will* blow the *Shofar,*" said the old rabbi.

"What! And risk getting shot? You know that they need only a little excuse to kill us. Why endanger our

indication of our hope for a sweet year. Many people avoid eating horseradish with their fish for this reason.

4. It is customary to eat the head of a fish or the head of a sheep and recite the verse *"Yehee Rotzon . . . She'Nihiyeh L'Rosh V'Lo L'Zanav"* ("May it be Thy Will . . . that *Klal Yisroel* should always be at the head, and not at the bottom, like the tail.")

5. We do not eat certain nuts because in Hebrew, the numerical value of the words "nut" *(egoz)* and "sin" *(chet),* are the same.

6. On the afternoon of the first day of *Rosh Hashono* (or on the second day if the first falls on *Shabbos),* we recite *Tashlich* near a body of water containing fish.

In order to recall the sacrifice of Isaac, we go to a stream of water on *Rosh Hashono* on the first day. It is told in the *Midrash* that when our father Abraham was on his way to sacrifce his son Isaac, the *Soton* turned himself into a large brook of water in the road. Abraham and Isaac attempted to wade through the brook, but the further they went, the deeper the brook became, so that the water soon reached up to their necks. Realizing that the Adversary had done this to keep him from carrying out the command of G-d, Abraham cried out: "L-rd rebuke you,

lives needlessly because of the *Shofar?"*

We are in danger no matter what we do. Even our bodies don't belong to us, for these murderers can do with us as they desire. Only our spirit remains with us. Let us not give that over to them too."

On the morning of *Rosh Hashono,* the small band of Jews arose very early. Never did this group of Jews pray so fervently as they did. When the time came to blow the *Shofar,* the assembled Jews held their breath while the rabbi put the *Shofar* to his lips and blew the loud blast of *"Tekiah"* followed by *"Shevorim"* and *"Teruah."*

Suddenly, the door of the barracks was smashed in, and a battalion of storm troopers appeared with leveled guns.

"Now I've caught you, you traitors," roared the commander. "You're sending signals to the enemy to bomb us. Now I know why we've been shelled so heavily the past few nights."

"This is not a signal," replied one of the inmates. "This is the sound of the *Shofar* and it is part of our holiday prayers."

"QUIET!" screamed the commander. "Tell me who smuggled in that horn and who was the Jew who blew it. The rest of you can go free."

No one responded.

"Answer me," the commander demanded "or else I'll choose twenty men from among you and shoot them immediately."

When they still remained silent, he gave the order to line up twenty men outside and shoot them. Then, just as

O Adversary." Terrified at the voice of Abraham, the *Soton* fled, and the place became dry land again so that Abraham and Isaac could proceed on their way to Mt. Moriah. It is to commemorate this bravery in the service of *Hashem* that we hold the *Tashlich* service by a steam of water.

We should choose a body of water that contains fish to remind us that we are like so many fish caught unawares in the net of judgment and justice. This awareness should impel us to sincere repentance. *(Levush)*

If it is likely that there will be very large crowds at *Tashlich* which may detract from the seriousness of the *Yom Tov*, then it is preferable to delay *Tashlich* until sometime during the *Aseres Yemei Teshuva*.

7. It is customary not to sleep during the afternoon of *Rosh Hashono*. If one is extremely tired and feels he must rest, he should do so for only a short while.

8. We do not say *Hallel* on *Rosh Hashono*, but we do say "*Avinu Malkeinu*" (except on *Shabbos*). We make sure to lengthen our *Tefillos* until at least mid-day.

9. Two *Sifrei Torah* are taken out. Five *Aliyos* are given out, followed by *Maftir*, and *Haftorah*.

10. If a *Bris Milah* takes place on *Rosh Hashono*, it is performed between *Krias HaTorah* and *Tekias Shofar* (the blowing of the *Shofar*).

---

the Rabbi was about to step forward, the air raid siren sounded. A raid! Everyone began to run, as a plane dove down upon them and dropped a bomb. The Germans fled for cover like scared rabbits, and many were killed. In the confusion, the Jewish prisoners managed to escape into the forest.

Later, when the inmates gathered around the rabbi to discuss this miracle of G-d, he said: "The Germans were right when they said that the *Shofar* was a signal. It was not a signal to the Allies, but to our Father in Heaven. We signaled Him that He should see our misery and punish our oppressors. *Hashem Yisborach* listened to our signal!"

"*Repentance, supplication and charity avert the evil decree.*" (New Year liturgy)

R. Abbahu said: "The reason why we blow a Shofar on Rosh Hashono is because Hashem said: 'Sound me a Shofar so that I may remember on your behalf the sacrifice of Yitzchok, the son of Avrohom, and I shall account it to you as if you had offered youselves to Me.'" (Rosh Hashono 16a)

Rabbi Isaac Luria, the renowned mystic, asked: "Why was the Confession phrased in the plural, so that we say 'we are guilt-laden' instead of 'I am guilt-laden' and so forth? Because Israel is one body of which each and every Israelite is an integral part. Hence it follows that all the members of that body are responsible for the whole, even as I am responsible for my brother. If my fellow Jew sins, it is as if I myself had sinned. Even when we

65

11. On the night of *Rosh Hashono,* we wish the following to a man, *"L'Shono Tova Teekosaiv V'Saichosem"* ("You should be inscribed for a good year") and *"L'Shono Tova Teekosaivee V'Saichosaimee,"* to a woman. The *Sephardim* say, *"Tizku L'Shonim Rabos"* ("You should merit many years").

12. One is not allowed to fast on *Rosh Hashono* since it is a *Yom Tov.*

13. Since the two days of *Rosh Hashono* are considered a single halachic day, it is doubtful whether or not the blessing *"Shehecheyanu"* can be said on the second night of *Rosh Hashono.* Therefore, during *Kiddush* on the second night one should wear a new garment or place a new fruit on the table, so that the *"Shehecheyanu"* can be related to one of these. If a new garment or a new fruit is not available the blessing should be recited anyway. Since this problem of the *"Shehecheyanu"* applies to the candle lighting and *Shofar* blowing of the second day, the same arrangement should be made when performing these *Mitzvos.*

Even in Israel, *Rosh Hashono* is celebrated for two days, and the two days are considered as one day.

14. One lights the candles before *Yom Tov* and recites the *Yom Tov Brocho,* and then *"Shehecheyanu."*

15. One says *Yaale V'yovo* in the *Shmoneh Esrei* and in *bentsching.*

recite the Confession alone, at home, 'Ashamnu' should be phrased in the plural, for we are all guarantors for one another. ." (*Yesod HaTeshuva,* Ch. 6)

THE SHOFAR'S MESSAGE
Many years ago, in a little town in Poland, there lived a poor orphan whom everyone lovingly called, "Yossele." While he was still young, he went to *Yeshiva* and learned *Chumash* like all the other boys, but when he grew older, he had to go out into the world to earn money to support himself. The townspeople got together and provided him with a basket full of merchandise and trinkets to sell. Yossele set out on his journey.

One cold day, Yossele was walking slowly down the snow-lined road, carrying his basket. He repeated the *Tehillim* that he knew by heart, and

tried to follow the road which was now completely covered with snow. Because of this, he took the wrong path and soon found himself lost deep in the woods.

He leaned against a broken tree and tried to keep himself from falling asleep, for fear that he would freeze to death. But slowly, his eyes began to close and . . .

A peasant farmer, passing in his sleigh, noticed the huddled figure of a boy almost fully covered with snow. He quickly ran over, brushed the snow off the frozen figure, and started massaging the boy's body until he finally saw him stir. He then carried him to his sleigh and drove off to his home in a nearby village.

After a few days, Yossele recovered completely and was grateful to the

HILCHOS SHMONEH ESREI:

1. One says *"Ha'Melech Hakodosh"* instead of *"Ha'kail Hakodosh,"* during the *Aseres Yemei Teshuva*, from *Rosh Hashono* to *Yom Kippur* inclusive.

2. If by error, one said *"Ha'Kail Hakodosh,"* but realized his mistake immediately *(L'toch K'Dei Dibur)* and before starting the next *Brocho*, he may correct himself. If not, he must start *Shmoneh Esrei* from the beginning.

3. On *Rosh Hashono* the custom is to recite the *Shmoneh Esrei* a bit louder than usual.

4. The following lines are to be added in the *Shmoneh Esrei* during the *Aseres Yemei Teshuva:*
a) *"Zochreinu L'Chayim Melech Chofetz Ba'Chayim ..."*
b) *"Mee Chomocha Av Ho'Rachamim ..."*
c) *"U'Ch'sov L'Chayim Tovim Kol Bnai Breesecha"*
d) *"B'Sefer Chayim B'rocho V'Sholom ..."*
The first two are said at the beginning of *Shmoneh Esrei* and the latter two are said at the end. If one forgets to say any of them, he need not repeat the *Shmoneh Esrei*.

kind farmer and his wife for their gentle care.

"What is your name?" asked the farmer's wife.

"I really don't know. I can't remember anything!"

"That's no problem," said the farmer. "We'll call you John."

Thus Yossele, or John as he was now called, became the farmer's adopted son, completely forgetting that he was a Jewish child.

Summertime came and John helped his "father" in the fields. One day, the farmer told him, "Tomorrow we shall go sell our produce in the market." John was very excited and could hardly wait for the next day.

Early the following morning, they rode into town, but when they got to the marketplace, they found it de-serted. As they passed a synagogue crowded with worshippers, the peasant farmer realized that it was a Jewish holiday. The farmer wanted to return home, but John asked if he could please stay a while and watch this fascinating sight. He felt an irresistable urge to look into the synagogue. The farmer agreed to meet him later, and went off to have a drink in the nearby inn.

John stood at the door of the synagogue, enchanted by what he saw. The worshippers wrapped in their beautiful, white *Talleisim* seemed very intent on their prayers. Many of them were weeping. John felt his heart beat faster. When had he witnessed this scene before? It all looked so familiar. The sight of the holy Torah scrolls being taken out of the Ark slowly brought back his memory.

INTRODUCTION TO TEKIAS SHOFAR

There is a biblical obligation to hear nine blasts of the *Shofar*. These should consist of three broken wails, each preceded and followed by an unbroken sustained blast. The sustained blasts, *Tekiahs*, should be at least as long in duration as the broken wail.

Because of a doubt as to whether the broken wail resembles a sighing sound, called *Shevorim*, or a wailing noise called *Teruah*, or a combination of both, three of each must be blown. Each is preceded and followed by a sustained blast, in order to definitely fulfill the biblical obligation. This requirement makes for a total of thirty blasts of the *Shofar*, 3 each of the following sequence.

Tekiah, Shvorim Teruah, Tekiah (4x3)
Tekiah, Shevorim, Tekiah (3x3)
Tekiah, Teruah, Tekiah (3x3)

The first thirty notes are blown after the reading of the Torah. Another set of thirty notes is blown during the *Chazan's* recitation of the *Mussaf Shmoneh Esrei*. Some blow also during the quiet *Shmoneh Esrei*.

An additional forty are blown at the end of *Mussaf* for a total of 100 sounds.

There was a tense excitement in the air as the silence was broken by the shaking voice of the aged cantor. The entire community joined in fervent prayer. For a while, the roar of the congregants praying seemed to shake the very walls of the Synagogue, and then gradually subsided into a solemn silence.

In the stillness of the air, the sobbing of the cantor became clearly audible, and Yossele (no longer "John") found himself crying too.

Suddenly he heard "*Tekiah-ah-ah,*" and the blast of the ram's horn pierced the air.

"*Shevari-i-im Teruah*" and again the broken sound of the *Shofar* seemed to stab Yossele's heart. "*Tekiah-ah-ah*" the *Shofar* called again.

"Yossele, you are a Jew," the *Shofar* seemed to say. "Yossele, you are a Jew. Hurry now . . . Now is the time to return to G-d . . . *Tekiah . . . Teruah-ah-ah . . .*"

Everything now became very clear to Yossele. "O dear G-d, forgive me" cried Yossele. The *Shofar* had called him back home.

"A person is obligated to prepare himself for judgment before G-d 30 days in advance with prayer and repentance and charity. One's whole body should be dedicated to serving G-d. "I am to my beloved and my beloved is to me" (Ani L'Dodi V'Dodi Li) stands for Elul, this symbolizes the closeness that we have to G-d at this time." (Chayei Adam)

When a person wishes to repent, the first thing he must do is to part from his wicked ways, and in the future to keep away from all those

68

HILCHOS TEKIAS SHOFAR

1. The *Baal Tokea* (one blowing the *Shofar*) should stand and not lean on the *bima* (podium) when blowing. The entire congregation must also stand. However, if one sits, he is still *yotzai*. Two *Brochos* are made before blowing the *Shofar*, "*Lishmoa Kol Shofar*" and "*Shehecheyanu.*"

2. One may recite the *Brochos* and blow for the congregation even if he himself had already fulfilled the *Mitzvah* of the blowing of the *Shofar*.

3. In most *Shuls*, the *Baal Tokea* says "*Shehecheyanu*" on the second day also, especially if the first day was *Shabbos*.

4. If he started blowing the *Shofar* but could not finish, another person may continue for him without repeating the *Brochos*. Even if the first person has not blown at all, the second one still need not repeat the *Brochos*.

5. It is best that the *Baal Mussaf* should not be the *Baal Tokea;* however, if there is no one else to do so, he may perform both functions.

6. After the *Brochos* are recited, one is not allowed to speak till after *Mussaf*. However, one person is allowed to announce the "*Tekiah, Shevorim, Teruah,*" for the one who is blowing.

7. The *Shofar* should be blown in the daytime after sunrise. One is not

things which lead man to sin. He should then labor very dilligently in the service of the L-rd and try to make amends for his past transgressions. Just as in war, a man cannot adequately attend to his wounds under a hail of bullets, but must remove himself from the battlefield to get a chance to nurse his wounds, so too, must one who wishes to repent sincerely of his sins remove himself from those paths which led him to sin in the first place."

"*Man is judged according to his actions at the time of judgment.*" (Rosh Hashono 16b)

"*The* Vavei Ha-Amudim *writes: 'It is good to shed tears during prayers. One whose heart is hardened and who cannot shed a tear should at least pretend to be weeping, for the Lord hath heard the voice of my weeping.'*" (Psalms 6:9).

MENDING OUR WAYS

Once, on *Rosh Chodesh Elul*, one month before *Rosh Hashono*, the *Tzaddik* Reb Levi Yitzchok of Berditchev (18th cent.) was standing at his window. A gentile cobbler passed by and asked him, "Have you anything to mend?"

At once the *Tzaddik* sat himself down on the ground, and weeping bitterly cried, "Woe is me, and alas my soul, for the Day of Judgment is almost here, and I have still not mended myself."

THE FIREMAN

Many years ago, before the advent of modern fire engines, when a fire broke out in town an alarm was sounded. The people who heard the alarm would form a human chain between the fire and the nearest well and pass on to each other pails of

69

yotzai if it was blown before *alos ha'Shachar* (early dawn).

8. One should not be *mafsik* (interrupt by talking) until after one has heard all the *Tekios*. However, if one did, he was still *yotzai*. If one interrupts before the blowing began, he must make a new *Brocho*.

9. One who is himself not obligated to hear the *Shofar* (e.g., one who is deaf, a boy under the age of 13, or a woman) cannot be *Motzee* others.

10. One who is only practicing to blow *Shofar* and is not blowing with the intent of fulfilling the *Mitzvah* of *Tekias Shofar*, cannot be *Motzee* others. One should not blow *Shofar* for practice unless he feels it is necessary for fulfilling the *Mitzvah* later on.

11. The one who is blowing the *Shofar* must intend to be *Motzee* the entire congregation or the individual for whom he is blowing.

12. On *Shabbos* one does not blow the *Shofar* and it is considered *muktzeh* (i.e. it may not be moved on *Shabbos*).

13. It is best to blow the *Shofar* and *daven Mussaf* after at least one quarter of the day has passed.

14. When blowing the *Shofar* for a congregation, one blows before, during, and after *Shmoneh Esrei*. When blowing for an individual, one blows all the sounds either before or after *Shmoneh Esrei* but only 30 are required.

water with which to put out the fire.

Once, a lad from a small village came to town for the first time and stopped at an inn. Suddenly, he heard the sound of a bugle. He asked the innkeeper what it meant.

"Whenever we have a fire," the innkeeper explained, "we sound the bugle, and the fire is quickly put out."

"How wonderful," thought the village lad. "Imagine how surprised my fellow villagers will be when I tell them about this."

So he bought a bugle and returned to his village. When the next fire broke out in his village, the lad ran to the scene of the fire with his bugle. "No need to be afraid of the fire any more," he exclaimed. "Just watch me, and see how quickly I put out the fire."

The lad began to blow the bugle with all his might, but the fire did not seem to care much for the music. It merely hopped from roof to roof until all the village was in flames.

The villagers now began to scold and curse the lad. "You fool!" they cried, "Did you think that merely blowing the bugle will put the fire out? It is merely an alarm to summon the people to the well ιo draw water and put out the fire."

* * * * *

Many people think like the village lad, that hearing the sound of the *Shofar* on *Rosh Hashono* solves everything. They think that there is no need to change their life and daily conduct; the *Shofar* sounded in the Synagogue will surely bring them a happy New Year. But, like the bugle in the story, the *Shofar* is only the sound of an 'alarm'. Its message is: "Wake

15. If one has not blown during the *Shmoneh Esrei*, he may blow those *tekios* at the end. In fact, if one thinks that he wasn't careful enough with all the *tekios*, then he may still blow additional ones at the end of the *Shmoneh Esrei*.

16. The *Shofar* should be from a twisted ram's horn. If it has any holes or cracks even if they have been glued, a *Rav* should be consulted.

17. One *davens* even if one does not hear the *Shofar*.

up, you sleepers. Think about your ways, return to *Hashem*, put out the 'fire' that is threatening to destroy your Jewish homes. Go to the Well, the Well of Living Waters, the Torah and *Mitzvos*. Hurry, before it is too late."

This is why, immediately after the *Shofar* is sounded, we exclaim: "Happy are the people who understand that the meaning of the sound of the *Shofar*; they walk in your light, Oh G-d." (*Tehillim* 89:16)

Why does the *Chazan* begin the *Shacharis* (morning) service on *Rosh Hashono* and *Yom Kippur* with the word *"Hamelech,"* the King?

A story is told about Rabbi Aaron Karliner who was officiating as *Chazan* for his congregation. When he started the davening with the word *"Hamelech"* he burst into bitter crying. Later, he gave the following reason for his emotional outburst.

"When I said the word 'King', I was reminded of the story told in the Talmud. When Rabbi Yochanan Ben Zakai appeared before Vespasian to ask for certain privileges, he referred to him as King. Vespasian, who was still only general of the army and was about to receive the news of his having been made Emperor replied, "If you call me King, why didn't you come to me before now?" (*Gitten* 56b)

"Today," said Rabbi Aaron, "when I cried out the word *King*, I imagined that I was being asked in Heaven, 'If this is so, why didn't you come before? Why did you wait so long before you repented before the Ruler of the Universe?'"

Resh Lakish said: "So great is *Teshuva*, that deliberate acts of wrongdoing are reckoned to have been committed without intent, as it is written: 'Return, O Israel, to the L-rd your G-d, for you have stumbled in your sin.' The Prophet speaks of intentional sin and yet calls it "stumbling." But, is this Resh Lakish's opinion? Has he not said that *Teshuva* transforms intentional acts into merits? There is no contradiction. When *Teshuva* is stimulated by fear of G-d, man's sins are deemed to have been without intent, but when this *Teshuva* is motivated by love of G-d, then his sins are reckoned as merits." (*Yoma* 86b)

"Rabbi Chama the son of Chanina said: 'So great is *Teshuva* that it brings healing to the world.'" (*Yoma* 86a)

 יום כפור

Yom Kippur

YOM KIPPUR—INTRODUCTION

"And it shall be a statute forever unto you: in the seventh month, you shall afflict your souls, and shall do no manner of work, the home-born or the stranger that sojourns among you. For on this day shall atonement be made for you, to cleanse you; from all your sins shall you be

YOM KIPPUR

TESHUVA

Teshuva is a very difficult concept to understand, yet it is vitally important to all G-d fearing Jews. Although *Teshuva* cannot really be defined in precise terms, it consists of three parts: (1) A person who is willing to do *Teshuva* must acknowledge that he has sinned, (2) He must take his wrongdoing to heart and truly regret what he has done, (3) He must commit himself not to repeat his improper activity.

Often, those who have erred, regardless of the degree of their transgression, mistakenly hesitate to do *Teshuva* because they feel that their Creator is not interested in the efforts of sinners. However, *Hashem* readily accepts the *Teshuva* of those who truly regret their sins, and he eagerly awaits their repentance.

A person who does *Teshuva* is considered in the eyes of *Hashem* as if he had never sinned. Furthermore, our Sages tell us, "Where those who do *Teshuva* stand, even the completely righteous cannot stand." (*Brochos* 34b) People who have done *Teshuva*

are, in a sense, greater than those who have never sinned, for they have had to work very hard to change their ways.

Our Chazal present us with a wide range of comments regarding *Teshuva*. Rabbi Meir said: "Great is *Teshuva!* For the sake of one man who repents, he and the entire world are forgiven!" (*Yoma* 86b) So great is the impact of a total *Teshuva* that the individual and all in his sphere of influence are now offered a new status, unencumbered by errors of the past.

If one sees his fellow man commit a sin or following an evil path, it is a *Mitzvah* to return him to the good, and to inform him that he had committed wrong through his evil deeds—as it is said: "You shall surely admonish your friend." Whoever admonishes his friend, whether in matters that are between themselves, or in matters that are between his friend and G-d, should do so in private. He should speak gently, with mild language, and should let his friend know that he speaks only for the latter's good, in order to lead him to the life of the World-to-Come. Whoever admonish-

clean before the L-rd. It is a Sabbath of solemn rest unto you, and you shall inflict your souls; it is a statute forever." (Vayikra 16:29-31)
Yom Kippur *(the Day of Atonement), the holiest day of the entire year, is the last of the Ten Days of Penitence, when the Book of Life is finally sealed on the tenth day of* Tishrei. *Beginning with the* Kol Nidrei *service just before sunset, all Jews, young and old, assemble in the synagogue to ask* Hashem *forgiveness of their sins, and fast from evening to evening.*
Yom Kippur *is set aside as a fast day for the purpose of repentance and rectifying the misdemeanors towards our fellow men and our Creator. Thus the establishment of the kingdom of* Hashem *on earth is furthered. Man asks forgiveness for his shortcomings from his G-d and resolves to live nobly and exemplify the ideals of his faith.*

es his friend should not speak to him so harshly as to embarrass him, for it is said: ". . . You shall not bear sin over him." Upon which the Sages commented: "One might think that he should admonish another even if the latter's face is altered. It is therefore taught: 'You shall not bear sin over him.' We learn from this that it is forbidden to shame a Jew, and all the more (is it forbidden to do so) publicly." Even though one who shames another does not incur *malkos* (the penalty of stripes), all the same it is a great sin (to do so). Thus did the Sages say: "He who causes his friend's face to turn white (with shame) has no share in the World-to-Come." (*Rambam Hilchos Dayos* 6:7-8).

A very important aspect of *Teshuva* deals with relationships between people. Although *Yom Kippur* atones for sins committed against *Hashem* alone, sins committed against people are not forgiven until the sinner has asked for forgiveness from his fellow-man.

In improving our attitudes towards others, charity plays a very important role. The giving of *tzedaka* to the needy on *Erev Yom Kippur* during

Mincha does much to make peace between Jews and their Father in heaven.

Showing compassion towards others is equally important at this time of year. The following story illustrates the compassion of a righteous Jew.

On the eve of *Yom Kippur*, the pious Rabbi Dovid of Lelov was proceeding to Shul to *daven Kol Nidre*, when he heard an infant crying. He entered the house and found a baby lying alone in his cradle. His parents had gone to Shul and left him without anyone to care for him.

Reb Dovid soothed the child and began rocking him. After the *davening* was over, the parents returned home to find this great man rocking their baby's cradle.

How great is the compassion the pious feel for their fellow-Jews! On *Yom Kippur* night, when everyone hurried to *Kol Nidre*, this pious man felt that easing the anguish of a Jewish child was more important than his praying with the congregation.

Rabbi Yisroel Salanter once went to a shoemaker to have his shoes repaired. The hour was late and dar-

73

I. HILCHOS ASERES YEMAI TESHUVA:
(The ten days of repentance from *Rosh Hashono* through *Yom Kippur)*

These ten days (including *Rosh Hashono* and *Yom Kippur)* are set aside for introspection and self-purification. Though one should behave properly throughout the year, he should be especially conscientious in his actions during the *Aseres Yemei Teshuva.* Therefore, during this period, one should make peace with his friends and neighbors, give charity and make special efforts to improve his behavior and attitudes.

The following laws and customs should be observed:

1. During these days we say extra *Tefillos* (prayers) and *Selichos,* including *"Avinu Malkeinu"* in the morning and afternoon.

---

kness had already descended. Noticing that the candle was burning out Rabbi Yisroel realized that the shoemaker might have trouble repairing the shoes in the dim light, and so he suggested that he perhaps could wait to do it until the next day.

"Do not despair," the shoemaker replied. "I can work very well by candlelight. As long as the candle burns, it is still possible to fix the shoes."

Rabbi Yisroel immediately realized the significance of the shoemaker's words. As long as the candle burned, he could still repair what was broken. And as long as the spark of life still flickers in a person, that person can still repair his sinful ways. One can never resign himself to spiritual doom.

AUSCHWITZ

Auschwitz was one of the most horrible of the concentration camps. Most of those who arrived there were killed outright. Those who were strong and healthy were kept alive for a while for slave labor. When they were too weak to continue, they too, were killed.

Among the laborers was a group of young Jewish girls. Their bodies were weak, but their will was strong. The

threats of their Nazi "masters" could not shake their loyalty to a higher Master, G-d.

To members of the camp, the days were one long blur. Each morning promised a worse experience than the previous one. Still, the girls somehow found out that *Yom Kippur,* the holy Day of Atonement, would take place during the following week. Despite their physical frailty, they were determined to fast. This was what the Torah commanded, and they still remained true to the Torah.

They summoned up the courage to approach their supervisor. She was an SS woman guard without a hint of human kindness. Their representative said, "Next week we Jews observe *Yom Kippur.* For us, it is one of the holiest days of the year. We would like permission to fast on this day, as we have always done."

The supervisor looked at them with her usual hatred. "So you dirty swines still believe in clinging to your stupid Jewish ways! Just for that, I should have all of you shot. Let me warn you, girls. Fast if you wish, but I will be watching carefully next week. If any-

74

2. One should not institute legal proceedings in a *bes din* (court).

3. One is usually not *Mekadesh* (sanctify) the new moon until after *Yom Kippur*.

4. Although it is permissible to eat Kosher bread manufactured by a non Jewish bakery throughout the year, during the *Aseres Yemai Teshuva* one should be careful to eat only bread baked by a Jew.

5. The *Aseres Yemai Teshuva* is a most opportune time to ask *Mechila* (forgiveness) from one's friends. If one isn't forgiven the first time he should still persist.

One should forgive a friend the first time that he asks for *Mechila*, just as he wants *Hashem* to forgive him immediately for his sins.

6. From *Rosh Hashono* until *Yom Kippur* the words *"Ha'Melech*

---

one of you faints or shows any weakness during your work on *Yom Kippur*, you will be killed on the spot. Let's see how your G-d can help you this time."

When *Yom Kippur* came, she announced the day's work assignment. It was physically more demanding than any work that they had ever done before. The supervisor enjoyed herself heartily as she noticed their reactions. They would obviously have to eat to get through the day, even though it was *Yom Kippur*. They would prove to be weak, miserable animals, as the Nazis had always claimed.

To make sure of this, the woman ordered the day's food rations brought in. They were much larger than usual, and included foods that the girls hadn't enjoyed in months. On any other day, they would have jumped at the sight. They were obviously undernourished, and needed the food desperately.

But today, they tasted not a bite. They simply looked at the food and then turned away. The supervisor waited for their wills to break, but the girls stayed strong. They simply went out to work as usual. "You had better finish digging that ditch by the time I

come back," she snarled, "or else!"

The girls set to work with a vengeance. They would show her; they would reveal the fiber of which Jews are made. They did the grueling work with vigor, and they helped each other out. Whenever a girl became too weak to continue, the others immediately came to her aid. They were unified against the enemy, unified in the service of *Hashem*.

Finally, the supervisor returned, expecting to have the last laugh. What she saw instead was a completely dug ditch, and a tired but triumphant group of girls smiling at her. All she could say was, "Back to your barracks." Then she stalked away.

The girls beamed with pride. Their bodies cried out for food, but the victory was theirs. By their fasting and adhering to their religion, they had proved that their will was greater than the enemy's, that the laws of the Torah were stronger than those of the Nazis. Oppression had only brought out the best in them. They were Jews, proud Jews, and a million Nazi guns could not take that fact away from them.

75

Ha'Mishpot" are said instead of *"Melech Ohaiv Tzedakah U'Mishpot."* If one makes a mistake here, he does not have to repeat the *Shmoneh Esrei.*

II. HILCHOS EREV YOM KIPPUR

1. This is the final day of preparation for *Yom Kippur,* and it is therefore somewhat of a minor holiday. It is a *Mitzvah* to eat all day.

2. *Tachnun, Lamnatzeach,* and *Mizmor L'Sodah* are not said on *Erev Yom Kippur.*

3. The custom of *kaporos* is observed either during the *Aseres Yemai Teshuva* or preferably on *Erev Yom Kippur.* This is the ritual of symbolically transferring punishment due one to a substitute such as a chicken

WHILE THE KING IS HERE

Scripture commands us to "cling to Him" (*Devorim* 11:22). We have to realize how fortunate we are, how exalted is our lot in this world, that we have been given the ability to cling to the blessed L-rd and be attached to Him. This great privilege is available to a human being only as long as he is alive on this earth—by keeping the Torah and its *Mitzvos.* Once he expires, however, and reaches the world of truth in the Hereafter, there are already many partitions and separations between him and the Holy Blessed One and he can no longer draw near to Him and cling to Him.

Let us explain with a parable: The owner of an inn prospered so much that he aroused the envy of his less wealthy neighbors, who wished to remove him and gain possession of the inn. They went to certain government officials and made false accusations against him, giving bribes to the "right" people to make sure they would be believed. Without bothering to call the inkeeper and question him, the official court of the emperor sentenced him to life imprisonment at hard labor.

The astounded man went into ac-

tion, to move heaven and earth in an attempt to save himself. He hired the most noted attorneys in the land. He sent people who knew the court judges to intercede and speak for him. He left no stone unturned—and got nothing for his pains. It was all in vain. The sentence could not be changed or removed.

Yet his friends told him not to despair. "There is still one more thing to do," they told him. "We see now that nothing else can help, except your going and presenting yourself to the emperor alone. It is well known that he is fair and merciful and will always listen to the plea of one of his subjects. If you can only succeed in convincing him of your innocence, you can be sure that he won't let any injustice be done to you."

The emperor had a custom that once a year he took off his royal garments and dressed in ordinary clothing, and thus he went wandering and traveling about in the land, letting no one know that he was the emperor. In this way he wished to have a good look at life and events in his country, to see if his subjects were prospering and how his subordinates were treating them.

or money. Some people perform *kaporos* by swinging a chicken or with money, which are then given to the poor.

4. It is customary for a man to use a rooster and for a woman to use a hen for *kaporos*. A pregnant woman uses two chickens for Kaporos, one male and one female.

5. It is customary before *Yom Kippur* to give more *tzedakah* (charity) than usual. It is also customary to pray at the graves of departed relatives or *Gedolim* (sages).

6. It is customary to go to the *Mikveh* on *Erev Yom Kippur*.

7. Part of the *Mincha* of *Erev Yom Kippur* includes *Veedui* (confession of sins) at the end of the *Shmoneh Esrei*. This must be recited while standing, and before the *Seuda Hamafsekes*.

By a stroke of "fate," his travels brought him to the town of the innkeeper, and one night he came to stay at the inn. No one had the least idea, however, of who he really was. Only after he left did the secret manage to leak out.

When the innkeeper learned that the emperor himself had been there, he was beside himself with grief. Here he was in desperate need of seeing the emperor and talking to him, to plead his case and convince the emperor of his innocence, and the emperor had been right there at his inn. He could have spoken to him face to face, and the emperor would have listened. And now the opportunity was gone, having slipped through his fingers.

He began tearing his clothing and shouting in agony. "Woe is me, woe is me. The great merciful emperor came right here, to my inn. I could have pleaded my case and implored him for mercy. And I missed the chance. How will I ever get to him now? He is locked away in his palace, guarded by hundreds of sentries without and within, who make sure that no uninvited guest can ever get in to see him."

This is exactly what happens with human begins on earth. While we are in the ten days, *Hashem* is here waiting for our repentance. There can be no better opportunity to approach Him (as it were) to pour out our prayer and beseech Him for all our needs, be it in regard to children, health or money matters. Yet how many simply miss the golden opportunity and let their great chance slip away. When they want to see Him in His heavenly mansion, in the Hereafter, it is no longer possible to do *Teshuva*. It is doubtful if they can ever succeed there in drawing close to Him.

Let every single member of Jewry bear this well in mind, so that he will know how to use his moments of opportunity, while the Divine Sovereign is with him, at his inn.

How does a person admit his sins on the day before Yom Kippur? *He should say, "I admit all evil that I did before You. I was standing in the wrong path. Whatever I did, I will not do again. May it be your will G-d my G-d that You forgive me for all my sins." (*Vayikra Rabbah 3)

8. In the *Mincha* of *Erev Yom Kippur*, the *Sh'liach Tzeebur (chazan)* doesn't repeat the *Veedui*. *Avinu Malkeinu* and *Tachnun* are not recited.

9. The final meal before commencing the fast is called the *seuda hamafsekes*. One finishes eating a short while before the actual onset of *Yom Kippur* (sunset).

10. If one intends to eat or drink something after the *seuda hamafsekes* he should keep this fact in mind before he recites the *bentsching* so that he has not yet accepted the *Taanis* upon himself.

11. One should not overindulge in eating on *Erev Yom Kippur* since it may cause him to feel uncomfortable on the *taanis*. It is also best to avoid eating spicy foods or other foods that will make it difficult for one to fast.

We say the words "forgive us" at the conclusion of *Yom Kippur*. This may seem to be a misplaced prayer, for hasn't one just spent the entire day asking for forgiveness? Why renew the plea so late in the day?

This situation can be compared to one in which a king was passing incognito, through a field. As he was doing so, one of the workers in the field came over to him, yelling that he had no business being in the field, and kicked him.

The men who were accompanying the king wanted to kill the man on the spot, but the king restrained them. "Let him be, for he did not know who I am," said the king. "If he knew me, he would not have done that. Instead, take him to the palace and teach him the meaning of respect and good manners. Then, we will see if he will change his ways."

The king's men did so, and after spending some time in the palace, the man came to understand the importance of respect. His head bowed in shame, the man approached the king, and pleaded, "Forgive me. When I kicked you, I was but a simple, ignor-ant person. It is only now that I understand how great my sin was."

If we have experienced *Yom Kippur* properly, then we have used it as an opportunity to grow in understanding. We might have begun the day ignorant of the effects of our sins. By the time *Yom Kippur* has reached its conclusion, though, we should have searched our souls sufficiently to realize the magnitude of our errors. We should have come to understand the importance of proper behavior, and, therefore, we should have felt our shame more intensely. Therefore, it is only appropriate to ask Hashem for forgiveness at the *end* of *Yom Kippur*, when the realization of what we have done is much clearer.

"The knowledge that a thing is evil, brings one halfway to repentance." (Meiri)

"The Jews said, "If our fathers sinned and brought a Korbon they were forgiven. Why do we not have any sacrifices now? G-d answered, 'I only want words of repentance and confession from you, and then I will forgive all your sins.'"

12. Before lighting the candles on *Erev Yom Kippur,* the woman recites the following *Brocho: ". . . Asher Kiddishanu . . . L'hadlik Ner Shel Yom HaKippurim."* If *Yom Kippur* falls out on *Shabbos* one includes *Shabbos* in the *Brocho.*

13. Besides the regular candles that are normally lit on *Yom Tov* additional candles are lit on *Erev Yom Kippur* in memory of departed ones.

14. On *Motzai Yom Kippur,* the candle used for *Havdalah* is lit from another candle that has been burning since *Erev Yom Kippur.*

III. HILCHOS YOM KIPPUR:

1. Since it is customary to wear white clothing on *Yom Kippur,* married men wear a *kittel* under their *Tallis.*

THE FORGOTTEN STORY

Shortly before the Baal Shem Tov was *"niftar"* (passed away), he bestowed a blessing upon his faithful follower and *"Gabbai".* The blessing was that the *"Gabbai"* would earn his livelihood by travelling from *'shtetl'* (small town) to *'shtetl'* relating stories of the wondrous Baal Shem Tov.

The *Gabbai* thought this was a strange 'blessing' but when the time came and he needed money to marry off his daughter, he followed the Rebbe's wishes. He found out that in a distant town, there lived a wealthy innkeeper who loved to hear stories about the Baal Shem Tov. He was also known to be a very generous man.

The *Gabbai* traveled to the distant city to meet this innkeeper. As soon as he introduced himself, the innkeeper served him a delicious hot meal and begged that he tell him an interesting story from the life of the Holy Baal Shem Tov.

For the first time ever, the Gabbai found that his mind was a blank. After all those years of traveling with the Baal Shem Tov, he couldn't recall a single story to relate.

"Don't let it bother you, my friend," said the innkeeper. "Rest here tonight, and perhaps tomorrow, when you'll feel refreshed from your journey, you'll be able to entertain me with an interesting story about the Baal Shem Tov. I always enjoy hearing them."

The next morning, the *Gabbai* davened and ate breakfast, but still could not think of any episode to relate. The innkeeper begged him to stay over Shabbos and perhaps in the interim he would be able to think of something. *Shabbos* passed and the Gabbai was very perturbed. After having spent most of his life accompanying his holy Master, the Baal Shem Tov, how was it possible that he still could not think of a single incident to relate to this innkeeper?

The innkeeper pleaded with him not to leave yet, but the *Gabbai* felt that he did not want to take advantage of his hospitality. He left the house and started crying, but just as he was about to board his horse and buggy, he suddenly remembered one story. He would now be able to fulfill his host's most fervent wish. He proceeded to relate to him the following

The reasons for this custom are as follows:
a) To show that we are free from sin like the angels.
b) To remind us of the white shrouds in which the dead are buried. (This realization should put us in a more serious frame of mind during this Day of Judgment.)

2. Once *Yom Kippur* starts, one is not allowed to eat or drink anything. This applies to girls and boys over the ages of twelve and thirteen, respectively, (although boys and girls aged 11 and 12 respectively should fast as a preparation.)

REMEMBER: This fast day is of Biblical origin and must be observed more stringently than other fast days, which are of Rabbinic origin. Thus, sick or very weak people must fast unless it may endanger their lives. Always consult a Rabbi in this case.

story, which had happened many, many years earlier.

"The Baal Shem Tov, who lived in Poland, asked me to join him one day on a trip to a distant city in Italy. We arrived on a day that happened to be a Christian holiday. The streets of the Jewish Quarter were deserted. No one dared venture outdoors for fear of inciting a pogrom.

"In the center of town, a big platform had been set up. People were pushing forward in the rush to get a front seat. As part of the holiday celebrations, the Archbishop of that province was going to be the guest speaker. Everyone wanted to hear him speak, since they were sure he would have a lot to say against the 'troublesome' Jews living in their midst.

"When we arrived in the town, the Baal Shem Tov and I rushed over to the inn at the Jewish quarter. The poor, frightened, innkeeper hesitated to open the door until the Baal Shem Tov assured him that all would be well.

"The doors and all the windows of the inn were tightly shut. Some were even boarded up. The Baal Shem Tov entered, and went to open one of the windows to observe the crowd of Christians that were massing outside. The frightened innkeeper pleaded with him to close the window, but the Baal Shem Tov again reassured him that all would be well. The Baal Shem Tov then called me to his side and asked me to undertake a most unique and frightening mission.

"The Baal Shem Tov told me to go out to the center platform just as the Archbishop was getting ready to speak, and to tell him, 'My Master, the Baal Shem Tov, wishes to speak to you.'"

"My friend, you cannot imagine the panic I felt in my heart. The Jews of that ghetto had barricaded themselves in their homes, fearing a pogrom, and here my Master was sending me out to speak to the Archbishop. I felt as if I were being thrown to the lions, but I could not refuse my Master's request.

"I walked out into the street with a prayer on my lips and a sincere hope in my heart that the Almighty in heaven would be with me. Of course, I didn't

3. Washing or smearing ointments is prohibited on *Yom Kippur.* If one's hands are dirty, he is allowed to wash off the dirt, since this is done for the purpose of cleaning and not for pleasure.

4. Upon awakening in the morning of *Yom Kippur,* one washes his hands three times up till the end of the knuckles and then recites the *Brocho, "Al Netilas Yodayim."* He can use the same water to wash the corner of his eyes.

5. One is not allowed to wash his face or his body.

6. One is not permitted to wear shoes made of leather.

7. Older children who have not yet reached the age of *Bar/Bas Mitzvah* and who don't fast the entire day should still be aware of the *taanis* and should abstain from food and drink at least during the night of

---

dare ask the reason for this mission. When I approached the Archbishop, all eyes in the crowd turned to me, since I was obviously Jewish. I walked over to him and whisperd in his ear that my Master, the Baal Shem Tov, wished to speak with him. To my utter amazement, he walked off the platform and followed me. He went in to speak with the Baal Shem Tov, and then he disappeared. I have no idea what they spoke about. I do know, however, that the pogrom that the Jews feared in that city never materialized."

As the Gabbai finished speaking, he saw tears in the eyes of the innkeeper. "Praised be the L-rd Who has seen fit to forgive my terrible sins of many years ago." Now it was the turn of the innkeeper to relate *his* story to the amazed looking *Gabbai.*

"As a young boy, I caused my parents a lot of anguish. Not only didn't I show any interest in my studies at the local *Cheder* (elementary Hebrew school) but as I grew older, I made the wrong kind of friends. Eventually I befriended a young man who was about to enter the Christian ministry. He convinced me to read and study his religion, and to follow in his footsteps. I committed the terrible crime of becoming a traitor to my religion. I rose rapidly in the Church hierarchy, and after many years of preaching and propagandizing against the Jews, I became the Archbishop whom you spoke to on that fateful day!"

The *Gabbai* gasped in amazement. He could hardly believe what he had just heard.

"When you told me to go speak to your master, the Baal Shem Tov," the innkeeper continued, "I felt such a feeling of relief in my heart—like one who has been drowning in the sea and is suddenly rescued. Now I can reveal to you the reason I followed you so readily so many years ago. For several nights before, I had been having a recurring dream in which I saw the face of my late father and the face of another who seemed like an angel. When I saw the Baal Shem Tov, I realized at once that he was the one who had been haunting my dreams.

"There I stood, a traitor to my religion and my people, yet the Baal Shem Tov spoke to me kindly. He made me remember my dear parents, whose early death I had caused. Realizing

Yom Kippur. On *Yom Kippur* day, they should abstain from eating non-essential foods.

8. One should consult a competent Rabbi as to whether a sick person must fast on *Yom Kippur.* When there is a *sakana* (danger to life), one is not allowed to fast. A pregnant woman who feels ill should also consult a Rabbi.

9. During *davening,* the phrase *"Baruch Shem K'vod Malchuso L'Olom Vo'ed"* in the *Shema,* which one normally says quietly, should be said out loud.

10. On *Shabbos* the *Krias HaTorah* is read with six *Aliyos,* a *Maftir* and a *Haftorah.* A *Bris Milah* on *Yom Kippur* is performed after *Krias HaTorah.* A *Brocho* is recited on wine and it is given to the baby to drink.

that in my body still beat a 'Jewish' heart, the Baal Shem Tov appealed to my emotions to return to my people. He assured me that if I did sincere Teshuva and started a new life—the life of a pious Jew living according to G-d's Commandments—then I would be forgiven for my past. He urged me especially to fulfill the *Mitzvah* of *Tzedakah,* giving charity to the poor and the needy.

"The Baal Shem Tov also gave me a sign so that I would know when and if my sins were forgiven. He told me that if ever someone came to my home and related this story to me, then I would know that my *Teshuva* had been accepted by the *Ribono Shel Olam.* That's why I always invite people to my house and ask them to tell me any stories that they know about the wondrous Baal Shem Tov."

R. Eliezer says, "Repent one day before your death." The students asked, "Do we know which day we will die?" He answered, "Then, of course, repent today because maybe you will die tomorrow." It is clear that all one's days should be full of repentance. (Shabbos 153a).

"There is no sickness in the world that has no healing. What is the healing of the evil inclination? Repentance." (Medrash)

RAV SAADIA GAON

A disciple of Rav Saadia Gaon once arrived at his home to find the saintly figure of the Gaon bent over in prayer and with an obvious look of pain and anguish on his face.

"Why is my master suffering so?" asked the disciple.

"I have just realized how insufficient my prayers and supplications are before *Hashem,*" answered the Gaon. The disciple could not understand how a person considered to be the greatest of his generation could speak thus of himself.

Rav Saadia Gaon proceeded to relate how he had learned a powerful lesson from another person. "I was a guest in the house of someone who did not know I was a scholar of the Torah and who extended the courtesy usually accorded to guests. Later when he found out who I was, he began to show me even greater honor. When I was about to leave his home, he fell to the ground, crying and pleading, 'Let the

82

11. If *Yom Kippur* falls on *Shabbos*, *"Vayechulu"* is recited at the end of *davening* on Friday night.
12. *"Tzidkoscho"* and *"Avinu Malkeinu"* are not recited if *Yom Kippur* falls on *Shabbos*. However, *Avinu Malkeinu* is recited on *Yom Kippur* if it falls during the week.
13. It is best to start *Mussaf* by *chatzos* (mid-day). By *Mincha*, *Krias HaTorah* is read with three *Aliyos*, with the last *Aliyah* reading *Maftir Yonah*. The day concludes with the added prayer of *Neilah*.

master please forgive the lack of honor I accorded him.' I said to him, 'You have honored me to the extent of your ability. What more could you have done?' He responded, 'I apologize for the first hour when I did not yet know of the identity of our master, and I did not honor him sufficiently.' "

"If that man was so concerned about honoring a human being in the proper manner, how much more so should we tremble with fear when we realize the honor that is due to the Almighty. Though I worship, fear and love Him more and more every passing day, I still have to pray and plead for Divine forgiveness for the shortcomings in my prayers in previous times."

* * * * *

RAV LEVI YITZCHAK OF BERDICHEV

The following story is told about the renowned Rabbi Levi Yitzchak of Berdichev. On the eve of the Day of Atonement, he and his attendant went to the synagogue, and there he bent down under the benches and desks, as if searching for something. He found nothing, but then with an expression of happiness and satisfaction, he prepared to begin his prayers. He raised his eyes to heaven, and addressed his Father in Heaven. "Sovereign of the Universe, look down at Your children and have mercy upon them. You have forbidden them to eat and drink on this day, but although they fulfilled the commandment, I have found no drunkard here nor any man suffering from gluttony, as is always true when other nations have their feasts. But here they are, all of them, waiting with awe and dread on the holy Day of Atonement. These are Your children. Take this into consideration and inscribe them all in the Book of Life."

* * * * *

SHEMA KOLEINU
"Shema Koleinu, Hear Our Voice, O L-rd."

The Gaon Reb Meshulam Yisochor Horowitz from Stanislow would open the Ark before he started the *Selichos* prayer, and with intense sobbing relate this story:

A king had an only son whom he brought up in princely fashion, denying him nothing. He loved him, had him well educated and, when the boy grew up, had him wed to a lovely princess. The king hoped to have his son follow a righteous path and eventually rule the kingdom. However, the son did not follow his father's advice. He mixed with bad company, who influenced him to concentrate on life's baser pleasures. Soon he left his wife, and became attracted to other women.

14. On *Motzai Yom Kippur*, we blow the *Shofar*, and we say *"Atoh Chonantonu"* in the *Shmoneh Esrei*.

15. *Havdalah* is made on a cup of wine and a candle. The *Brocho* is recited on the candle. *Besomim* (spices) are not used on *Motzai Yom Kippur*. When *Yom Kippur* falls out on *Shabbos*, most authorities advocate using *besomim* for *Havdalah*.

16. *"Vihee Noam"* and *"Atoh Kodosh"* are not recited on *Motzai Yom Kippur* even if it also happens to be *Motzai Shabbos*. This is because *Sukkos* follows *Yom Kippur*, and one does not recite those *Tefillos* when there is a *Yom Tov* during the following week.

This caused his parents great heartache, so much so, that in time, the father banished him from the palace. The son left the place of his birth and wandered from city to city all over the world. His clothing became tattered. The features of his face changed so that it was impossible to recognize him, let alone believe that he was once a prince.

Years passed. The former prince suffered greatly. He began to think about the causes for his exile and his great suffering. He regretted his behavior and decided to turn over a new leaf. He planned to return to his father and beg forgiveness, and after many difficulties, he succeeded in reaching his father's palace. When he approached the king, he fell to his knees sobbing and pleading for forgiveness for his mistakes. But his father did not even recognize him because conditions had so changed his physical features. In desperation, the son exclaimed, "Father, if you don't recognize my face because of the change in me, surely you recognize my voice. My voice has not changed." The father listened carefully and did recognize it. He had mercy on his only son and took him back into the palace.

"So it is with us," the *Tzaddik* continued. "We are the children of the holy L-rd. He loves us, takes pleasure in us, exalted us above all people, escorted us under the wedding canopy at Mt. Sinai, gave us the holy Torah that teaches righteousness. But we turned away from His commandments and were exiled from our land. The multitude of our sins has caused our original features to change and become unrecognizable. But now that the Holy Days have arrived, we are indeed sorry for our misbehavior. We want to return to the L-rd. We therefore exclaim, "Hear our voice." If you do not recognize our features, please recognize our voice because we are Your children. Spare us and have mercy on us and accept our prayers in mercy and with favor."

CHOFETZ CHAIM

One of the Jews who lived in Radun (the town of the Chofetz Chaim) became severely ill, and the doctors gave their opinion that it would endanger the man's life to fast on *Yom Kippur*. Fearing that this man might stubbornly disobey the physicians and insist on fasting, the Chofetz Chaim went personally to see him right in the middle of

17. *Motzai Yom Kippur* is a partial *Yom Tov*. *Kiddush Levana* (blessing of the new moon) is recited. It is best to start working on the *Succah* right after *Yom Kippur* to show that we start off the New Year with a *Mitzvah*.

the holy day, bringing him some food. The pious sage cut this into small pieces, each of them smaller than a *kezayis*. Then he explained to the sick man, carefully and precisely, how to eat them—that is, how much time to leave between one bite and the next. Only after the sick man promised him that he would follow his instructions did the Chofetz Chaim return to the place of prayer. As he departed, he told the man that he would pray that his eating should be accepted by the Almighty as equal to fasting and that he should merit to receive *Hashem's* pardon, forgiveness and atonement. (After *The Chofetz, Chaim, His Life and Work*, p. 918)

"*If it were not for* Yom Kippur, *the world would not exist, because* Yom Kippur *forgives in this world and the next world. Even if all* Yomim Tovim *would cease to be,* Yom Kippur *will always be.*" (Pirkei DeRav Elazar)

"*Rav Levi said: 'Great is repentance, for it reaches as far as the Throne of Glory.'*" (Yoma 86A)

סוכות
Succos

SUCCOS—INTRODUCTION

"On the fifteenth day of the seventh month, when you have gathered the fruits of the land, you shall keep the feast of the L-rd seven days; on the first day shall be a solemn rest, and on the eighth day shall be a solemn rest. And you shall take to you on the first day the fruit of goodly trees, branches of palm trees and boughs of thick trees, and willows of the brook, and you shall rejoice before the L-rd your G-d seven days. And you shall keep it a feast unto the L-rd seven days in the year; it is a statute forever in your generations; you shall keep it in the seventh month. You shall dwell in booths seven days; all that are home-born in

SUCCOS

We are taught by our Sages that dwelling in the *Succah* serves as a reminder that this world is but a temporary one. Our behavior should, therefore, be of the kind that one adopts under temporary circumstances. Our goal in life should not be merely to possess and cherish wordly goods, but rather to serve G-d.

The Torah requires us to rejoice on the holiday of *Succos*. In addition, we are to feel charitable towards others who do not have the luxuries we are blessed with. Leaving our homes to dwell in the *Succah* reminds us of those less fortunate than we.

Although our religion is not merely symbolic, nevertheless, there are *mitzvos* which carry strong symbolism. The Four Species, *Arba Minim*, have a beautiful symbolic interpretation:

The *Esrog*, which is edible and emits a pleasant fragrance, is symbolic of those people who do good deeds and are learned in Torah. The *Lulov*, which has no fragrance but which comes from a date tree bearing fruit, is compared to those people who are learned in Torah but lacking in good deeds.

The *Hadass* (myrtle) which has a pleasant fragrance but grows on a bush that bears no fruit, is compared to those who do good deeds but are ignorant of Torah. The *Aravoh* (willow) which has neither taste nor aroma represents the Jew who, unfortunately, has neither good deeds nor the knowledge of Torah to his credit.

The Torah tells us to gather these four species which represent four types of Jews, and hold them together. This symbolizes the importance of Jewish unity, as it is written in the *"Amidah"* prayers of *Rosh Hashono,* "And they (Israel) shall all form a single band to do Your will with a perfect heart."

Israel shall dwell in booths; that your generations may know that I made the children of Israel to dwell in booths, when I brought them out of the land of Egypt; I am the L-rd your G-d." (Vayikra 23: 39-43).

The Feast of Succos is the third pilgrimage festival which the Torah specifically devotes to rejoicing. It is the time when the farmer rejoices after he has gathered in his produce after the autumn harvest. His granaries are overflowing and he is full of thanks for his good fortune. Thus the festival is also known as Chag Ha-Asif, *the ingathering of the harvest.*

The cardinal principle of the festivity is to forsake your convenient home and dwell seven days in a hut or booth. You abandon a home of comfort made of brick or stone and you find shelter in a frail booth which the rain may flood and the wind overturn. On entering this hut, you indicate the implicit faith and trust you have for your Maker.

Succos *(Tabernacles) is celebrated beginning the 15th day of* Tishrei. *During the seven days of this joyous festival we dwell in a* Succah *(small hut) as a reminder of the movable huts in which the Jews dwelled during their desert wanderings, when Hashem protected them. We also use the Four Species (*Esrog, Lulav, Hadassim *and* Arovos*).*

"Sit as if it is your living quarters." From here they learned, "All seven days a man makes the Succah *his residence and his house only temporary." How? By bringing nice vessels and tablecloths into the* Succah, *eating, drinking, walking and sleeping in the* Succah. *(Succah 28b)*

The reason why the Lulov *is waved several times in the service is because this signifies a gesture of triumph. Just as kings hoist their flags over territory they have won from their enemies, so too do we wave our own standard to proclaim that we have been victorious over our accusers on* Yom Kippur. *(Abudraham)*

"We should have in mind when sitting in the Succah *that G-d commanded us to do so in remembrance of the exodus out of Egypt*

and the Clouds of Honor that surrounded the Children of Israel in the Wilderness." *(Bach)*

THE UNIQUE ESROG

It was the first morning of *Succos* in the city of Lisensk, and the rabbi, Rabbi Elimelech, was obviously disturbed by something in the Shul's air. He constantly stopped in the middle of *"Hallel"* to sniff.

After *davening,* Rabbi Elimelech started investigating all of the congregants' *Esrogim.* An hour of searching brought no success until the rabbi came to a stranger sitting in a corner near the exit. When the rabbi smelled this man's *Esrog* he heaved a deep sigh of satisfaction.

"This is the one!" he exclaimed. Turning to the owner of the *Esrog,* Rabbi Elimelech said, "Tell me, please. Where did you acquire this *Esrog*

HILCHOS SUCCAH

1. It is a *mitzvah* to start building the *Succah* immediately after *Yom Kippur*. If this is not possible, the building can be done before *Yom Kippur*.

2. The walls of the *Succah* have to be at least 10 *tefochim* high (38 inches).

3. A *Succah* whose top is higher than 20 *amos* (35 feet) is *possul* (invalid).

4. The walls of the *Succah* have to start at least within three *tefochim* (11 inches) from the ground.

5. If a *Succah* is smaller than 7 by 7 *tefochim* (25-27 inches) it is *possul*.

6. Any material can be used for the walls so long as it can withstand the normal winds. (Therefore certain materials must be tied securely to the framework.)

7. A *Succah* that was not made *"L'shem Succah"* (e.g., a garage with a removable top) is kosher, so long as it was made for shelter.

8. One fulfills the *Mitzvah* with a borrowed *Succah*.

---

which radiates the fragrance of *Gan Eden?*"

"Well, it's a rather lengthy story, rabbi," the stranger said sheepishly. "Actually, until this very moment, I felt rather embarrassed at having only a little *Esrog.*"

This is the story that he told:

"I live in Strelisk, and although I am not very well off, I am content. Every year, before *Succos*, I save up enough money to buy myself an expensive *Esrog*, because I value that *Mitzvah* very highly.

"This year, as always, I took the fifty gulden I had saved and made my way to Lemberg to buy an *Esrog*. "I stopped over for the night at a roadside inn, and as I prepared for bed, I heard a commotion from the street. I hurried downstairs to see what was happening.

"When I reached the lobby, I saw a burly man, almost hysterical, begging the innkeeper to help him. The inn-keeper explained to me that the man was a *Baal-Agalah,* a wagon-driver, and the horse which he relied on for his income had broken its leg. Now the *Baal-Agalah* was forced to buy a new horse to replace it. The innkeeper offered to sell him a horse for fifty gulden but the *Baal-Agalah* had nowhere near that sum with him.

"So I told the innkeeper that if he would give the *Baal-Agalah* the horse, I would give him forty-five gulden in cash. The innkeeper agreed, and the *Baal-Agalah* was speechless with gratitude.

"The next morning I continued on my way to Lemberg. I bought the nicest *Esrog* I could for five gulden and returned home. My wife agreed with me when I said that we couldn't stay for *Succos* in Strelisk, where everyone would make me feel ashamed of my *Esrog*, so we came to Lisensk for *Yom Tov.*"

Rabbi Elimelech eagerly followed all

9. The *Succah* should have at least 3 walls. If it has fewer than 3, a rabbi should be consulted.

10. A *Succah* should not be built under any projection (e.g. a ledge or overhang.) One must be careful that tree branches do not extend over the *Succah*, and one must not eat under those branches if they do. (In these cases, a *Rav* should be consulted.)

11. As befits a *mitzvah*, the *Succah* should be tastefully decorated. If any part of the *Succah* or its decorations falls, one may not use them in any manner until after *Simchas Torah*. (They can, however, be rehung on *Chol Hamoed*.) Hanging decorations should be hung within four *Tefochim* of the *S'chach*.

S'CHACH (Roofing)

1. The *Succah* must be constructed first, and only then is the *S'chach* placed on top.

2. *S'chach* is material of plant origin, detached from the ground, which is not subject to the laws of *tumah* (ritual impurity). Branches, bamboo poles, or narrow wooden slats are usually used. Edible fruit should not be

---

the details of the tale and when the stranger had finished, he exclaimed, "That is truly a remarkable story, my friend. Now I understand why I have been smelling the scent of *Gan Eden* all through davening. You truly deserve it. Let me hold your *Esrog* a moment before you go home."

The Vilna Gaon was known to be especially particular about finding perfect *Esrogim* and *Lulovim* for *Succos*. Once, messengers were sent to find a perfect set but they returned empty-handed. One messenger, though, came back to report that he had found a most beautiful set. However, it was in the possession of a certain man who refused to sell it. When the man learned that the *Lulov* and *Esrog* were to be used by the great Vilna Gaon, he changed his mind. "I will sell it to you on one condition, that when the Vilna Gaon uses this set, I get the reward for the *Mitzvah*."

When this was related to the Vilna

Gaon, he smiled. "May *Hashem* be thanked for arranging matters in this way. I do the *Mitzvah* for the sake of *Hashem*, not just for the reward. I will gladly do it even without the reward since I am doing what *Hashem* desires."

They say of the saintly Rabbi Levi Yitzchok of Berdichev that on the first day of *Succos*, without realizing it he broke the glass case wherein the *Esrog* lay, such was his eager devotion to performing the *Mitzvah*. He also did not realize that his hand was bleeding until after he had made the *Brocho*.

The Esrog *numerically equals 610; with the other 3 "minim," we have 613.* (Zohar)

"He who buys a nice Esrog *and a* Lulov *merits this world and the next."* (Maharal)

The Esrog *is shaped like a heart. It symbolizes the hope of Divine forgiveness for the illicit desires of our hearts. The* Hadas *is shaped*

89

left on the branches. The *S'chach* may not contain any sort of receptacle. Stolen *S'chach* may not be used.

3. The *S'chach* should be placed on the walls of the *Succah* itself. If the walls are metal, a *Rav* should be consulted as to how to place the *S'chach*. This problem may arise with a prefabricated *Succah*.

4. The *S'chach* must shade the majority of the area of the *Succah*. However, it should not be dense enough to provide total protection from heavy rain. The pieces of the *S'chach* should be sufficiently separated so that the stars are visible from inside the *Succah*. If they are not visible, it is still kosher.

5. There must not be a gap of three or more *tefochim* between the pieces of the *S'chach*, or between the *S'chach* and the wall. If part of the *Succah* is roofed, that area is not considered part of the *Succah*. Therefore, when eating in the *Succah*, one must stay only under the *S'chach*. It does not always make the *Succah possul*, but one should not eat under the roofed part.

6. *S'chach* which is wider than four *tefochim* (14 inches) should not be used for the *Succah*. Anything bigger than that would look like a permanent roof, and is not permissible.

like an eye, symbolizing the hope of Divine forgiveness for greed and envy. The Aravah *is shaped like a mouth, symbolizing the hope of Divine forgiveness for idle talk and falsehoods. The* Lulov *has only one spine and symbolizes Israel's single-hearted loyalty to G-d. (Sefer Ha-Manhig)*

Rabbi Naftoli of Ropshitz told the following story:

"A certain wealthy scholar bought a beautiful *Esrog* for a considerable sum of money. Someone asked to borrow the *Esrog* so that he, too, could fulfill the mitzvah. The borrower dropped the *Esrog* and it was damaged, rendering it unfit for use. The owner of the *Esrog* thought to himself that if he yelled or showed displeasure to the borrower, this would be displeasing to G-d. He therefore accepted the dam-

aged *Esrog* without a word of reproach."

THE SANZER REBBE

During the period preceding *Rosh Hashono* and *Yom Kippur,* people are careful about giving charity to the poor. Unfortunately, after the two sacred *Yomim Tovim,* we become lax. But it is over the long *Succos* holiday that the poor are especially in need of help.

The Sanzer Rebbe, Rav Chayim, Zt'l, was especially careful not to forget the needy at this time of year. Instead of spending great sums of money on *Noy Succah (Succah* decorations) he donated the money to the poor. He even borrowed money from the *Esrogim* dealers to distribute to the poor. When his son, himself a well-known Rav, asked him if one actually has to borrow funds to give to the poor, the

HALOCHOS OF EATING IN THE SUCCAH

1. If it rains on the first night of *Succos*, one must wait a reasonable amount of time for the rain to stop. If it does not, then one must make *Kiddush* in the *Succah*, wash and eat a small *kezayis* (size of an olive) of *challah* and not make the *Brocho*, *"Leishev BaSuccah."* If it then stops raining after one has eaten indoors, one must go out to the *Succah* again, wash, and make the *Brocho*, *"Leishev BaSuccah"* and eat in the Succah.

On the second night of *Succos*, one does not have to wait as long to make *Kiddush*, but one must still try to eat a *Kezayis* of *Challah* in the *Succah*. On all other nights, it is not necessary to wait until it stops raining, but one can eat inside the house. If the rain interferes with the normal use of the *Succah*, then one eats inside.

2. The first night of *Succos* we make a *Borei Pri Hagofen*, then *Kiddush*, then the *Brocho* of *Leishev BaSuccah*, and then *Shehecheyanu*. The second night of *Succos*, we make a *Borei Pri Hagofen*, then *Kiddush*, then a *Shehecheyanu*. There are different customs as to when one makes the *Brocho*, *"Leishev BaSuccah"* on the second night

---

Sanzer Rebbe replied, crying bitterly, "You know that your father doesn't know how to learn the Holy Torah. In me, there isn't a drop of *yiras shomayim* (fear of Heaven). There is only one *Mitzvah* left that I can observe, and that is the giving of *tzedakah*. Do you want to take that from me too?"

THE SPECIAL SUCCAH

It was the day before *Succos*, and the rain was splashing down like ocean waves. "I hope the rain ends before tonight, so we can eat in the *Succah*," Rabbi Mordechai of Lechovitz said to himself as he gazed out the window.

Then he noticed an old man limping slowly to the door. He quickly opened it and invited the man inside. "I am sorry to bother you," the visitor said, "but I am a poor shoemaker, and I have no lumber to build my *Succah*. I have heard that you are kind enough to buy boards and give them to the poor for their *Succahs*."

"Yes," said the Rabbi, "but they have all been distributed already. I am afraid that I have none left."

The old shoemaker nodded sadly. "Well, thank you anyway. I don't want to take up any more of your time." With that, he rose and slowly and despondently departed.

Rabbi Mordechai watched him in anguish as he trudged along. "Almighty G-d," he said to himself, "see how Your people obey Your commandments. Here is a poor, lame man who comes in the rain to find a way to build a *Succah*, and see how he suffers because he cannot!"

Suddenly, Rabbi Mordechai had an idea. He called out to his son, "Yossie, quickly dismantle our *Succah* and place all the boards here. We are going to bring them somewhere!"

The rain soon stopped—almost miraculously, it seemed. And so, that night, Rabbi Mordechai and his family were able to eat in the *Succah* after all. Only the *Succah* was not near their

of *Succos*. Some make it before the *Shehecheyanu*, like the first night, and some make it after the *Shehecheyanu*, as the last *Brocho*. After *Kiddush*, during the day, there are two customs of when to make the "*Leishev BaSuccah.*" Some make it after *Hagofen* and others make it after *Hamotzee*. On *Chol Hamoed*, the *Brocho* of *Leshev BaSuccah* is said after making *Hamotzee*.

3. Throughout *Succos*, it is forbidden for males to eat any meal of bread or cake outside of the *Succah*. Although one can eat fruit outside of the *Succah*, it is best to eat as much as possible in the *Succah*.

4. At every meal eaten in the *Succah*, following the *Hamotzee* or *Borei Meenei Mezonos*, we add the *Brocho*, "*Leishev BaSuccah.*" If we remain in the *Succah* from one meal to the next, it is not necessary to repeat the *Brocho*.

5. Until *Simchas Torah*, it is not permissible to use either the boards of the *Succah* or the *S'chach* for any other purpose.

6. One should eat and drink everything in the *Succah* during all of *Succos*. If possible, one should even sleep there. In colder climates,

own home. It was next to the home of the poor shoemaker, who was celebrating the most joyous *Succos* of his life, thanks to Rabbi Mordechai's generous gift.

Even though the Jews went out of Egypt in Nissan, *and that is when they started to utilize their* Succos *G-d did not command us to build* Succos *in that month since the weather is warm and it might seem that they are being built for shade. G-d therefore commanded us to make a* Succah *in* Tishrei *when it is cold, to make sure that we are building the* Succah *for the sake of the Mitzvah.* (Tur 625)

Rabbi Levi Yitzchok of Berditchev used to invite all his neighbors, including those of lower social strata, to eat with him in his *Succah*.

Once, he asked why he went out of his way to invite poor people. He replied with good humor, "In the future, in the World-to-Come, when all the

Tzaddikim will be invited to the *Succas Ohr Shel Livyoson*, (the *Succah* that will be created out of the skin of the Leviathan), I, Levi Yitzchok, will also wish to enter. No doubt, the angel stationed at the entrance will stop me and demand angrily why I, a nobody among great personalities, have the nerve to force my way into the *Succah*.

"I will answer, 'Please do not be angry with me. In my own *Succah*, I also spent the *Succos* holiday with very ordinary people and I was not at all ashamed of them.' "

MAH NISHTANA ON SUCCOS??

Rabbi Zvi Hirsh Lewin was once confronted by a Christian deacon who was determined to prove that Jewish customs are strange. "Tell me, Rabbi. How is it that on the night of Passover the youngest child asks *Mah Nishtana* at the *Seder*? Why doesn't the child ask the *Mah Nishtana* on *Succos* night instead? During this holiday, a

however, one need not sleep in the *Succah* if inclement weather causes undue hardship.

7. Women, very small children and sick people are exempt from eating in the *Succah.*

8. Proper respect should be shown to the *Succah.*

ARBA MINIM

There is a biblical commandment to hold in one's hands on the first day of *Succos* the following four minim (species): an *Esrog* (citron), a *Lulov* (palm branch), three *Hadassim* (myrtle branches), and two *Arovos* (willow branches).

LULOV—Palm Branch

1. The *Lulov's* central shaft or "spine" *(shedra)* terminates into one doubled leaf which is called the *teyomes.* A *Lulov* is unfit for use *(possul)* if:

(a) It is dry and white, or if the top of the *Lulov* is cut off or broken.

(b) The leaves are completely detached, or even just spread apart and hanging from the spine.

(c) The leaves are not doubled, or one side of the *Lulov* has leaves and the other side is bare.

person changes his entire living pattern. He leaves the comforts of his home to live in a temporary dwelling where the wind blows through the fragile walls. In general, it makes for a most uncomfortable way of life. The child should ask, 'Why is this night of *Succos* different from any other night of the year?' "

Rabbi Lewin explained, "At the *Seder,* the child sees his father sitting like a *melech* (king) at the head of a beautiful table set with wine and good food. Everyone is at ease, showing not a trace of worry or sadness. This is a most unusual scene for Jews in *Golus* (exile) and the child cannot understand the reason for this joy and happiness. In surprise, he asks, 'Why is this night different from any other night?'

"But during *Succos*, the child sees his family away from the security of their home, eating in a hastily constructed hut with the cold wind blowing through the walls. 'This,' says the child to himself, 'is the life of a Jew in *'Golus.'* He's not surprised, and therefore, he doesn't raise any questions."

The holiday of Succos *is a climax of festivities which commence with the High Holidays. (22B)*

THE APTER RAV

Although it was the day before *Succos,* it did not seem so at the home of the Apter Rav, Rabbi Avrohom Yehoshua Heschel. The customary delicious fragrances of *Yom Tov* food cooking were absent, for there was no food in the house. The *Succah* was

(d) Most of the leaves are split more than halfway down to the spine.

(e) The center top double leaf is split more than half-way down to the spine. However, if it split after the first two days of *Succos*, it is still usable.

(f) The center top leaf is split only a *tefach* (approximately 3 inches), but it is V or Y-shaped.

(g) The top leaf is single, or the *Lulov* has thorns.

(h) The *Lulov* is bent like a hunchback or to the side—(but if it is only slightly curved, then it is still kosher.)

(i) The *Lulov* has shrunk or shriveled.

2. The spine of the *Lulov* must be at least four *tefochim* (15 inches) long. The top of the *Lulov's* spine should also be at least one *tefach* higher than the *Hadassim* or *Arovos*.

already built and decorated with greens, but the family had nothing to eat there.

In the afternoon, a prosperous look-ing stranger arrived at the rabbi's house and politely said to the rebbet-zin (rabbi's wife), "I live in a distant city and can't possibly make it home on time for *Yom Tov*. Would you be good enough to allow me to spend *Succos* with your family?"

The rebbetzin could hardly hold back the tears as she replied, "Our house has always been open to guests and we would be honored to have you join us but . . . you see . . . things were a bit difficult this year and we have no money with which to buy wine, fish, chicken or meat for *Yom Tov*. I don't even have two candles to light in honor of the holiday."

"Is that all?" smiled the stranger good-naturedly. "I thought someone was sick. Money—that's no problem. Here, take these funds and go to the market. Buy whatever you wish *l'ko-vod Yom Tov* (in honor of the holi-day)."

The rebbetzin could not believe what she had heard. She thanked the

man for his generosity and rushed off to purchase all that she needed for the holiday without having time to tell her husband the news.

Toward evening, the stranger went to *Shul*. After *davening*, he ap-proached the *Rav* and asked if he could join his family for the *Seudas Yom Tov* in the *Succah*.

"We would be honored to have you as our guest. We are always eager to have guests at our table, but this *Yom Tov*. . . ." The *Rav* was too embar-rassed to continue. The stranger walked behind the *Rav* as he headed for his *Succah*.

"*Succah, Succah*," said the Apter Rav in a sad voice. "I did all that I could. I built you and trimmed you with all kinds of greens. Now I feel ashamed to enter you. But let me at least fulfill the *Mitzvah* of sitting in a *Succah*, even though I have nothing to eat."

The *Rav* entered the *Succah* with the stranger following behind him. His eyes lit up at what he saw. There on the table stood tall, glowing candles, two large *challahs*, a bottle of wine and a sumptuous *Yom Tov* dinner.

ESROG (Citron)

1. An *Esrog* is *Possul* if:

a) it is shriveled and dried up, or if something is missing.

b) it is spoiled or rotten.

c) it is cooked or preserved, or if it is soaked in water for 24 hours or in vinegar even for a few minutes.

d) it is completely round.

e) there are either black, white, or red spots covering the surface of the *Esrog*, or there is one large spot in these colors. If so, it should not be used unless there is no other alternative. A Rav should be consulted in case of such spots.

f) If it has been grafted with a lemon, an orange or with any other fruit. The result is a *Murkav* (hybrid). There are three visible signs of a *Murkav:*

1) Its outer skin is smooth.

2) The stem is on the surface of the fruit.

3) The skin is thin and its fruit is large and juicy. The skin of the kosher *Esrog* is thick and its fruit is small and contains very little juice.

The *Rav* did not ask where all these good things had come from. With great joy he bid his family "Good *Yom Tov*" and asked the stranger to please join them. They made *"Kiddush,"* ate the delicious foods, sang the holiday melodies, and recited *"Birchas Hamazon."*

After the meal, the *Rav* remarked that *Hashem* had provided him with the material needs for the *Yom Tov* but that he still lacked the required *Lulov* and *Esrog*. Once again, the stranger came to their rescue.

"I happen to have with me a most beautiful *Esrog* and a nice green *Lulov.*"

Now the Apter Rav knew that his *Yom Tov* was truly perfect and his joy was boundless. He embraced the mysterious stranger who had been sent like an angel from *Heaven.*

Early in the morning, the Apter Rav left for *Shul* alone, expecting his guest

to come a bit later. However, when he returned after davening, he found the man in bed, dangerously ill and unable to talk. He never found out who his generous benefactor was, for the man died several hours later.

After that time, the Apter Rav, his children and grandchildren made it their custom to light a *"Yahrtzeit"* candle every *Succos* in honor of the mysterious guest who had done so much to make their *Yom Tov* a beautiful and happy one.

SUCCOS IN JEOPARDY

Many years ago there was an epidemic in the city of Nadvernoh. In an effort to halt the spread of the deadly disease, doctors cautioned residents to be most careful about the cleanliness of their homes. All this happened a few days before *Succos* and Rabbi Mordchele of Nadvernoh had already erected his *Succah* in his yard.

95

2. Additional Laws:

a) If the entire *Esrog* is red, consult a Rabbi. If it is a reddish-brown color, it is permissible.

b) The size of an *Esrog* should displace at least 3 ozs. of water, according to Rav Moshe Feinstein, Shlita.

3. An *Esrog* should be as clear as possible and have bump-like elevations so that it does not have the feel of a lemon.

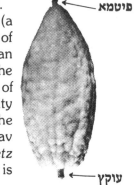

פיטמא →

4. Some *Esrogim* grow naturally with a *pitum* (a protrusion at the opposite end from the point of detachment from the tree). Some do not. If an *Esrog* naturally grows with the *pitum*, then the *pitum* should be whole. If the entire *oiketz* (point of detachment from the tree) broke off and a cavity remained, the *Esrog* is *possul* (not usable). If the entire *oiketz* broke off but the cavity is filled, a Rav should be consulted. If the entire cavity of the *oiketz* is filled and a part of it remains above the *Esrog*, it is kosher.

עוקץ →

Nadvernoh had a judge who hated the Jews and caused them much hardship whenever possible. When he heard about the *Succah*, he sent a policeman with orders that it be torn down, claiming that it was a threat to public health.

The rabbi refused to obey, and the judge sent the local police chief to carry out his orders. The rabbi still refused to comply, stating, "I have built this *Succah* to stand, not to be destroyed."

The judge decided to attend to the matter in person. He felt his own presence would make the rabbi back down, but he was wrong. He grew red with fury as the rabbi repeated his statement, "I built this Succah to stand, not to be destroyed. By the way, do you know that Reb Meyer'l of Premishlan was my great uncle?"

"Who cares who your uncle was?" screamed the outraged judge. "I order

you to remove this hut or you will spend your holiday in jail!"

"Your honor," Rabbi Mordchele said in a respectful tone, "please take a moment to sit down and listen to an interesting story." Reluctantly, the judge agreed.

"Once there was a nobleman who was blessed with ten strong, healthy sons. He also owned a beautiful garden full of trees. He decided to plant a flower bed to enhance the beauty of his garden. However, there was no vacant land available, so he ripped out the trees and planted flower beds in their place.

"As soon as he had completed this change, his sons became deathly ill. One after another, they passed away, until only the youngest remained alive. He, too, was very sick and it seemed that he too would soon follow his brothers to the grave.

"All the efforts of the doctors were

5. It is a *mitzvah* to seek a beautiful *Esrog (Pri Etz Hadar)*. One should spend up to one third more than the minimum price to acquire a beautiful *Esrog*.

AROVOS (Willow Branches)

1. The *Arovoh* tree should have reddish twigs. Its leaves should be smooth and have long edges.

2. The top of the twig and the top leaf should be intact.

3. All the leaves should be fresh without any dryness or wrinkles.

4. All the leaves within the full *shiur* of three *tefochim* should be present, and each leaf should be whole.

5. Some *Poskim* hold that one should try to obtain *Arovos* which actually grew near water.

6. If the twig is still green it is kosher, as long as it is not white. One that is dried out (i.e., when most of the leaves within 11 inches have dried up, or fallen off) is *possul*.

7. If the three *tefochim* on top are kosher, the *Arovoh* is kosher even if the bottom part, (below the three *tefochim*) is dried out.

---

of no avail. The boy was going to die! Finally, someone advised his father to go see the famous Rabbi Meyer'l. The nobleman had no alternative. He desperately wanted to save the life of his last remaining son, and so he made the long trip to Premishlan. With a broken heart and a crushed spirit, he related to Rabbi Meyer'l the tragic story of his nine sons and pleaded for a miracle to save the life of his last child.

"The rabbi scolded him for destroying G-d's trees in order to plant a flower garden. 'A tree is like a human being and should not be wantonly destroyed,' Rabbi Meyer'l told him. 'However, since you do show remorse, perhaps it's not too late. I will pray to the Al-mighty G-d that He spare the life of your youngest son.'

"By the time the nobleman returned to his home, he found that his son had recovered from the terrible illness."

Rabbi Mordchele turned to the judge. "Be advised," he said, "that you are the son. I therefore ask you: Is this the way to repay us for the debt you owe my great-uncle who saved your life?"

The judge fell at the feet of the saintly Reb Mordchele and said, "I know that all you have told me is true. Please forgive me. You may erect as many *Succahs* as you please."

Because of *Hashem's* action, the Jews and their *Succahs* enjoyed the official protection of the judge and they enjoyed a very happy *Succos. (Sipurei Chassidim)*

THE BEAUTIFUL GIFT

"You know, Rabbi," a man told the great *Dubno Maggid* (Preacher of Dubno), "there's one question about *Simchas Torah* that has always bothered me. Why don't we celebrate it together with *Shavuos*, the holiday which marks the Giving of the Torah?"

HADASSIM (Myrtle Branches)

The *Hadass* is a myrtle branch which has a group of three or more leaves encircling the twig. In each group one leaf should not be lower than the others.

Selecting The Hadass:

1. The *Hadass* should be fresh, green and moist—not dry or withered. If the leaves of the *Hadass* are dried out, it is *Possul*. The leaves are considered dried out if they are white.

If most of the leaves of the *Hadass* are dry, but one group of fresh leaves which are *Meshuloshim* are on top of each of the three *Hadassim*, the *Hadassim* are kosher. The reason for this is that the top of the *Hadass* provides the main image of the *Hadass*—because one's eye observes the top first. Thus, if the top leaves are dried out, they are not the most preferred, and the *Mitzvah* has not been fulfilled. Where the entire *Hadass* is not dry but the top leaves have whitened, the dried leaves should be removed.

The Maggid answered with the following *moshol* (parable): "There once lived a king who ruled over many lands and possessed vast treasures. Yet, he was never really happy for he had no children. The greatest doctors in the land were summoned to help but nothing succeeded.

"One day, the king heard about a saintly Jew who lived in the forest and who could perform miracles. The king decided to seek the help of the holy man. After hearing the king's request, the pious Jew walked to the corner of the room and prayed briefly. He then turned to the king and promised that his prayers would be answered and that a daughter would soon be born to him. However, there was one condition. No person excluding the king and queen, would see or speak to the young girl before she married. The king was surprised, but realizing that he had no choice in the matter, he agreed to the condition.

"As soon as the king returned to his castle, preparations for the little princess began. He set aside an island where only he and his wife would take care of her. Sure enough, nine months later the child was born. She was a beautiful girl, and as the years went by, it was obvious that she would be a beautiful and educated woman—truly fit to be a princess.

"When she reached her eighteenth birthday, her father was ready to give his daughter's hand in marriage. Many princes and lords wanted to be the king's son-in-law. When they found out, however, that they would not see the princess until after the wedding, they feared that something was wrong. They all refused to marry her; all except one young man whose father was the chief steward of the king. He could not dare insult the king. Although he secretly feared that his future wife might be handicapped, he agreed to become engaged to the young princess.

"After the strange wedding cerem-

2. All three *Hadassim* should be *Meshuloshim* (three leaves growing out from the same spot), for the entire length of the *shiur* of three *tefochim* (11 inches). All leaves should emerge from their buds on the same level.

3. If more than one half of the entire length of the *Hadass* is not *Meshulosh*, then the *Hadass* is *Possul*. If one is unable to obtain three *Hadassim Meshuloshim* he may use one which is *Meshulosh* and two which are not *Meshuloshim* if he can't obtain anything else.

4. The leaves should be straight and lying on the branch so that the branch is completely covered by the leaves. The top of the branch and the top leaves should be whole. If part of the top of the twig broke off, it is best to use a different *Hadass*. However, if there are not other *Hadassim* available, it may still be used if the leaves cover the top of the twig.

5. The leaves should be whole, not torn or broken.

6. The *Hadass* should not have more berries than leaves, even if the berries are green. However, with green berries, the *Hadass* is still kosher even if there are more berries than leaves. If the berries are red or black and they are more numerous than the leaves, then the *Hadass* is *possul*.

---

ony where no people were present, the lad finally got his first glimpse of his new bride. To his great surprise and immense delight, she was the most beautiful and intelligent girl he had ever seen.

"When the couple returned from their honeymoon, the young husband asked the king if they could now make arrangements for a great wedding feast. The small ceremony had not done justice to the lovely bride. A great celebration was made—worthy of the occasion and the charming bride.

"So too in our case," explained the Maggid, "The Torah was offered to all the nations, but they refused it, fearing the hardships that its observance may entail. But the Jews who had served *Hashem* from the beginning accepted it unconditionally. Only after months of study could the Jews truly rejoice in the treasure they had received.

"They celebrate it with a great wedding feast—none other than the joyous *Simchas Torah*."

The Torah does not mention "happiness" in connection with *Pesach*. It does so only once regarding *Shavuos*, yet it is mentioned 3 times in connection with *Succos*. The reason for this is as follows: *Chazal* say that the world is judged on four occasions: the grain crop, on *Pesach*; fruit, on *Shavuos*; man, on *Rosh Hashono*; and water on *Succos*. Since *Pesach* comes at the beginning of the year, before all other judgments have been made, the Torah does not mention happiness. On *Shavuos*, since one judgment day has passed (*Pesach*), the Torah mentions happiness only once. On *Succos*, three judgment days have passed (*Pesach, Shavuos* and *Rosh Hashono*) so the Torah can say "*Simcha*" (happi-

7. The *Hadassim* should be longer than three *tefochim* (11 inches) according to Rav Moshe Feinstein.

When Do We Perform The Mitzvah of the Four Minim?

The four species are taken on all seven days of *Succos* except on *Shabbos*. All four are required to fulfill the *Mitzvah*. If one does not have all the *Minim*, he should use whatever he has so that the *Mitzvah* of the four *Minim* should not be forgotten. A *Brocho* is said only when the *Mitzvah* can be done correctly with all four minim.

1. Beginning with the first day of *Succos* (if it's on *Shabbos*, we begin with the second day) through *Hoshana Rabba*, we must make the blessing over the *Lulov* and *Esrog* every day, except on *Shabbos*.

2. The *Mitzvah* of the four species must be performed during the daytime, i.e. between sunrise and sunset. If necessary, one may take the four species before *Hanetz* (sunrise) and after *Alos Hashachar* (the break of dawn.) If one did not have a *Lulov* and *Esrog* in the morning, he can still recite the blessing at any time during the day. If one has not yet taken the four species before twilight, which is right after sunset, he should do so then, but should not recite the blessing.

---

ness) three times. *(Rabbeinu Be-chaye)*

> *We beat the* Aravos *on the ground on* Hoshana Rabbah *to symbolize our hope that all evil will be ground into the dust so that it will exist no more.* (Tolaath Yaakov)

> *He who did not see the happiness of the* Simchas Bais Hashoeivah *did not see happiness in his days.* (Succah 51b)

> *The reason we are so joyous on* Succos *is that after we are cleansed from our sins on* Rosh Hashono *and* Yom Kippur, *we can serve G-d with true happiness.*

DANCING UNDER FIRE

The *Hakofos*—dancing around with the *Torah*—were in full swing—livelier than ever. No one realized that they had already been dancing for three hours. Someone would start a lively tune and the dancers, holding each other by the hand or shoulders, would quicken their pace even more.

Although I had come only to watch, I came too close to the circle and I was pulled into the mass of dancers. At first, I couldn't get the beat, but I, too, was soon singing and dancing excitedly with all the rest. What a great feeling—rejoicing with the Torah on *Simchas Torah!*

I looked up to glance at the man who had pulled me in. He appeared to be in his seventies, and it was wondrous that such an elderly man could dance with such vigor. I know it may seem astonishing, but tears were actually streaming down his cheeks.

Finally, the *Hakofos* were over and everyone sat down to relax. I followed my elderly friend and took a seat next to him. Seeing my interest, he remarked, "It's a long time since I had such inspiring *Hakofos*. The last time

GENERAL LAWS OF THE FOUR MINIM

1. To fulfill the *mitzvah* of the *Arba Minim,* one must hold the Four Species, and two blessings are made on the first day: (1) *Al Netilas Lulov* (2) *Shehecheyanu.* On subsequent days, only the first blessing is made.

2. Before saying the *Brocho,* the *Lulav* (to which the *Haddasim* and *Aravos,* the twigs of myrtle and willow, are bound) should be taken in the right hand and the *Esrog* in the left, and the blessing *"Al Netilas Lulov"* is recited.

When the Four Species are taken for the first time, the *Brocho* is followed by the *"Shehecheyanu."*

3. One takes the *Esrog* in his left hand and the other three items in his right hand (if he is right-handed). The *shedra* (central spine of the *Lulov)* should face the person. The *Lulov, Hadassim* and *Arovos* are bound together with *Lulov* leaves. The knots tying the *Lulov* together must be made from the same material.

The *Hadassim* should be on the person's right and the *Arovos* on his left. The *Hadassim* should be higher than the *Arovos.*

4. Since the blessing must immediately precede the performance of the *mitzvah,* one should pick up the four species with the *Esrog* upside down, make the blessing, and then turn the *Esrog* upright. There are some that solve this problem by picking up the *Lulov* after the *Brocho.*

5. One should stand when he recites the blessing and takes the four species. After taking the Four Species, one waves them according to his own custom, in each of the four directions, and up and down.

was over 30 years ago. Would you like to hear the story?"

Seeing the interest on my face, he didn't bother waiting for my answer, and continued. "It was during World War II and the Germans were trying to get control of my hometown, Riga. The nationalist forces were trying to defend the city but things were going badly for them. They suspected everyone of treachery and espionage. Almost everyone they arrested was shot on the spot.

"Can you imagine that night? The whole city was blacked out. Suddenly, the sentries saw a light coming from the top floor of our building. They hurried to investigate, but not finding anyone in the building, they rushed into the cellar, screaming, 'Where is that spy?'

"Let me explain to you about the light. We had in our community a man named Berel. He was one of the poorest people in the community, but he didn't know what it meant to be sad. In the cellar that night, everyone was silent, afraid to utter a sound. Berel

6. On the first two days of *Succos* one must legally own the four species. One may make a gift of the four species to his friend on *Yom Tov* to allow him to fulfill the *mitzvah*, and one may stipulate that the gift must be returned. Merely borrowing the 4 *minim* is insufficient. Even if the four species are bought in partnership, a stipulation should be made that each partner will acquire exclusive title to the Four Species when he takes them to perform the *mitzvah*.

7. A member of a synagogue may use the set belonging to his synagogue, because he is considered a partner in the set and we assume that the other members waive their shares to him to allow him to perform the *mitzvah*.

8. If one allows a child to use his *Esrog*, it is better that everyone else use it first since children can acquire property but cannot transfer it. (Therefore, if possible, each child should be provided with his own Four Species.)

could stand it no longer. He got up and shouted, 'It's *Simchas Torah* tonight. Let's rejoice!'

"His words fell on deaf ears. Suddenly, remembering something, he remarked, 'You need a little schnapps to wake you up. Wait, I'll get some from upstairs.'

"We looked at Berel in amazement. In the middle of the heaviest bombardment of the month, he was actually going to go up six floors, to his apartment—just for a bottle of whiskey. Before we could stop him, he was on his way.

"After he got the bottle, he took a candle and lit it so he could see his way downstairs. Berel was in such high spirits that he literally danced down the steps. It was this candle's light, seen by the sentries, which caused the commotion.

"There we were, ready to start the *Hakofos* when the guards burst in. We were horrified, and remained speechless. The sentry began shouting, 'Where is the spy who was sending signals to the enemy a few moments

ago? If you don't turn him in now, we'll shoot all of you!'

"Just then Berel stepped forward and said calmly, 'It was I whom you saw with a light, but . . .' Before he could finish the sentence, they marched him off.

"Many of us began to cry. We were sure that Berel would be shot. We pledged to support his widow and orphans. Everyone had a good word about Berel. The hours dragged by slowly.

"Suddenly, we heard footsteps and in walked—Berel. We thought it was a ghost, but there he was in the flesh. We all rushed to embrace him, but he stopped us. 'We have time for that later,' he said. 'Let's dance *Hakofos*.' But we wouldn't start until he told us the miracle that had just happened to him.

" 'Don't I always tell you that we have a great and mighty G-d? When I was brought to headquarters, the officer behind the desk said, 'Shoot him,' without even looking up.

" 'Staring at that officer, a thought

9. Women are not required to hold the Four Species on *Succos*, but if they choose to do so, they do fulfill a *mitzvah*, and therefore should make the blessing.

10. There should be no separation between one's hands and the Four Species. Thus, if one puts on *Tefillin* during *Chol Hamoed*, he should remove them before taking the Four Species.

11. Some have the custom of taking the Four Species and reciting the blessing in the *Succah*.

12. One may not eat a meal before reciting the blessing over the Four Species.

13. During the week of *Succos*, the *Arba Minim* may be used only for the purpose of the *Mitzvah*.

14. On *Shabbos*, one is not allowed to pick up the *Lulov* because it is *Muktzeh*.

15. The *Lulov* is shaken during *Hallel* when *"Hodu LaShem"* and *"Ana Hashem Hosheea Na"* are said. There are various customs concerning the exact directions in which to wave the *Lulov*.

---

flashed through my mind. 'Vladimir,' I said. 'Don't you remember me?'

" 'He looked up and smiled. "Berel! It's been a long time! I remember coming to your house on Saturday to light the fire in the winter. You rewarded me with a big, delicious piece of challah. You were always nice to me, Berel. You really are lucky. I wasn't even supposed to be on duty tonight. Tell me, what's this spying business? And what's the bottle of whiskey in your hand? Is tonight *Purim?'* he asked me.

" 'Vladimir, you should be ashamed of yourself,' I said. '*Purim* is later in the year. Tonight is *Simchas Torah.'*

" 'Oh, now I remember,' laughed Vladimir. 'You make a big circle and dance the whole day. Go home now Berel, and say a prayer for us, too.'

"That was Berel's story. When he returned we had *Hakofos* that I'll never forget."

Then the old man took my hand, pulled me up to dance and began singing this lively melody:

"Swing your feet and raise your voice,
With the Torah we rejoice. . . ."

Once a man who was not a follower of Rabbi Levi Yitzchok of Berditchev observed him dancing *Hakofos* and frowned disapprovingly at it. He felt that this was below the dignity of a religious Jew and so he remained aloof from the festivities. Rabbi Levi Yitzchok noticed this and came over to him.

"Does the Torah not tell us to rejoice on our festival?" he asked. "This is why I feel so ecstatic. Had we not been commanded to enjoy the holiday I would not behave in this manner. My happiness is obvious because I am observing the commands of *Hashem* in the way that He wants them performed—with great zeal and spirit."

DAVENING ON SUCCOS

The seventh day of *Succos* is *Hoshana Rabba*, the eighth day is *Shemini Atzeres*, and the last day is *Simchas Torah*.

1. All nine days including *Shemini Atzeres* and *Simchas Torah*, "*Yaale V'Yovo*" is inserted in the silent *Shmoneh Esrei* and in *Birchas Hamazon*. On *Shemini Atzeres* and *Simchas Torah*, "*Yom Hashmini Chag Ho'atzeres Hazeh*" is substituted for "*Yom Chag Hasuccos Hazeh.*"

2. On all seven days of *Succos*, *Hoshana* prayers are said immediately after the *Mussaf Shmoneh Esrei* according to *Nusach Ashkenaz*. (According to *Nusach Sefard* they are said after *Hallel*.) It is customary that a *Sefer Torah* is taken out and that everyone in the synagogue who has a set of the four species joins in a procession counterclockwise around the *bima* during the *Hoshanas*. One who is in mourning should not participate in the procession but could give his *Arba Minim* to someone else to use. On *Shabbos* there is no procession or *Sefer Torah*

KOHELES

The Book of *Koheles* which was written by *Shlomo Hamelech* (King Solomon), is read on *Succos*. Among its wise sayings is, "Cast your bread upon the waters, for you shall find it after many days." (*Koheles*, 11:1) This is interpreted to mean that one should always be ready to do a good deed even if he doesn't expect a reward for it, for some day, the fitting reward will come.

The following story is a good illustration of this principle:

Bar Kappara, one of the scholars who lived at the time of Rabbi Yehuda HaNassi, was once walking along the seashore of Caesaria, when he noticed a shipwreck in the distance. As he stood and watched, he saw a man swimming from the wreck towards the shore. Although the man was a good swimmer, he was on the verge of collapse when he reached the shore.

Bar Kappara rushed to his aid. Had he not been there at the time, the man would probably have died of exhaustion and thirst. Bar Kappara brought the man safely to shore and gave him food and water. When Bar Kappara saw that the man was completely recovered, he gave him some money so that he could continue his trip.

"Why have you done this for me?" asked the man. "We are total strangers, yet you showed me the kindness of a brother."

"We are all G-d's children, and should help one another," answered Bar Kappara. "I feel privileged to have helped save a human life. Go in peace, and may G-d be with you for the rest of your journey."

Many years later, the Jews of Caesaria found themselves in difficulty with the local authorities. To ease their plight they decided to petition the Governor, and Bar Kappara was chosen to intercede on their behalf. At the palace, Bar Kappara was ushered into the presence of the Governor. To his great astonishment, he recognized him

taken out during the *Hoshanas*. On *Hoshana Rabbah* the custom is to take out all the *Sifrei Torah* and to go around the *bima* seven times.

3. It is customary to say the *Shacharis* for *Yom Tov* on *Hoshana Rabba*, except that *Mizmor L'Sodah* and the weekday *Shmoneh Esrei* should be said and *"Nishmas"* is omitted.

4. In the *Tefillah* of *Hoshana Rabbah*, we recite all the *"Hoshana"* prayers, after which we strike the floor five times with the bundle of *"Hoshanos"* (a bundle of five willow twigs).

5. The eighth day of *Succos* is *Shemini Atzeres* and the ninth day is *Simchas Torah*. On both days, *"Shehecheyanu"* is recited over Kiddush (and by women, upon lighting the candles) since it is a festival in its own right.

6. Beginning with *Mussaf* on *Shemini Atzeres*, *"Mashiv Horuach U'morid Hagoshem"* is recited in the blessing of *"Mechaye Hamaisim"* in every *Shmoneh Esrei* until *Mussaf* on the first day of *Pesach*.

7. There are differing customs regarding sitting in the *Succah* on *Shemini Atzeres*.

8. *Yizkor* is said on *Shemini Atzeres*.

---

as the same man whose life he had saved on the shores of Caesaria.

It was obvious that the Governor was pleased to see his savior.

"What can I do for you, my friend?"

Bar Kappara begged the Governor to use his authority to help the Jews of Caesaria. The Governor listened carefully to all that Bar Kappara had to say. Then he replied:

"I am glad that our paths have crossed again. I will gladly do this favor for you, because when I was in a desperate position, you helped me without seeking any reward. Because of those unselfish and kind acts you have done for me, I will heed your request and help your suffering brethren."

Bar Kappara had brought a large sum of money as a gift to the Governor from the Jewish community. The Governor, however, gave the money back to Bar Kappara, saying:

"Although the sum of money you gave me after I was shipwrecked was not as great as this, it meant everything to me at that time. Keep your money as a gift from me. You may return to your people and tell them that I am helping them out of gratitude to you."

Bar Kappara joyfully returned to his fellow Jews who were eagerly awaiting the results of his mission on their behalf.

Their rejoicing at Bar Kappara's good tidings was great, and they all acknowledged the wisdom and truth of *Shlomo HaMelech's* teaching:

"Cast your bread upon the waters, for you shall find it after many days." *(Koheles Rabba)*

SIMCHAS TORAH

This happened on the last *Simchas Torah* in Warsaw, in 1942. Only a handful of Jews had remained alive

CHOL HAMOED

The *Mitzvah* of *Simchas Yom Tov* applies to *Chol Hamoed*, so that fasting in general is forbidden on these days.

I. MELACHA ON CHOL HAMOED

1. There are five cases in which *Melacha* (work) is permitted on *Chol Hamoed:*

a) *Ochel Nefesh* (work involving preparation of food)

b) *Tzorchei Hamoed* (needs of the *Yom Tov* other than *Ochel Nefesh*)

c) *Tzorchei Rabim* (needs of the community)

d) *Poel She'ein Lo Ma La'achol* (one who lacks money even for food.)

e) *Davar Ha'Aved*—It is permitted to do a *Melacha* on *Chol Hamoed* to prevent a probable loss to something which is already in one's possession. For example, an employee whose position would be jeopardized if he missed work on *Chol Hamoed* may go to work. (He should, however, try to arrange to take his vacation during *Chol Hamoed* even though a different time might be more attractive for personal reasons). Other examples would be fixing the lock on the front door (to prevent theft) and picking fruit from one's own tree if it might spoil if left unpicked. When in doubt, consult a Rabbi.

II. CUTTING HAIR AND WASHING CLOTHES

1. It is not permissible to take a haircut and wash clothes on *Chol Hamoed* since the Rabbis forbade these two activities to ensure that they would be done *Erev Yom Tov*. One of the exceptions to this rule is in the case of hostages or prisoners who have just been released.

2. It is permissible to wash clothing which are dirtied continually, such as diapers or children's clothing. It is also permissible to remove a small stain locally, but not to clean the entire garment.

out of the five hundred thousand formerly in the Polish capital.

Twenty Jews were gathered in the home of Rabbi Menachem Zemba, the last remaining rabbi in Warsaw, to observe *Simcas Torah*. Among them was Judah Leib Orlean, former director of the Beth Jacob's Teacher's Seminary, who had devoted his life to religious education. At the proper time, they brought forth the Scrolls of the Torah; and, sorrowfully reciting the verses, which in former years had been joyously chanted, they wearily plodded the *Hakofos* about the table.

Suddenly a boy of twelve appeared in the room. This was astonishing, for the Germans had already slain or deported for extermination all the Jewish children in the ghetto. Who

III. OTHER LAWS OF CHOL HAMOED

1. There is a difference of opinion whether *Tefillin* are to be worn on *Chol Hamoed*. (Generally, *Misnagdim* put on *Tefillin* and *Chassidim* do not, but the Vilna Gaon also held that *Tefillin* are not worn and many *Misnagdim* follow his view). One should follow the custom of his father.

2. If one forgets *Yaaleh V'yovo* and has completed *Shmoneh Esrei*, then he must say *Shmoneh Esrei* again. If he remembers before he has finished *Shmonei Esrei*, then he returns to *R'tzei*. If he remembers before commencing *Modim*, then he says *Yaale V'yovo* at that point.

3. During the Birchas Hamazon, if one forgot to say *Yaaleh V'Yovo*, he does not repeat the *Benching*.

4. "Half" *Hallel* is said on *Chol Hamoed Pesach* and full *Hallel* is said on *Chol Hamoed Succos*.

5. *Mussaf* for *Yom Tov* is said every day and when *Chol Hamoed* falls on *Shabbos*, we include the *Shabbos Mussaf* as well.

6. One should not write on *Chol Hamoed*. If one must, he should do so with a "variation."

7. One should not buy clothes or fix one's house on *Chol Hamoed*.

could he be, and where had he come from? No one knew.

Orlean ran to the boy, and embracing him together with this Torah, cried out, "Young Jew with the holy Torah!" swept him along in an exultant hassidic dance. The others joined the dance one by one until all had formed a circle about the unknown boy, Orlean, and the Torah.

Bereaved fathers who had lost their entire families danced, with tears rolling down their faces, while the great educator reiterated, "Young Jew with the holy Torah! Young Jew with the holy Torah!"

This was the last dance of the Jews on their last *Simchas Torah* in Warsaw.

חנוכה
Chanukah

CHANUKAH—INTRODUCTION

When the Jews returned to the Land of Israel from the Babylonian exile (which had lasted seventy years) in the year 3408, they were not only permitted to rebuild the Bais Hamikdosh (Holy Temple), but were also allowed religious freedom. Thus, they were able to reestablish their homeland on a sound foundation of Torah. This tranquility, however, did not last.

Forty years later, the Near East was conquered by the Greeks, under Alexander the Great. Greek culture began to make inroads into the Jewish way of life. Greek generals now ruled over Judea. The most cruel and wicked tyrant to rule over the Jewish People during this period was Antiochus. He issued many harsh decrees against the Jews in an effort to force them to abandon their religion and adopt the Greek

CHANUKAH

Why is the emphasis in the celebration of Chanukah on the lighting of the candles? Why isn't more emphasis placed on the victorious battles that the Maccabees fought?

The answer to these questions teaches us an important lesson. If we were to celebrate only our victories over the Greeks, years later people would say that the reason we were victorious was because we were better soldiers. They would stress the human side of it and forget that it was G-d who was responsible for the victory. Hashem, therefore, had to perform a miracle that was impossible to explain logically so that everyone would have to admit that it was from G-d. Through this, everyone would come to realize that all the events of

Chanukah are attributable to Hashem.

We find that this is true even in our times. When Israel was victorious in her wars against the Arabs who were far superior in weapons and in numbers, we tended to forget that these victories were due to G-d; we could not win without Him. It is only when we forget that we are Jews and think that we are like all other nations, that Hashem has to remind us that we will not be victorious, unless He so decides.

It is unfortunate that it took another terrible conflict like the Yom Kippur War of 1973 to prove that it is not "Kochi V'Otzem Yadi" (man's strength) that makes the Jews victorious, but rather "Yisroel B'tach Ba'hashem"—Israel must trust in G-d. (Tehillim 115:8)

culture. *Religious practices, particularly* Bris Milah *(circumcision) and the observance of* Shabbos, Rosh Chodesh *and* Yomim Tovim, *were all prohibited under penalty of death.*

Many Jews chose to die as martyrs rather than accept the pagan culture and idol-worship of the Greeks. Others, however, chose to revolt against this oppression. This marked one of the first times in the history of mankind that a nation fought for freedom to worship their own religion. With the help of the Almighty, and under the leadership of Yehudah Maccabee and his brothers, the Jews were victorious over their enemies, who logistically were far superior to them.

After the military victory, the Jews turned to restoring and rededicating the Bais Hamikdosh, *which had been desecrated by the Greeks. When they came to light the* Menorah, *they could not find any pure olive oil which had not been defiled by the Greeks. Finally, one small bottle of oil was found with the seal of the High Priest still intact. It was sufficient to burn for only one day. By a miracle, it lasted for eight days, which was long enough for a fresh supply to be obtained from the territory of the Tribe of Asher, which was a four-day journey from Yerushalayim. An additional four days was needed for the return trip. Therefore,* Hashem *made the small bottle of oil miraculously burn for eight days, until the*

Chanukah is a reminder that this fire which the Jews had lit when they were willing to go to war on behalf of *Hashem* and His commandments, will *never* be extinguished. No matter how superior the enemies may seem, we will still be victorious if we deserve to be. *"Aileh Ba'rechev, V'aileh Ba'susim"* (they have horses and chariots) *"Va'anachnu B'shaim Hashem Elokainu Nazkeer"* (but we will call on the name of *Hashem). (Tehillim* 20:8)

THE HERO'S ATTEMPT

After the wicked Antiochus died, his son Eopater became king of Syria. Eopater was no better than his father. He controlled the biggest army ever known up to that time. It was composed of 100,000 infantry men, 20,000 horsemen, and 32 trained war elephants. All the soldiers had armor and helmets and were veterans of previous wars. When the sun rose and shone upon the glittering array of armor, the reflected light dazzled the eyes for miles around.

The Jews, under the leadership of Yehuda Hamaccabee, were determined to fight to the last man. They prayed to *Hashem* to help them in their holy cause.

The Maccabees fought bravely, destroying one battalion after another, but there seemed to be no end to the swarming masses of the enemy.

Suddenly Elazar, Yehuda's brother, noticed a war-elephant that was more elaborately decorated than the others, and heavily guarded.

"That elephant must bear the king," thought Elazar. "If I kill him, the victory will be ours." With no thought for his own life, Elazar rushed in the direction of the elephant. He fought his way

new supply of olive oil reached the Bais Hamikdosh. Chanukah *comemorates these miracles.*

HILCHOS CHANUKAH

1. The eight days of *Chanukah* begin on the 25th day of Kislev. On these days we celebrate with festive meals to commemorate the miracles that *Hashem* performed for us in the days of the Maccabees. In order not to detract from the joy of *Chanukah,* one is forbidden to fast or eulogize during these days.

2. We light the *Menorah* on each of the eight nights of *Chanukah.* The first night we light one oil or candle light, the second night two lights, and so forth, until all eight lights are lit.

3. Candles are placed on the right side of the *Menorah.* Each night the new candle is lit first, so that the *Menorah* is lit from left to right.

WHO SHOULD LIGHT THE MENORAH:

1. Ideally, each member of the household should light *Chanukah* candles. The *Menorahs* should be separated from one another to avoid confusion to the observer as to the number of candles being lit.

2. A woman generally fulfills her obligation through her husband's *Menorah* lighting.

(A) A woman may be *motzee* (perform the *Mitzvah* on behalf of) her

---

through the guard, killing right and left, until he reached the decorated elephant. Elazar then drove his spear into the underbelly of the elephant. The huge animal came crashing down killing its rider. But here the heroic Elazar lost his life, also being caught beneath the crushing weight of the elephant.

It wasn't the king whom Elazar had killed, but one of his top generals. Nevertheless, Elazar's act of bravery inspired his brethren, and they fought on. The odds were too heavily against them, however, and they found themselves in grave danger.

Suddenly, a messenger brought news to the Syrian king of an uprising back in his own land. His son was attempting to overthrow him. Antiochus Eopater decided to call off this battle and make peace with Yehuda.

Thus, the land of Israel was once again saved at the very moment when all seemed lost.

* * * * *

MENORAH TO THE RESCUE

Our story takes us to the home of a poor Jewish family in Toledo, Spain, in the late 1400's. The impact of the Inquisition was already being felt by the Jews in Toledo, but so far, this family had not been put to the supreme test of faith.

Don Manuel, the elderly head of the household, was dying. He called in his only son, Isaac, to give him some personal instructions before his death.

"Isaac, my son," said Don Manuel, "I shall be leaving you soon. As you know, it has become very difficult to remain Jewish in Spain. If you find your lives are endangered, leave the country as soon as possible.

husband if he is unable to light; if so, they should both have the intention to fulfill the *Mitzvah* through this.

(B) If in the above case the husband is able to light the *Menorah* later, he should do so.

3. A child who has reached the age at which he understands the *Mitzvah* of *Chanukah* should light *Chanukah* candles.

THE MENORAH:

1. Every *Menorah* must have a *shammash* (service candle) by which the candles are lit. The *shammash* should be placed somewhat higher than the other lights so that it is obvious that it is not one of the *Chanukah* lights. Its purpose is to light and protect the other candles so that if any light is used from the *Menorah* it should be from the *Shammash* and not from the candles.

2. The lights of the *Menorah* itself may not be used for any purpose other than the commemoration of the miracle.

3. It is best to use olive oil or candles for lighting the *Menorah*. Any kind of wicks may be used for the *Menorah,* and they may be used repeatedly.

Oil that was stolen may not be used for the *Chanukah* lights, because this would be a *Mitzvah Habah B'Aveira* (a *Mitzvah* that is the result of a transgression).

"I have no great wealth to leave you except for this *Menorah*. It was my father's and his father's before him. Do not sell this *Menorah!* It has a tradition of miracles behind it. Take it with you wherever you move. You will not be sorry if you do."

Isaac, of course, agreed. Don Manuel passed away during the night, and the family was thrown into despair. What did the future hold for them?

The following evening, the neighborhood priest made a surprise visit to Isaac.

"How kind of you to take the time to visit us, Father Jose. Is there anything I can do for you?"

"I heard about your father's death," the priest said, "and I've come to bring my condolences."

"Thank you, Father Jose," Isaac said.

"Isaac, you know I've always been friendly to the people of the Jewish faith, and particularly with your father. I've come now to warn you. The Inquisition will begin concentrating its efforts in Toledo. I know you and your family will not convert to Christianity, and you may be forced to undergo a lot of suffering. Therefore, I suggest that you leave the country as soon as possible."

"But I haven't any money for the journey," said Isaac.

"I'm sorry I can't help you there," said the priest. "I can only warn you of the trouble ahead. Good night and good luck!"

The priest left a troubled and frightened Isaac staring after him into the

4. The lights must be in a straight line. They should not be lit in a circle because then the lights would look like a torch.

Each of the lights should be separate. Similarly, the wicks of the *Menorah* may not draw oil from one central source because then the *Menorah* would also resemble a torch. However, if the oil basin has a cover on it so that the wicks stick out from different spouts, it is permitted as long as it is not a circle.

5. An electric *Menorah* cannot be used for the *Mitzvah* of *Hadlokas Ner Chanukah* unless no other *Menorah* is available. In such a case, it should be lit without a *Brocho*.

WHERE TO LIGHT THE MENORAH:

1. One should place the *Menorah* at a window where people can see it, so that one fulfills the *Mitzvah* of *Pirsumei Neesah* (publicizing the miracle).

2. The *Menorah* should be placed between three and ten *tefochim* (between one and three feet, approximately) from the floor so that it will be visible to passersby.

It is permissible to place the *Menorah* higher than ten *tefochim*. However, if it is placed twenty *amos* (approximately 36 feet) above one's level ground, then one has not fulfilled the *Mitzvah*.

dark night. Isaac had heard stories about the treachery of the Inquisition. It gave him the chills to even think about it. But without any money how could he ever get away from his homeland that now threatened doom? Unless . . .

The next morning, *Erev Chanukah*, Isaac decided to bypass the *Shiva* (seven days of mourning for his father) in order to visit the captain of a certain ship, who was spending the night with his relatives in Toledo.

"Sir," Isaac said, after introducing himself to the captain, "you have earned a reputation for being kind to the Jews in their times of misery. It is urgent that I leave Spain with my wife and two children immediately, or we will be caught in the clutches of the Inquisition."

"I am sure that you are prepared to

pay," said the captain.

"Well, that's a problem. I haven't any cash available right now. However, I have a wealthy cousin in Holland who will be glad to pay any amount you request, if you could take me there."

The captain smiled sadly, and shook his head. "I'm sorry, but there are too many risks involved in making such a journey, and I cannot rely on promises of payment."

"But, I *will* pay . . ." Isaac began.

"If I don't see the money tomorrow morning," the captain interrupted, "I will sail without you."

Isaac went home depressed, and on the verge of tears. Where could he get money? No one would lend him any; he had no collateral. Should he sell the *Menorah*? No, he couldn't do that. *Chanukah* was starting that very

3. If one is traveling and it is possible for him to light the *Menorah* there, he should do so only if it will burn a half hour, even though in the vehicle he is travelling the *Menorah* may be higher than twenty *amos* from the ground outside. This is also true about lighting in a hospital, or on a high floor in an apartment building.

4. The *Menorah* must remain in the place where it is lit.

5. If a person is sick and cannot leave his bed to go to the window to light the Menorah, he should light it at his bedside.

6. If one normally eats in one place and sleeps in another, a Rav should be consulted as to where the candles should be lit.

7. If one is going to a friend's or relative's house for a *Chanukah seuda* (meal), he should light the *Menorah* at home because that is where he normally eats and sleeps.

8. If a person is staying at someone else's home during *Chanukah,* he should give his host a coin in order to participate in the *Mitzvah* when his host lights candles. However, it is always best to light his own candles.

9. A guest who does not have his own candles should watch the host lighting the *Menorah.* However, if he did not do so, he has still fulfilled the *Mitzvah.*

night, and he felt that he wanted to light his precious *Menorah* with more love and devotion than ever before. But was the *Menorah* worth the lives of all his family? He could readily sacrifice himself for his father's wish, but should he also sacrifice his family?

When Isaac returned home, he brought out his *Menorah* and stared at it for a long time. Of what use was this *Menorah?* He didn't even have enough spare money to buy oil to light it. He would have to choose between supper and the *Mitzvah* of lighting the *Chanukah Menorah.*

Suddenly, the *Menorah* appeared to be the symbol of salvation. He remembered all the stories he had heard of Jewish martyrdom. He remembered his father's face as he warned him on his deathbed, "Do not sell this *Menorah.* It has a tradition of miracles behind it."

Isaac began to polish the *Menorah,* in preparation for its use that night. He rubbed and rubbed until the old *Menorah* began to shine brilliantly. In the course of the polishing, he exerted pressure on a certain spot that cause the bottom of the *Menorah* to slide open. Dozens of gold coins clattered to the floor. Isaac couldn't believe what he saw—enough gold coins to pay for his family's safe passage out of Spain! *Chanukah* was indeed a time for miracles.

Isaac ran back to where the captain was staying. He gave him all of the gold coins, except for one. That one he saved to buy oil for his *Menorah.*

The next day Isaac and his family left Spain. They left all their household possessions behind, except for one item. They brought the *Menorah* with them, and it remained the family's most cherished possession for centuries after.

10. The *Menorah* must also be lit in shul with a *brocho* between *Mincha* and *Ma'ariv,* though one is not *yotzai* (does not fulfill his obligation to perform) the *Mitzvah* of lighting the *Chanukah* candles through the lighting of the *Menorah* in shul.

11. Because of *Pirsumei Neesah,* one should light the *Menorah* in every public place where Jews congregate; e.g. wedding halls.

WHEN TO LIGHT THE MENORAH:

1. One should light the *Menorah* right after dark, or at sunset, according to one's custom. The lights should last at least until a half hour after the stars come out.

2. On Friday, the *Chanukah Menorah* is lit before the *Shabbos* candles. On this day there must be extra oil or larger candles in the *Menorah* to make sure that the lights will still burn until ½ hour after the stars come out.

3. If a woman kindles the *Shabbos* candles before the *Chanukah* lights her husband may still light the *Menorah.* However, if there is no one else at home, she should be *yotzai* with someone else's *Brocho* and lighting of the candles.

4. On *Motzai Shabbos,* it is questionable whether the *Havdalah* candle or *Menorah* is lit first. In Shul, the *Menorah* is lit first and then *Havdalah* is made. At home, one follows the custom of one's family.

A SPARK IN THE DARK

"My fellow Jews, it's *Chanukah* today! Granted, this is an unholy place, but we mustn't neglect to kindle the *Chanukah* lights, right here in this concentration camp."

"You can't be serious," someone yelled.

"Go ahead! Light your candles. Pure olive oil and ritually acceptable wicks," another person said, laughing scornfully.

"Look over there," a third person cried out. "Those fires out there, they are waiting for us," and he pointed at the burning ovens of the crematoria of the concentration camp.

"Nevertheless, today is *Chanukah,* my fellow Jews," the old Rabbi spoke up again. "Who needs oil and wicks? Every Jew is a candle, as it is written,

'The soul of man is the light of the L-rd.'" (*Mishlei* 20) It was obvious that the old Rabbi had more to say. But just then, the hated chief Kapo of the camp burst into the cabin.

"Filthy Jews! It's your holiday today. A good meal is waiting for you. I will give regular hotel and restaurant service—to fatten you up. But first, I will teach you a lesson in the good manners we observe in this camp.

"Rule one: We have prepared boiling soup for you, and we will pour it into the palms of your hands. Rule two: Every ten men will get a whole loaf of bread. You will divide it into equal slices without using a knife. Rule three: Two grams of margarine will be given to each one of you tonight. You will lick it off your fingers, at my order."

THE BROCHOS RECITED ON CHANUKAH:

1. When one lights the *Chanukah Menorah*, the following *Brochos* are recited:

(a) . . . *L'Hadlik Ner Shel Chanukah.*

(b) . . . *She'asah Nissim La'vosainu Bayomim Ha'haim, Bazman Ha'zeh.*

(c) . . . *Shehecheyanu (only on the first night)*

Haneiros Hallalu and *Maoz Tsur* are then sung.

2. If one missed one night of lighting, he continues the next night with a Brocho and with the lighting of the proper amount of candles for that night.

3. If one forgets to light the *Menorah* on the first night of *Chanukah*, he should say *Shehecheyanu* on the second night.

4. If one made a *Brocho* on the *Chanukah Menorah* and then realized that there was no oil in the *Menorah*, he does not have to make another *Brocho* if he has oil right in front of him. If, however, he has to go somewhere else to get oil, he has to make another *Brocho* when he lights the *Menorah* later.

5. A *Ger* (convert) also makes the *Brocho* ". . . *She'asah Nissim* . . ." even thought it contains the phrase "our fathers," which does not directly apply in his case.

The starved and degraded crowd seized upon the promise of food, like a drowning man grabbing for a straw. The chief Kapo and his assistants began to distribute the dabs of margarine.

"Each ration of margarine is 700 calories, enough for doing one week of work. Each pat is a day of life," the Kapo explained. He was determined to destroy the last spark of humanity in the hearts of the starved inmates, and to instigate fights among them. "Every able-bodied Jew will get a double portion," he added, just as he was about to give the old Rabbi his portion.

"You, grandpa, I'll give a double portion," the Kapo laughed loudly, and in his mirth he dropped bits of margarine on the floor and ordered

the old man to pick them up.

"A miracle, a miracle!" the old Rabbi whispered. He quickly went down on his knees, carefully picked up the crumbs of fat from the floor, and put them inside the flap of his long coat.

"Ha, ha, ha, you old glutton," the Kapo laughed at the degradation of the old Rabbi. The crowd of humiliated Jews stood there, not understanding the Rabbi's intentions.

"The bread and the boiling soup you will get in exactly one hour. In the meantime, you can lick the fat which is melting on your fingers."

The Kapo left the cabin and went to get his friends to let them share his enjoyment of watching the Jews being degraded.

"My dear friends, this is truly a mir-

6. If one comes home late at night when no one else is awake (either at home or on the street), he must still light the *Menorah* at that time (with a *Brocho*).

7. If one is unable to light the *Menorah* on a given night, and he sees someone else's lit *Menorah,* he should say the *Brocho,* "*She'asah Nissim . . .*" (and *Shehecheyanu* if on the first night) over this *Menorah.*

8. If one lights the wrong number of candles, he does not make the *Brocho* when adding or subtracting additional candles on the same night.

ADDITIONAL TEFILLOS ON CHANUKAH:

1. The complete *Hallel* is said on all eight days of *Chanukah.*

2. "*Al HaNissim*" is added in *Shmoneh Esrei* and *Birchas Hamazon.*

3. (A) If one forgets to say "*Al HaNissim,*" he can go back and say it if he hasn't said *Hashem's* name in that *Brocho.*

(B) If he did not remember to say it at all, he does not have to say *Shmoneh Esrei* or *Birchas Hamazon* again. However if he remembered in the *benching* before *Harachomon Hu Yezakeinu,* he inserts it there.

4. On each day of *Chanukah,* three people *(olim)* are called to the Torah, and four are called on *Rosh Chodesh.* If *Rosh Chodesh* occurs on *Shabbos Chanukah,* then three *Sifrei Torah* are taken out from the *Aron Kodesh;* otherwise, two are taken out on *Shabbos Chanukah.*

---

acle!" the voice of the old Rabbi trembled. "I picked up the crumbs for a holy purpose. We can now light *Chanukah* candles if we are willing to give up all our margarine. I will light my portion. It's truly a miracle from heaven."

"A *Chanukah* candle! A *Chanukah* candle!" the words aroused shouts of joy.

The old Rabbi pulled some threads from the lapel of his coat to be used as wicks. He held up the bits of fat, not knowing where to put them.

"I have a small spoon which I had been hiding," someone called out from the crowd.

"Perhaps you can use some buttons?" a man said, as he pulled the buttons off his coat.

"Excellent idea! A true *Mitzvah.*"

The old Rabbi smiled and took the few buttons. They were made of tin, and after the cloth lining was removed from them they became containers for the melted fat.

As preparations for lighting the *Chanukah* lights were completed, the Rabbi's face shone: "My friends, the whole purpose of lighting the *Chanukah* lights is to publicize the miracle, for in the end the forces of holiness will overcome and triumph over the forces of evil. So let's light the *Chanukah* candles on the window sill, so that the villainous enemy will know that his end is near. . . ."

The old Rabbi stood before the window through which he could see the smoke of the ovens rising up to heaven, and he recited the blessing over the miracle of the oil, kindling the holy flame in everyone's heart.

As the Rabbi sang "Haneiros Hallalu," many joined in. Just then the Kapo burst in, shouting at the top of his lungs. The light in the window had caused a general alarm.

"You will all pay dearly for this," the Kapo screamed with disappointment, seeing that his plan had not worked.

In their hearts, the Jewish inmates of the concentration camp felt that the small flickering lights on the window sill had scored a victory over the chimneys of the giant crematoria, and even over death itself.

THE EXTRA MIRACLE

The question is an old one: Why do we celebrate the miracle of Chanukah for eight days? After all, if there was enough oil for one day, and it lasted for eight days, the miracle took place for only seven days, and not eight!

There are a number of answers. Some explain that the oil that was found was divided into eight parts, yet each day this small amount of oil burned for a full day. Therefore, it was a miracle each of the eight days.

Others say that the very discovery of the bottle of pure oil was a miracle in itself. If it had not been found, there would not have been any miracle of Chanukah at all. To explain this, the following Moshol (parable) is told:

A wealthy merchant was traveling to the market with eight bags of gold coins. Suddenly, a band of robbers fell upon him. They galloped away with seven of the bags, overlooking one.

When the merchant reached his destination, he hired a search party with some of the money he had left, telling them to find the robbers. He promised that if his money was recovered, he would donate one-tenth of all the money to charity.

Sure enough, his hired hands were successful. The bandits were rounded up, and the money was recovered. The people in charge of the town's charity asked the man to fulfill his pledge.

"Fine," he said. "I'll give you one-tenth of the money from the seven bags I got back."

"I thought you said you would give 1/10 of all the money, including the eighth bag?" they asked.

"That wasn't part of the deal."

"Not so!" they replied. "After all, if it hadn't been for the eighth bag, you wouldn't have had any money to hire a search party to find the other seven bags, so it is certainly included in your pledge."

The same idea applies to the miracle of Chanukah. If the bottle of oil had not been found on the first day, there would not have been any light at all on the other days. Therefore, the first day of Chanukah is as much a part of the miracle as the other seven days. That is why we light the Menorah for a full eight days.

* * * * *

The custom of kindling the Chanukah lights not only in the home but also in the synagogue was instituted by the Rabbis for the benefit of transients who ate and slept in the synagogue (Levush 671:8). The reason the custom is still followed today is to enable the ignorant to hear the blessings recited correctly and so to learn to recite the prayers properly themselves. Another reason is because the original miracle of the bottle of oil occurred in the Temple, and the synagogue today is considered a "Temple in miniature." Another reason is to publicize the miracle (Pirsumay Neesah).

פורים

Purim

PURIM—INTRODUCTION

Purim *is the Hebrew word for "lots." The evil Haman cast lots to decide the date on which he would exterminate the Jews. The date he chose was the thirteenth day of the Jewish month of Adar.*

It was on the fourteenth day of Adar *that the Jews of Persia were saved by* Hashem *through the efforts of Esther and Mordechai, from*

PURIM

The **Jewish people's** miraculous survival throughout history, despite persecution and exile, their outliving of empires and nations much mightier than them, calls to the mind the words of the prophet, "Take counsel together, and it shall be brought to naught, speak the word and it shall not stand; for G-d is with us." Sooner or later all conspiracies contrived against Israel are annulled and brought to naught by the L-rd. A philosopher once asked Rabbi Eliezer, "Is it not written, 'They shall build, but I will throw down'? Now all the buildings still stand upright."

Rabbi Eliezer answered, "It was not said with respect to the buildings but to the plots and wicked counsels which you are always contriving against us. You build up your plans and He destroys them immediately."

The philosopher agreed.

"It is indeed so. Every year designs are made to exterminate you, but something always intervenes and you always seem to survive."

APPROACHING EXECUTION

Over 300 years ago, during the reign of Emperor Ferdinand II of Hapsburg, a new governor was appointed over Bohemia, which included the famous Jewish ghetto of Prague. Among the things the governor brought with him to Bohemia was a chest containing gold brocade curtains. He intended to present them at some later date as a gift to the Emperor.

One day, word reached him that the chest containing the priceless drapes was missing. The governor instructed that no one should be allowed to leave the city until a thorough search for the chest had been made.

Hradek, the palace chamberlain, suggested that a sharp eye should be kept on the Jewish-owned stores, and that a thorough search of the ghetto should be conducted.

The governor, given an excuse to torment the Jews, jumped at the opportunity. The Jews, naturally, were terrified. The search party showed no consideration for the inhabitants of the homes they searched. The con-

118

Haman's wicked plot to destroy them. This story is read in the Megillah *(a small parchment scroll) on the evening and morning of* Purim. *The festival is a joyous one with much merrymaking and fun.*

The dramatic impact of this miraculous rescue on the Jewish people was so great that its commemoration through the Feast of Purim *has become an integral part of Jewish tradition.*

I. HILCHOS PURIM

1. *Megillas Esther* must be read twice on *Purim*, once in the evening and once more during the day.

2. In the evening, it must be read after *tzais hakochavim* (when the stars become visible).

3. After sunset and on, one is not supposed to learn Torah, eat, or do any work before the reading of the *Megillah*.

tents of closets and cupboards were strewn about haphazardly.

When they came to the home of Enoch Altschul, the councillor of the ghetto, they forced the trembling old man to lead them to his secret vault where he kept his most precious merchandise. Sure enough—there they discovered the glittering gold curtains. Enoch Altschul was put in chains and taken to the palace for questioning. The Jewish community feared for his safety and for their own.

"So, the 'honest' Jew has been caught as a thief," sneered the Governor. Explain yourself, if you can, Jew."

"I gave my word of honor to a noble member of your court that I would keep quiet about this," replied Enoch Altshul. "I cannot explain the presence of those curtains in my house, unless he gives me permission to do so."

"Take this man away," screamed the Governor, "and see if twenty lashes of the whip will loosen his tongue."

That night, poor Enoch Altschul tossed in pain. What should he do? He prayed sincerely for heavenly guid-

ance, and finally fell into a deep sleep. In his dream, he saw his beloved teacher and friend, the revered Rabbi Yehuda Loewy (the *Maharal* of Prague), who came to tell him not to worry. With G-d's help, everything would be all right.

Enoch Altschul awoke in the morning full of hope. He davened *Tefillas Shacharis* in his cell while waiting for the guards to come and bring him once again before the Governor.

The Governor was in an even worse mood this morning than he had been the day before, and threatened to destroy every house in the ghetto, if Enoch Altschul didn't reveal the truth.

Suddenly, there was a stir, as Hradek, the chamberlain stepped forward.

"Your honor," he said to the astonished Governor, "I am the one who stole the curtains. You see, several months ago I was desperately in need of 25,000 gold ducats to repay a gambling debt. I hit upon the idea of pawning your gold curtains. I went to Enoch Altschul, for I knew him to be a wealthy Jew who readily did favors for

4. Although one is permitted to read the *Megillah* all night, it is best to do so as soon after *tzais hakochavim* as possible.

5. In the daytime, one can begin reading the *Megillah* at sunrise. However, if a person must leave his home early in the morning, and might not have time to read the *Megillah* later on, he may begin as early as *alos haShachar* (approximately 72 minutes before sunrise.)

6. If a person forgot to hear the *Megillah* during the day and remembered during *bain hash'moshos* (twilight), he should read it then without a *Brocho*.

II. WHO IS OBLIGATED TO HEAR THE MEGILLAH?

1. Even though women are normally exempt from *Mitzvos Assai She'Hazman Gromma* (positive precepts that apply only at a specific time), they are nevertheless obligated to hear the *Megillah*. This is

those in need. He gave me the money, but then I threatened him that his Jewish friends and neighbors would suffer if he ever mentioned this incident to anyone.

"I would not have said a word about this, were it not for the fact that last night I had a most terrifying dream. I saw the famous late Rabbi of the Prague ghetto, Rabbi Loewy, who warned me that I must come forth and tell the truth. I was filled with the same fear that was felt years ago by those who tried to frame the Jews with blood libels. I knew I had no choice but to come forward and confess."

As he talked, Hradek kept clutching at his throat as if he were choking. When he finished, he fell down dead. Those who witnessed this scene were terrified by the realization that the G-d of the Jews had saved them from destruction, and had killed their enemy.

The Governor had no choice but to free Enoch Altschul and to give orders that the waiting mobs be dispersed. The Jews were to be left in peace. It was on the 22nd day of *Teves* that this miracle happened in Prague. For many years this day was celebrated by the

Altschul family and the Jews of Prague as the "Purim of the Curtains," for on that day their sadness had been turned to happiness as during the *Purim* of old.

The lesson of *Purim* seems to repeat itself throughout Jewish history. A tyrant arises to destroy the Jewish people. The situation seems hopeless, but the Jews are saved. No matter how many Hamans arise in each generation, *Hashem* will always remember the Jewish people and come to their aid in time of need if they turn to Him honestly and sincerely.

THE MASTER PLOT

It was a cool spring day in the year 568 C.E. The Jews of Baghdad lived a life of peace and tranquility. They were respected by their neighbors, and most importantly, they had been befriended by the Sultan. What the Jews were not aware of, however, was that the peace they enjoyed was about to be shattered.

Prince Rhamad, second advisor to the Sultan, had been troubled for some time by a very pressing problem. The problem was Rav Aharon, first because all Jews—men, women, and children—were under the threat of annihilation by Haman. It also serves to remind us of the great part played by Queen Esther in the story of *Purim*.

2. Even if a woman knows how to read from a "kosher" *Megillah* (one that is written on parchment with the proper ink), it is best for her to hear it read by a man.

3. If there is no one to read it for her, she may read it herself and make the *Brocho*, "*Lishmoa Mikroh Megillah.*"

4. A *koton* (child under the age of 13) should be brought to *Shul* to hear the *Megillah* in order to educate him to do *Mitzvos*. Young children should be supervised so that they do not make noise that would interfere with others hearing the *Megillah*.

5. Although a *koton* must listen to the *Megillah*, he cannot be the one to read it for other people.

advisor to the Sultan. Rav Aharon was the head of the Jewish community and he was admired by all for his brilliant mind and humble character. The Sultan valued every word of advice that Rav Aharon uttered, and it was therefore no surprise that he should be chosen as the Sultan's close confidant. At first, Rhamad and Rav Aharon held equal positions in the High Court. As time passed, however, Rav Aharon's ability and wisdom as advisor became more and more apparent, and Rhamad slipped farther and farther into the background. One day he decided to take action to reverse this trend. . . .

"Rhamad, are your sure?"

"The evidence is before you, Your Highness. Aharon and his henchmen are planning a takeover of your government. I am aware that until today you trusted in him and so I was always afraid to reveal my suspicions to you. With the discovery of these secret plans to overthrow you and your regime, however, my suspicions have been confirmed."

"Yes, Rhamad, the evidence is very convincing. To tell you the truth, I never would have suspected Rav Aharon of planning such a scheme. Why, up until today, I considered him the most honest and decent man in my entire empire. In any case, I am very grateful to you, Rhamad, for your work in uncovering these plans. You will be justly rewarded, and Aharon and his friends will be executed tomorrow. Send two of my guards to Rav Aharon's house and have him brought to my palace at once."

Rhamad had it all planned. He must see to it that Rav Aharon was executed *before* he had a chance to speak to the Sultan, for Rhamad knew that Rav Aharon was wise enough to prove that he and his friends had been framed.

"Excuse me, Your Highness, but I don't think it would be a good idea to bring Rav Aharon to the palace."

"Why is that, Rhamad?"

"Well, you see, Rav Aharon is such a sly fellow, that I wouldn't be surprised if he somehow eludes the guards before they have a chance to

III. HALACHOS OF READING THE MEGILLAH:

1. One may read the *Megillah* either standing or sitting. However, if one is reading on behalf of a congregation, he should stand.

2. It is best to have a *Minyan* present when the *Megillah* is read. If there is no *Minyan*, one can still be *motzee* other people (include them in the *Mitzvah*).

3. If two people read the *Megillah* out loud, one who listens to both of them fulfills the *Mitzvah*. An example of this is when the *Baal Korai* reads from his *Megillah* and another person in *Shul* reads out loud along with him from a "kosher" *Megillah*. If this would occur during *Krias HaTorah* one would not be *yotzai* (fulfill the *Mitzvah*) because one cannot concentrate if he hears two voices. However, the *Megillah* is so special that he will make an effort to listen even in such circumstances.

bring him to the palace."

"You are right once again, Rhamad, I can no longer afford to underestimate him. What do you suggest?"

"Ah" thought Rhamad, "and now comes the final part of my plan."

"I have something in mind, Your Highness," he said. "Why don't you send a simple messenger to Rav Aharon's house and have him tell Rav Aharon that he brings with him an important request from the Sultan. The Sultan asks that Rav Aharon go to the royal vineyard and ask the guard on duty if the king's order was done. At the same time, your Highness, a messenger should be dispatched to the royal vineyard. The guard there should be informed that the first person to inquire as to whether the king's order was done should be executed on the spot. This way, Rav Aharon will suspect nothing and will finally meet the end that he so justly deserves."

"Rhamad, I must confess that not until today did I realize how wise you are.

I will not waste any more time in rewarding you for your honorable

deeds. You are hereby proclaimed first advisor to the king."

"What a strange request," thought Rav Aharon when he heard it. "The Sultan has to ask his first advisor to inquire as to whether an order of his was carried out in the royal vineyard. What could be so important in the royal vineyard? No matter, however. If the Sultan asks this deed of me, I must be loyal to him and fulfill his command."

"Rav Aharon, Rav Aharon!"

"I am sorry, Yitzchok. I have no time now. I am on my way to carry out an order of the Sultan."

"But Rav Aharon, this is an emergency. I'm sure you remember my brother, Reuven, the one that lives in the suburbs of the capital. His wife gave birth to a baby boy eight days ago and the *Bris Milah* is supposed to be today. The problem is that the Mohel who was supposed to perform the *Bris* is ill, and you are the only *Mohel* close enough to reach my brother's house before sundown."

"Travel to your brother's house now? But I told you already, the Sultan

4. The *Baal Korai* should read word-for-word from the *Megillah,* and should not recite any words by heart.

5. One is allowed to continue reading from a *Megillah* that was found to be missing some words. (This is unlike the case of a *Sefer Torah,* where one missing letter makes it *posul,* requiring that it be replaced with another *Sefer Torah.*)

If the missing word or letter was in the opening or closing lines, then the *Megillah* is *posul.* One has not fulfilled the *Mitzvah* then and he must read everything from another *Megillah.*

If the missing letter or words happened to be in the middle of the *Megillah,* then the reading is valid as long as it was not a major part. However, it is best, if at all possible, to use a different *Megillah.*

6. If a person does not have a "kosher" *Megillah* he should not read

has sent me on an errand which I must fulfill immediately."

"The Sultan has sent you on an important errand? What is the command of a mere Sultan worth when compared to the command of the King of all Kings, *Hashem?* I am asking you to bring a Jewish child into a Covenant *(bris)* with G-d, and you tell me about errands that you must fulfill?"

"Yitzchok is right," thought Rav Aharon. "If I don't perform the *Milah,* the child will not have the *Bris* on the 8th day, as commanded in the Torah. Yet, how can I dare disobey the order of the Sultan? He will certainly be enraged when he discovers that I defied his order. Still *Bris Milah* is more important than my position as first advisor to the king. I will perform the *Bris* and put my trust in *Hashem* that He will work things out for the best."

Rav Aharon and Yitzchok were on their way . . .

"It is almost sundown," thought Rhamad. "Rav Aharon must have reached the royal vineyard about three hours ago. Rav Aharon is certainly a dead man by now. But you never know with that sly Jew. I had better go down to

the vineyard myself and see that the guard did, indeed, execute him."

The guard at the gates of the vineyard recognized Rhamad. "Good afternoon, Prince Rhamad. Can I help you?"

"Yes. Tell me, was the Sultan's order carried out?"

As soon as he heard these words, the guard carefully drew his sword, and . . .

Rav Aharon finished telling his story to the Sultan.

"Rav Aharon, I never should have doubted you. You have proved conclusively that the plans were forged by Rhamad. Well, he has already met his death, the very same death that he had planned for you. You, Rav Aharon, shall be rewarded with the highest honors befitting a royal prince."

Once again, we see how a "Haman" who stood up against the Jews, was foiled in his plans by the intervention of *Hashem,* and faced a fitting death.

"Every year designs are made to exterminate the Jews but Hashem *brings them to nought."* (Yalkut Shimoni, *Malachai 1*)

along with the *Baal Korai*. (That is why the latter repeats out loud those lines that the congregation says in unison.)

7. There are four *pesukim* (sentences) that are read out loud by the *tzeebur* and then repeated by the *Baal Korai:* (1) *Ish Yehudi* . . . (2) *U'Mordechai Yatza* . . . (3) *La'Yehudim Hoysa* . . . (4) *Kee Mordechai* . . .

8. If the reading of the *Megillah* is interrupted for a short period of time (even by talking), the *Baal Korai* may continue afterwards. However, if the *Chazan* made a long interruption, a *Rav* should be consulted.

9. If a person talks between the *Brochos* and the reading of the *Megillah,* he won't be *yotzai* with the *Brochos* unless the talking was in connection with the *Megillah* reading; only then is it not considered a *hefsek* (interruption).

10. The *Megillah* has to be read in the proper order. If someone

No nation has the ability to completely annihilate *Hashem's* Chosen People. This is one of the reasons Jews are spread throughout the earth. (*Pesachim* 87b). If one nation persecutes its Jews, the Jews of another nation will still survive. Certainly many countries have done their best to rid the Earth of Jews, but none have succeeded and none ever will. For the Jews have a special "weapon" on their side, as was pointed out by Rav Yehoshua. The Roman Emperor Hadrian once praised the resiliency of the Jews by remarking, "the lamb who stands against seventy wolves." But Rav Yehoshua replied, "How great is the Shepherd that guides and watches this lamb." (*Midrash Tanchuma, Parshas Toldos 5*).

The Jews have witnessed many miraculous salvations throughout the ages when they deserved it. In this connection, it is written that if someone reads the *Megillah* backwards, he has not fulfilled the *Mitzvah* of *Megillah*. (*Megillah* 17a). What is the meaning of reading a *Megillah* backwards? One explanation is that if someone says that the events of the *Megillah*

happened in the past but can no longer occur, then he is looking at the *Megillah* in a backwards manner and he has not fulfilled his obligation of believing in *Hashem's* eternal assistance. *Hashem* is always aware of plots against Jews, during any era, and He will continue to defend the Jews.

Everyone has to regard the miracles done to the Jewish nation in the past as being directly relevant to his own day. As Reb Baruch of Mezbiz used to say, "Just as everyone must look upon himself as if he himself had been delivered from Egypt, so too, everyone must feel as if he had been through the miracle of Mordechai and Haman." (*Sippurei Hassidim.*)

DANGER

Haman was a smart and a sinister man. His plan to wipe out the Jews was well-prepared. It seemed that no one could stop him, not even Mordechai or Esther.

But he was wrong. He did not realize the power of the *teenokos shel bais rabban,* the Jewish children who learn Torah.

Mordechai, of course, realized this.

Purim

skipped a word by mistake, he must return to the place where he made the error and continue from there. He cannot simply add the part he missed at the end.

11. One is *yotzai* the *Mitzvah* of hearing the *Megillah* even if he doesn't understand it. Of course, it is best to study it beforehand so he can understand it.

12. A person who is drowsy while listening to the *Megillah* is not *yotzai* because he may have missed a few words due to his drowsiness. However, if he was reading along with the *Baal Korai* then he is *yotzai*. Many people bring a "kosher" *Megillah* to read along quietly with the *Baal Korai* and not have to worry that they may have missed a word.

13. Before beginning to read the *Megillah*, the *Baal Korai* should have in mind to be *motzee* everyone in *Shul*.

He gathered the thousands of Jewish children of Shushan into the large synagogue, and said, "Our nation is on the brink of destruction, and it is up to you, children, to save us. You must pray to *Hashem* and promise Him that we will mend our ways and will observe all His Commandments. If not, Haman will kill us all."

For three days and three nights these children remained in the *Shul* and prayed to *Hashem* for mercy. It was during this time that Queen Esther risked her life for the sake of her people. Because of the sincere prayers and repentance of the children, the Almighty's decree changed direction from the Jewish nation to Haman and his children.

The special message of *Purim* is clear. Whenever *Bnai Yisroel* are in danger, the Jewish children, through the power of prayer and repentance, can always arouse the mercy of Heaven and save the Jewish nation.

TEAMWORK

On *Purim* Eve, it is customary to give half-dollars to recall the "Half-Shekel" that the Jews gave in the month of *Adar* in ancient times. The giving of the half-*Shekel* in the desert was for the purpose of counting the people. But why half a *Shekel*, rather than a whole one? Why not have each individual show that he is whole and complete?

Giving only "half" emphasizes the fact that no individual is complete when alone. No man and certainly no Jew, is an island. He can reach the ultimate heights of spirituality only when he associates and cooperates with other Jews. If he goes out of his way to help others, to learn from others, to join others in positive group efforts, then he is a true member of the Jewish nation.

The importance of working together is best illustrated in a tale of a man who lost his way in a huge, dense forest. He kept walking around in circles until eventually he came upon a second person, also seeking his way out of the forest.

"Can you show me the way out of the woods?" he asked.

"No, not yet," said the second man. "However, through my travels I have

125

14. It is best that the *Baal Korai* read the list of Haman's ten sons in one breath, starting from *"Chameish Me-os Ish . . ."* through *"Aseres . . ."*

15. The *Megillah* used for the *tzeebur* should be folded like a letter while being read publicly and not rolled up like a scroll. If one reads for an individual only, he may leave it as a scroll.

16. When Haman's name is mentioned we stomp our feet and make noise in order to blot out his name. (Caution! One should be certain to stop making noise when the *Baal Korai* is ready to continue reading.)

17. If one finds out that he heard the *Krias Megillah* from a scroll that had been borrowed without permission, then he was still *yotzai*.

18. The *Baal Korai* recites three *Brochos* prior to the reading of the *Megillah*, both in the evening and in the daytime: (1) *Al Mikroh Megillah*.

---

already found out which roads not to take. Maybe together we can find the right way."

So it was! By pooling their knowledge, they soon found their way out of the forest. Had each remained alone, he would have wandered on forever.

The day before Purim is observed as *Taanis Esther* (Fast of Esther) in order to recall that Queen Esther fasted and declared a public fast in order to merit *Hashem*'s Mercy when the Jews were in danger of annihilation. A public fast is supposed to impress upon us that the Almighty is near to those who are in great difficulty and engage in fasting and *Teshuvah* when they are in great difficulty.

MEGILLAH

Hashem's name is omitted from the *Megillah* because of two reasons.

1. Originally, the *Megillah* was sent out as "letters" to the various Jewish communities. As such, it was thought that they might be thrown away, causing degradation to the Holy Name. Even though the *Megillah* was later included in the Sacred Writings of the *T'nach*, it was still considered proper to retain the original wording of the document as written by Mordechai and Esther.

2. Rabbi Samson R. Hirsch suggested that the Holy Name was purposely omitted in the *Megillah* to teach us that the Hand of G-d is ever-present in the history of man, even when we fail to see it openly, as is the case in the events which led to the miracle of *Purim*.

Hallel is not recited on *Purim* because of the following reasons:

1. The Talmud states that these Prayers of Thanksgiving are recited only for those miracles that occurred in the Land of Israel. (*Purim* occurred in Persia.)

2. *Purim* does not require the recital of *Hallel* since the very reading of the *Megillah* is a superior form of *Hallel* and Thanksgiving.

3. Because the Jews still remained under the rule of Achashverosh. (*Megillah* 14a)

When we say the *Shehecheyanu*, we have in mind the following:

The special *Mitzvos* of *Purim*, (1) *Matanos L'Evyonim* (gifts to the poor), (2) *Mishloach Monos* (sending food

(2) *She'Osoh Nissim* . . . (3) *She hecheyanu* . . . *When the Baal Korai* recites the *She'hecheyanu* in the morning, he and the *tzeebur* should have in mind to include with this *Brocho* the other *Mitzvos* of the day: (1) *Matanos L'Evyonim* (gifts to the poor) (2) *Shalach Monos* (sending of food gifts to friends), (3) *Seudas Purim* (the *Purim* meal).

19. If he forgot the *Brochos* he is still *yotzai* with *Krias Megillah*.

20. If a person is reading the *Megillah* for a group of women, then the *Brocho* that is to be recited is *"Lishmoa Mikroh Megillah."*

21. The *Brocho* that is recited after the reading of the Megillah is said only when there is a *Minyan.* The paragraph, *"Asher Hai-nee . . ."* following the final *Brocho* is recited only in the evening. *"Shoshanos Yaakov"* must be said in the evening and morning.

portions to friends) (3) *Seudas Purim* (feast of *Purim*), which are performed during the day time do not have any particular blessing. We, therefore, keep in mind the performance of these special *Mitzvos* at the time when the *Shehecheyanu* is recited in the morning.

AMALEK'S HATRED FOR ISRAEL

The hatred which Amalek has for Israel is not comparable to the hatred of all other anti-Semites. The hatred of other anti-Semites subsides at times. Amalek's hatred never subsides, and as long as he exists, he constantly plans only our destruction. Our other enemies accept bribes and are placated. When other nations rose against Israel and saw the hand of G-d inflicting punishment upon them, they at times experienced awe and fear, and submitted. In the case of Amalek, even the sight of G-d's mighty wonders on behalf of Israel, and the vengeance He exacts from His people's enemies—even the knowledge that his attack against Israel would bring him to grief and destruction—would not deter him. For the very essence of Amalek is hatred of Israel without

prospect of self gain, hatred without cause or motive, hatred for the sake of hatred alone, a hatred which never ceases.

"And Mordechai would not kneel or bow down." (*Esther* 3:2) Why did Mordechai endanger his people by arousing Haman's anger? The Sages have said that an idol hung on Haman's heart, in order to trap Israel into sinning while bowing down to him, and idolatry is one of the three transgressions which one may not commit even on penalty of death.

Why is it said, "He *would* not kneel or bow down," in the future tense, rather than, "He *did* not kneel or bow down"? We learn from this that Mordechai sought to let Haman know that he would never bow down to him. Mordechai could have escaped Haman's wrath by avoiding his presence. Instead he intentionally appeared before Haman to demonstrate his refusal to bow down to Haman and his idol.

The following story is told in the Talmud: The disciples of Rabbi Shimon ben Yochai asked their master: "By what sins had the Jews incurred

IV. ADDITIONAL TEFILLOS ON PURIM:

1. *"Al HaNissim"* is added to the *Shmoneh Esrei* and *Birchas Hamazon* (grace after meals) both at night and during *Purim* day. It is not said on *Shushan Purim* unless one lives in a city where the *Megillah* is read on *Shushan Purim*. (e.g. Yerusholayim)

If one forgets *"Al HaNissim"* in *Shmoneh Esrei* or *Birchas Hamazon*, he does not have to repeat the prayer.

2. *Hallel* is not recited on *Purim*.

3. *"Tachanun," "Lomnatze'ach"* and *"Kail Erech Apayim"* are not said on *Purim* or *Shushan Purim*.

4. The portion read in the Torah is *"Vayavoh Amalek"* (the end of *Parshas B'Shalach),* even though there are only nine *pesukim.* On *Purim* day, we read the Torah before the *Megillah.*

V. SPECIAL MITZVOS ON PURIM:

1. It is customary to give three half-dollars to charity in *Shul* to commemorate the *Machatzis Hashekel* that was given in the month of *Adar* during the time of the *Bais Hamikdosh.* It is given right before the reading of the *Megillah* on the day before *Purim,* unless that day happens to be *Shabbos.*

---

the decree of Haman (to kill all the Jews)?"

"How would you explain it?" the master asked of the disciples in reply.

"Because the Jews also participated in the feast arranged by Achashverosh, the pagan king," the disciples suggested.

"If this were so," the master countered, "only those who lived in Shushan the capital, and who partook of this feast should have suffered. Why then did the Jews in the provinces have to suffer as well? It must be because they knelt before the idol that stood in the king's banquet hall."

"In that case, they were actually guilty of a grave sin. Why then, were they saved from destruction?" the students asked.

"They bowed to the image not because they wanted to sin, but only for appearance's sake," their master explained. "As a result, the Holy One also decreed their destruction only for appearance's sake, to frighten them into repentance. He actually had no intention of destroying them."

(*Megillah* 12a)

"It is to commemorate the 'pretended' nature of G-d's evil decree that we today change our outward appearance by putting on masks and disguises." (Bnei Ysaschar).

"Rabbi Meir Shalom of Porisov would make it a point to distribute money to the poor the day after Purim. *He would say, 'Since there is a special obligation to give gifts to the poor on* Purim, *people neglect this commandment the day after* Purim. *It is especially important to perform a neglected* Mitzvah.'"

2. *Matanos L'Evyonim* (gifts to the poor) are given to two different people. It is best to give either ready-made food or money that can be used to buy food. This *Mitzvah* is even more important than the *Seudas Purim* and *Shalach Monos*, as Maimonides says, "There is no greater joy than to gladden the hearts of the poor."

3. One should give *Tzedakah* freely and generously on *Purim*.

4. One is supposed to rejoice and have a special *Seuda* (feast) on *Purim* but the *seuda* must be held during the day. One should make a small *Seuda* on *Shushan Purim*.

5. One must be sure that the *seuda* is started while it is still day.

6. Even if the *seuda* extends into the night, one still says "*Al HaNissim*" in the Birchas Hamazon, since the beginning of the *seuda* was in the daytime.

7. The *Mitzvah* of *Shalach Monos*:

(a) One is supposed to give *Shalach Monos* (the sending of portions of food) to at least one friend.

(b) The *Shalach Monos* should consist of at least two different foods which are ready to be eaten on *Purim*.

(c) If *Purim* occurs during the twelve-month period of mourning for one's parents, the mourner sends *Shalach Monos* but one does not send *Shalach Monos* to him.

(d) Women are also obligated to give *Matanos L'Evyonim* and *Shalach Monos,* and participate in the meal.

פסח
Pesach

PESACH—INTRODUCTION

"And the L-rd said: 'I have surely seen the afflication of My people who are in Egypt, and have heard their cry on account of their taskmasters; for I have known their suffering; and I am come down to deliver them out of the land of the Egyptians; and to bring them up out of that land unto a good land, unto a land flowing with milk and honey; unto the place of the Canaanite, and the Hittite and the Amorite, and the Perizzite, and the Hivite and the Jebusite.' " (Shemos 3:7-8)

"And Moses said unto the people, 'Remember this day on which you came out from Egypt, out of the house of bondage, for by strength of hand the L-rd brought you out from this place; no leavened bread shall be eaten. This day you go forth in the spring month. And it shall be when the L-rd shall bring you into the land of the Canaanite, and the Hittite, and the Amorite, and the Hivite, and the Jebusite, which he swore unto your fathers to give you a land flowing with milk and honey, that you shall keep this service in its month. Seven days you shall eat unleavened

PESACH
THE SPECIAL SEDER

Rabbi Levi Yitzchok of Berditchev hadn't finished the *Seder* until it was almost morning of the following day, for he was most exacting in the performance of every custom that had to be followed. He was still sitting at that table feeling very happy because everything had gone so smoothly, when he heard a heavenly voice say, "Why are you so excited with your *Seder?* The *Seder* that Chaim the water-carrier performed was much more acceptable than yours."

The Rabbi immediately sent people in search of Chaim the water-carrier. They found that he lived in an old hut

in the poor section of the city. They knocked on the door and asked the wife if they could speak with Chaim. She told them it wasn't possible, since her husband had drunk so much wine at the *Seder* that he had become quite tipsy and was now sleeping it off.

The messengers wouldn't take 'No' for an answer. "The Rabbi told us to bring him and we will." They entered the house, awoke Chaim from a deep sleep, and carried him to the rabbi's residence. He was brought to the rabbi's chambers, and was seated at the head of the table next to the Berditchever.

In a soft voice, the Rabbi asked, "My dear Chaim, please tell me what hid-

bread, and on the seventh day shall be a feast to the L-rd. Unleavened bread shall be eaten throughout the seven days; and no leavened bread shall be seen with you throughout your borders." (Shemos 13:3-7)

Pesach *starts on the 15th day of* Nissan *and celebrates the liberation of our ancestors from Egyptian slavery. During this eight day festival we have the* Pesach Seder *on each of the first two nights (outside of* Eretz Yisroel). *At this special home service, we retell the story of the exodus from Egypt (as stated in the Torah) by means of certain symbols that are placed on the festival table. We eat* matzos *instead of bread throughout the entire eight days, since all foods containing leaven are forbidden.*

The three Mitzvos Aseh *which apply to the observance of* Pesach *nowadays are:*

a) Disposing of leaven on the fourteenth day of the month of Nissan.

b) Eating matzoh *on the night of* Pesach.

c) Relating the story of the exodus from Egypt on the night of Pesach.

HILCHOS PESACH—THE MONTH OF NISSAN

1. The month of *Nissan* is also referred to as the month of *Aviv*. One reason is that the Hebrew letters in the word *Aviv* may be divided into two words, "*Av*" meaning father, and "*Yud Veis*", the numerical symbol for "twelve." In other words, *Nissan* is the "Father" of the twelve months of the year. This is the month in which the Jews were granted spiritual freedom. Another reason is that *Pesach* must be in the spring *(Aviv)*. *(Binath Moshe*, by Menachem, Rebbe of Koznitz.)

den thoughts you had in your mind the day before *Pesach* when you cleaned your home of all *chometz*."

The sleepy man opened his eyes and said, "I had no particular thoughts in mind. I looked in all the corners, gathered all the pieces of *chometz*, and placed them in a wooden spoon."

"What thoughts did you have in mind the next day when you burned the *chometz*?"

"*Oy vay!* Now that you brought that up, I regret that I have to tell you that I forgot all about the *chometz*. It's still in the wooden spoon under the beam in my house."

The Rabbi was baffled, but con-tinued. "Tell me please, how did you perform the ceremony of the *Seder*?"

Now the man was awake, more alert. In a low voice he said, "Rabbi, I want to tell you the entire truth. Yesterday evening, when my wife asked me to perform the *Seder*, I said to her, 'What do you want? Why do you bother me? You know that I am an uneducated person. My parents couldn't afford to send me to a good school and I don't know how to perform a *Seder*. I don't know what to do and what not to do. This much I do know: Our forefathers and mothers were slaves in Egypt. We have a great G-d who redeemed them and made us

2. The reason why the Special Daily Supplication *(Tachnun)* is not recited throughout the month of *Nissan* is that most of the month has a festive character. When Israel was in the wilderness the twelve tribal leaders offered special sacrifices, each on one day of the month of *Nissan*. *(Bamidbar 7)*. Each of these days was considered a festive occasion for the leader who was scheduled to offer this sacrifice on that day. The twelve days of offering were followed by *Erev Pesach,* and then by *Pesach* itself, ending with *Isru Chag,* the day after *Pesach*. Consequently, most of the month of *Nissan* bore the stamp of festivity and holiness. *(Beis Yosef,* Ch. 429)

3. The *Shabbos* before *Pesach* is called *Shabbos Hagadol,* "The Great *Shabbos."* This is because of the miracle that took place on the *Shabbos* before the first *Pesach*. G-d commanded the Israelites to offer up lambs for the Paschal service. This was a dangerous thing to do since the lambs were regarded as idols by the Egyptians, who might have killed anyone attempting to harm these animals. Still, the Israelites did as they were told. Then a miracle came to pass. The Egyptians were paralyzed with sudden terror so that they could do nothing to protect their sacred lambs. This miracle took place on the tenth of the month of *Nissan,* which fell on a *Shabbos* that year. (See *Tosfos, Shabbos* 87b sub voce, "Ve-asa").

BEDIKAS CHOMETZ

1. The Torah does not allow one to have *chometz* (leavened bread) in his possession on *Pesach*. There are two methods of disposing of this

a free nation. But look what happened! We are in bondage again! But I'm certain that our great G-d will eventually redeem us once again."

"Then I saw that my wife had set the table with a tablecloth as bright as the sun. On the table were platters with *matzos,* eggs, and all kinds of delicacies. My wife and I ate the *matzos* and the eggs, and drank the delicious red wine.

"When I had enough, I was happy and lifted my cup of wine toward heaven and exclaimed, 'Ribono Shel Olam, You see this cup of wine. I drink it for you. L'Chayim! And now, please,

dear G-d, bend Yourself toward us and redeem us from bondage.' Then we ate and drank some more and said the *Haggadah* quickly and rejoiced in honor of *Hashem,* until I became exhausted and fell asleep. This, honored Rabbi, is the entire truth."

"Now I understand," said Rabbi Levi Yitzchok. "Your *Seder* may have been short, but it captured the essence of *Pesach* perfectly."

HASHATA HACHA

"*Hashata Hacha* ... This year we are here, next year may it be in the land of Israel! This year, slaves, next year—free men."

Chometz. a) *Biyur Chometz*—Actual destruction of the *chometz* in one's possession, or removing it from there. b) *Bitul Chometz*— Renouncing one's title to the *Chometz* in one's possession.

By Rabbinical decree one is required to use both of the above methods.

2. As a prerequisite to *Biyur Chometz,* one must thoroughly search for *Chometz* in one's house on the night before *Pesach,* preferably immediately after the stars appear. If *Erev Pesach* is *Shabbos,* the search is done Thursday night. Every room is searched thoroughly, as are the pockets of one's clothing, one's place of business, one's basement, garage, automobile, etc. Any *chometz* that has been found is put in safekeeping until the time prescribed for the burning of the *chometz* on the following morning.

3. Anyone leaving his residence within thirty days before *Pesach* and not planning to return until after *Pesach,* must perform the search before leaving. The same laws concerning the search apply but no blessing is recited. One should not start eating a meal or start performing a job within a half hour before the time when the stars come out.

4. The search should be done by the light of a candle containing a single wick, or a flashlight.

5. Some have the custom to place ten pieces of bread throughout the house before commencing the search. The reason is that since the *Brocho* is made on the burning of the *Chometz,* we want to make sure we find *Chometz* after the *Brocho.* (Some people don't put out the *Chometz* because they follow the authorities who believe that the *Bro-*

Why is this wish stated at the beginning of the *Haggadah* before the actual recital is even started? The Dubno Maggid clarifies it with the following *moshol* (parable).

A poor man who earned so little that he had to live on bread and water suddenly acquired great wealth. He opened a large warehouse, bought goods and sold them all over the world. For years he lived in luxury. But in order not to become arrogant or forget his past misery, he was accustomed after his elaborate meals to dip a piece of bread into water and eat it.

Unfortunate business dealings caused this man to lose most of his great wealth. He was still owed large sums of money but the debts were not yet due. Thus, he was forced to live in poverty once again while awaiting the day that he would receive his payments.

One day, he was invited to be the guest of a rich gentleman where he ate amidst great splendor. At the end of the meal, he requested a piece of bread and a glass of water. His amazed host asked for an explanation. The man replied that he was accustomed to do so after an ample meal to remind himself of his former misery.

cho is made on the searching and not on the finding of the *Chometz.)* The search should not be merely a cursory ceremony in which these pieces of bread are collected, but rather a thorough search. Immediately prior to the search, the blessing *Al Biyur Chometz* is recited. One may not speak between the recitation of the blessing and the beginning of the search. It is also proper not to speak during the entire search, unless this is necessary for the search itself.

6. Following the search, *"Kol Chamirah,"* which constitutes *Bitul Chometz,* is recited. It is a statement renouncing title to any chometz other than that set aside for breakfast, sale, or destruction the following morning. It is important to understand the formula of *Bitul Chometz.* Therefore, if one does not understand Aramaic, he should recite the following English version: "All *chometz* and sour dough (leavening) in my possession which I have not seen and have not destroyed shall be considered nullified and ownerless to me, even as the dust of the earth." The Torah prohibits deriving any benefit from *chometz* from midday of *Erev* (the day before) *Pesach* until the end of *Pesach.* Furthermore, the Torah commands us to destroy all of our *chometz* by midday of *Erev Pesach.* By rabbinical decree, it is forbidden to eat *chometz* after one-third of the day has passed, and it is forbidden to derive benefit from *chometz* after 5/12 of the day has passed.

7. Thus *chometz* found during the search as well as any other *chometz* still in one's possession must be destroyed the next morning, preferably by burning it. After this *Biyur Chometz* has been performed, a more

---

The rich host couldn't understand this answer. If the man was rich, he would need a reminder, but certainly not now, after he had lost his wealth.

"Why are you still keeping your old custom?" asked the host. "Aren't you as poor now as you were before?"

"No," replied the guest. "I believe my present circumstances to be temporary. I still have large amounts owed to me and I am sure that they will be repaid on the dates due. Then I shall be a rich man once again."

We Jews have suffered in a manner similar to this man. In Egypt we were poor and miserable toiling as slaves. Our oppressors gave us "the bread of affliction" *(lechem oni)* to eat. Then *Hashem* freed us from slavery, brought us to *Eretz Yisroel,* and made us a great nation. But we retained the custom of eating *Matzoh* and *Maror* on *Pesach* to remind us of our past afflictions.

Now that we are again in *Golus,* scattered all over the world, why do we need reminders of past afflictions? Aren't there still Jews suffering today all over the world? Haven't we lost everything?

No! Not everything! We still possess the sacred teachings of the *Torah* and *Mitzvos.* It is the Torah that has sustained us throughout the years of

inclusive version of *Bitul Chometz* is said including all *chometz* ("whether I have seen it or not seen it; whether I have destroyed it or have not destroyed it. . . ."). Both the *Biyur Chometz* and the *Bitul Chometz* should be done before 5/12 of the day has passed; for, as soon as it is forbidden to derive benefit from *chometz,* it is no longer within one's power to renounce title to it, and *Bitul Chometz* cannot be done.

8. Dishes, pots and pans and anything else that is stored over *Pesach* should be locked up in a closet or pantry until after Pesach. (They should be cleaned from *chometz* before storage.) Any *chometz* that is discarded,(besides that which is to be burned) should NOT be put into the garbage cans unless the Sanitation Department will pick it up by morning's end. Since the garbage cans either belong to us or are on our property, putting *Chometz* into them would actually be retaining the chometz in our possession. It is, therefore, best to put out any garbage containing *chometz* in a plastic bag and leave it outside as *Hefker* (unowned). If one finds *chometz* in his house on *Chol Hamoed,* he should destroy it immediately. If one finds it on *Yom Tov* or *Shabbos,* he should not move it, but he should cover it with a vessel until the conclusion of *Yom Tov* or *Shabbos,* when he must destroy it.

SALE OF CHOMETZ

1. There is a Rabbinical decree forbidding one to derive benefit from *chometz* which was in a Jew's possession on *Pesach*—even if he performed *Bitul Chometz* and was totally unaware that he had this *chometz* on *Pesach.*

Golus. We know that it is only a matter of time till the Moshiach will come and end this *Golus. L'SHANA HA-BA'AH BE'YERUSHALAYIM!*

THE GREAT Z'CHUS OF RIGHTEOUS WOMEN

Rabbi Akiva said: "As reward for the deeds of the righteous women who lived in that generation, the Jewish people were redeemed from Egypt. What did these heroines do? When they went to draw water, G-d arranged that small fish should enter their pitchers, so that the pitchers they drew were half full of water and half full of fish. They would then set two pots on the fire, one for hot water and the other to boil the fish. These they carried to this husbands in the fields, washed them, anointed them, fed them, gave them drink and lived with them. When the time came for them to give birth, they did so in the field beneath the apple tree. G-d sent His divine messengers to wash the infants, straighten their limbs and provide them with honey and oil. When the Egyptians noticed the children, they went to kill them, but a miracle occurred and the ground swallowed and preserved the children." (*Sotah* 11b)

2. This Rabbinical decree does not apply to *chometz* which one sold to a non-Jew before *Pesach,* since it was not in the possession of a Jew during *Pesach.* The following points should be understood by one who sells his *chometz* to a non-Jew:

a. The rabbi is appointed as an agent of the owner of the *chometz* to sell it to a non-Jew.

b. One not only sells to the non-Jew the *chometz* in his possession, but also gives access to the property on which the *chometz* is located.

c. The procedure must be a bona fide sale in accordance with both Jewish and civil law. There may be no condition attached to the sale, but one may promise the non-Jew that he will buy back the *chometz* at a profit to the non-Jew, as long as this is not a condition attached to the sale. Since there are several complexities of Talmudic law concerning this sale, only a reliable rabbinical authority should be appointed as one's agent to sell the *chometz.*

d. The sale must be made before 5/12 of the day of *Erev Pesach* has passed. If one is going away for *Pesach,* he should instruct his Rabbi to sell his *chometz* before 5/12 of the day has passed at his *Pesach* location.

e. *Chometz* utensils (pots, pans, dinnerware) should not be included in the sale, since it may necessitate ritual immersion of these utensils before use after *Pesach,* but the *chometz* absorbed in the utensils can be included in the selling.

3. Since it is forbidden to derive any benefit from *chometz* which was in a Jew's possession during *Pesach,* one should take care to obtain chometz after *Pesach* only from a non-Jew or from a Jew who sold his

---

The *Avnei Azel* (in *Mayonoh shel Torah* by Alexander Zusha Friedman, Ztl') clarified and interpreted the above Talmudic passage as follows:

When the ruthless regimen of work ordered by their Egyptian slavemasters drove the men to such a state of despair that they felt utterly demoralized, it was the valiant Jewish women of that era who inspired their husbands with faith and courage. They transmitted to them their own indomitable spirit to live so that even under these seemingly hopeless conditions they continued their normal family lives. In this way, the Jews could continue to thrive. The women did not follow the false notion that under such extremely adverse conditions it was best to have fewer children. Instead, they had full faith in G-d, believing that it is within His power to sustain and feed all in a miraculous manner.

It is in such indomitable faith and valiant deeds that the piety of the Jewish women of that generation manifested itself, and it is thus that they truly influenced and hastened the Redemption.

Shortly before Pesach, a poor man came to Rabbi Yosef Dov Soloveitchik and asked him, "Does a per-

chometz to a non-Jew before *Pesach.* If in doubt in a particular case, one should wait before buying from a Jew until he is reasonably certain that a new stock of *chometz* has been acquired. However, if there is a doubt whether a Jew has sold his *chometz,* one must check it out, and if one can't, it is still permissible to be eaten.

LAWS OF EREV PESACH

1. It is forbidden to eat *Matzoh* on *Erev Pesach* because by his doing so, he would not be able to eat the *Matzoh* at the *Seder* with a full appetite and desire.

2. If a person is a first-born male, he should fast on *Erev Pesach,* because we recall the fact that when the firstborn of Egypt were slain, the firstborn of Israel were spared. However, if he partakes of a *Seudas Mitzvah,* like that of a *Siyum,* (a meal at the completion of a portion of Torah) then according to most authorities he is permitted to eat for the remainder of the day.

3. One may eat moderate amounts of fruit, meat, etc., if this will not adversely affect one's appetite for the *Seder.*

SPECIAL PROCEDURES WHEN EREV PESACH FALLS ON SHABBOS

1. If *Pesach* falls on *Motzai Shabbos,* the *Bedikas Chometz* is done Thursday night, and afterwards we are still allowed to eat, up till, and including *Shabbos* morning, the *chometz* which has not been sold through a *Rav.* But one must make sure that it is eaten very carefully, and that no crumbs fall on the table or on the floor. It is a good idea to eat

son fulfill the obligation of drinking the *'Arba Kosos'* (four cups of wine) at the *Seder* if he uses milk instead of wine?"

"No," replied the Rav, and he handed the man a considerable amount of money. Afterwards, Rabbi Soloveitchik was asked why he gave such a large sum, since all the person apparently needed was money to buy wine.

"Since he wanted to drink milk at the *Seder* I understood that he not only lacks wine for *Pesach,* but also meat," he replied. "I therefore gave him enough money to buy both."

Exceptional care is taken to carry out every detail involved in baking

hand *Shemura matzos.* In their eagerness to fulfill this *Mitzvah,* the people may become angry or raise their voices against others engaged in the same *Mitzvah.* We might shout at a fellow-worker who is not nimble enough at his task. We must remember that there is no *Mitzvah* so important that it overrides the prohibition against showing anger and offending our fellow-man.

Our Sages have warned all who bake *"Matzos Mitzvah"* after mid-day on *Erev Pesach* to refrain from bitterness and anger, so as not to introduce the sin of anger into the *matzos,* for

the piece of *Challah* over a tissue or napkin. When we finish the *"Hamotzee"* on the *Challah* eaten over a napkin, all signs of *chometz* are cleared away from the table. The napkin with the crumbs should be flushed down the toilet. (Be sure NOT to leave it in your own garbage can.) Then we eat only *Pesach* products for the remainder of the meal.

2. Foods for this *Shabbos* are to be cooked and prepared in *"Pesach-dike"* pots and pans.

3. It is best to use disposable forks and knives for this meal, in order to avoid problems.

4. One also has the option of avoiding any type of chometz on *Shabbos* by using egg *matzohs* for 'Lechem Mishna'. However, he must make sure to eat at least one whole egg *matzoh*, (preferably two); which is the amount needed to wash and say *Birchas Hamazon*.

5. For *Shalosh Seudos,* one has the option of eating fruit later in the afternoon. If, however, he wishes to wash and eat *Challah*, he should finish the first meal and say *"Birchas Hamazon"*. He should then take a short break before he washes again, make *"Hamotzee,"* and eat *Shalosh Seudos*. He must finish the *Challah* before 1/3 of the day has passed and then clear away all traces of *chometz* before 5/12 of the day.

6. The *Bitul Chometz* must be performed by 5/12 of the day, with the recitation of the *Kol Chamira*.

CHOMETZ

1. *Chometz* is the product resulting from one of the five types of grain (wheat, barley, spelt, rye, oats) remaining in contact with water for a

this is as serious as introducing *chometz* in the *matzos*.

"Why is matzoh *called bread of affliction? Because of the pain with which we were afflicted in Egypt"* (Mechilta)

FOOD FOR THOUGHT

Rabbi Shmuel Mohliver of Bailystok used to supply kosher meals to Jewish soldiers stationed nearby so that they would not have to eat the non-kosher food from the army's kitchen.

It happened one year that shortly before *Pesach*, Rabbi Mohliver was informed that due to the unusually high prices of food that year it would not be possible to supply the Jewish soldiers with kosher *Pesach* meals.

"In that case," said Rabbi Mohliver, "I will have to allow the use of peas (normally prohibited on *Pesach)* for this *Pesach*."

"That's a wonderful idea," said the head of the congregation. "Here I was so worried about supplying the Jewish soldiers with food and you've already solved the problem." "Oh no!" said Rabbi Mohliver. "Peas for the Jewish soldiers? Never! You, I, and the entire city will eat peas for *Pesach*, but the Jewish soldiers will be supplied with the best foods available."

period of time (normally 18 minutes, though sometimes even less), before baking.

2. The Torah forbids eating or deriving any benefit from *chometz* on *Pesach*. In addition, one is prohibited by the Torah from having any *chometz* in his possession on *Pesach*.

3. A small amount of *chometz* mixed with other food particles renders the entire mixture *chometz*, and one is forbidden to eat or own this on *Pesach*. Since *chometz* prohibitions usually extend to even the slightest amount, extreme care must be taken in ascertaining that commercially available food products are free of all *chometz* derivatives. Therefore, only foods produced under strict rabbinical supervision should be used.

4. Everyday foods, such as dairy products, soda, ketchup, mayonnaise, and cider vinegar must have a reliable *Hashgacha* (rabbinical supervision).

5. Postum and other coffee substitutes are made with grain, which is *Chometz*, and they therefore cannot be used on *Pesach*.

6. Paper products may be used for *Pesach*, although some plastics can contain grain starch and should be checked.

7. Products which were never fit for human or animal consumption, such as chemicals, turpentine, ink, shampoo and soap, can be used on *Pesach*, without Rabbinical supervision.

8. Wood alcohol may be used on *Pesach*. Ethyl alcohol which is not synthetic, however, is *Chometz*. This substance is found in many cosmetics and toiletries. Since it is questionable whether these products are fit for human consumption, it is best to put them away with the rest of the *chometz*, to be sold.

Many years ago, in a small town in Europe, Rabbi Meir Margulies was walking along a muddy street towards the river, carrying a large pitcher. Rav Yaakov Yosef, the Maggid of Ostroah, was likewise on his way towards the river, but he rode in a wagon. He noticed the Rabbi and stopped his wagon to ask him, "Why do you walk on this muddy road?"

Rabbi Margulies replied, "The *Mitzvah* of drawing water for the baking of *matzos* comes but once a year. I do not want to lessen it by sharing it with a horse." The Maggid descended from his wagon and walked beside the Rav to the river.

THE EXTENDED PESACH

Rav Yecheskel Landau, also known as the famed *Nodeh B'Yehudah*, once noticed a gentile boy shivering and crying in the winter cold. Rav Landau tried to calm the boy, and asked what was the matter. The boy replied that he had been sent by his parents to sell some wares, but several of the local ruffians had stolen all the money he had made. Now he was afraid to return home to face his parents with-

9. Although toothpaste is not eaten, it is best to use *Kosher L'Pesach* toothpaste because it comes in contact with the mouth. This rule applies to mouthwash and liquid medicines as well.

10. Ashkenazic Jews (of European descent) have the *minhag* (custom) not to eat *kitniyos* (beans, rice, kasha, corn and legumes) on *Pesach*. Sephardic Jews, however, do eat these foods. They may be kept in the house over *Pesach* without being sold to a gentile. Lecithin, a derivative of *kitniyos,* should not be used on *Pesach*, according to most customs. One should note that some candies and milk chocolates made for *Pesach* contain lecithin. Under many circumstances, medicine or baby's food made from *kitniyos* may be used. Cottonseed oil is questionable.

11. The use of peanuts on *Pesach* is questionable. However, if the *Minhag Hamakom* (custom of the community) permits it, then they may be eaten. In such cases, it is also permissible to use peanut oil. The juice from *kitniyos* is also questionable and is used only if it is the custom to eat *kitniyos.*

12. Medicines should be checked, since many contain *chometz.* Medicine tablets which are coated and liquid medicines containing grain alcohol must be checked with a Rav as to their usage.

MATZOH

1. *Matzoh* is made of one of the five types of grain, (wheat, barley, spelt, oats, and rye) kneaded with water and immediately baked.

2. There is a biblical commandment to eat *matzoh* on the first night of

---

out a penny. Taking pity on the young boy, Rav Landau gave him some of his own money, which the boy accepted most gratefully.

Many years later, while the Jews of Rav Landau's *'shtetl'* (little town) were busily preparing for the coming *Yom Tov, Pesach,* he himself had a strange feeling that something dangerous was threatening the Jewish community. This feeling, no doubt, had something to do with the strange dreams he was having, warning him to be on the alert.

It was *Erev Pesach* and Rav Landau was preparing for a *Seder,* when he heard a knock at the door. He opened it to find a tall gentile youth there—a

most uncommon sight on *Pesach* night.

Rav Landau was afraid that the youth was there to rob him. He was about to shut the door, when the young man said, "Don't you remember me, Rabbi? I'm the boy you once comforted by giving me money in the street. I never really thought that I would have a chance to repay you. Now, I have come to return the favor, which I have never forgotten.

"I overheard the non-Jewish bakers talking about how Jews always buy bread from them the day after *Pesach* when they have none of their own. Several of the bakers said that this

Pesach. On the remainder of *Pesach* it is not a requirement to do so, but some say that one fulfills a *mitzvah* when one eats *matzoh* on the rest of *Yom Tov.*

3. The Torah says that one should eat *Matzoh Shemura* (commonly known as *Shemura Matzohs*). These *Matzohs,* according to most customs, should be supervised from the time of harvesting. (For at least the first two nights of *Pesach,* one should try to obtain *matzoh* that has been under supervision from the time the grain was cut. If necessary, supervision from the time the wheat was ground is sufficient.)

4. Although machine-made *matzohs* are generally acceptable for *Pesach* use, there are various opinions concerning the suitability of using machine *shemura matzohs* for the *mitzvah* of *matzoh* on the first two nights of *Pesach.*

5. Egg *matzoh* or *matzoh* kneaded with any liquid other than water should not be eaten on *Pesach.* Aged or sick people not capable of eating regular *matzoh* may eat such *matzohs* on *Pesach,* but they may not be used to fulfill one's obligation on the first two nights of *Pesach.* A *Rav* should be consulted in such cases.

SEDER

1. The food for the *Seder* table should be prepared and set in place before the *Yom Tov,* to allow the start of the *Seder* immediately after one returns home from *Shul* after nightfall. The reason we begin the *Seder* promptly is to be certain that the children should be awake and able to ask the *Mah Nishtana.* This allows the father to answer their questions,

---

year they were planning to poison the bread, and in this way kill all the Jews."

Rav Landau felt a chill as he listened to the boy's words. He now realized the reason for those frightening dreams and that feeling of impending doom. He was about to suggest going to the police when the boy continued speaking.

"Rabbi, I felt the need to warn you, since all these years I have felt grateful for the way you had helped me in my time of need. However, I must ask a favor of you. Under no circumstances are you to go to the police about this. No one is to know that I was your source of information. You see, the

bakery I spoke of belongs to my mother!"

Rav Landau was stunned by the boy's revelations. How was he to save the Jewish community while at the same time protecting the identity of his informant? Turning to the boy, he said, "Go in peace and may G-d Bless you for your kind-hearted help. You need not worry. Your secret is safe with me."

A few days later, Rav Landau informed his congregation that, because of an error in the calendar, they had started celebrating *Pesach* a day early that year. They would, therefore, have

thereby fulfilling the *mitzvah* of *Sippur Yetzias Mitzrayim* (relating the story of the exodus from Egypt). We use elegant vessels at the table to symbolize that we are free men and members of spiritual royalty. The reclining during the meal is also symbolic of this.

2. There is a *minhag* for men to wear a *kittel* (white robe) at the *Seder* for two reasons: Firstly, it resembles the garments of the angels; secondly, it resembles shrouds, reminding us that even though we are like royalty on this night, we should not become overbearing and haughty. If a person is in mourning, or, according to some customs, if he is in his first year of marriage, he does not wear a *Kittel*.

3. The *Seder* plate is placed before the master of the house, and the others of the household obtain their *Seder* foods from him. According to the individual custom, the *Seder* plate is brought to the table either before or after *Kiddush*.

The placement of food on the *Seder* plate is done according to custom. It consists of three *matzohs, marror* (bitter herbs), *chazeras* (romaine lettuce), *karpas* (greens), *charoses* (mixture of nuts, apples and wine) and two cooked or roasted foods, like a shankbone and egg. The salt water is left on the table.

The reason we place three *matzohs* rather than two on the *Seder* plate is because they represent the three parts of Israel: the top one is called *Cohen*, the middle is called *Levi* and the bottom one is called *Yisroel*. (There are those who use only two *Matzohs (Grah)*).

4. The *Kiddush* must not be recited until after nightfall. The *Kiddush* is the first of the four cups of wine drunk during the *Seder*. All four cups must be drunk while reclining on the left side.

to refrain from eating bread for an additional day.

When the bakers heard the Rabbi's ordinance, they were furious. They complained to the Governor that their business would be ruined. After all, so much extra bread had been prepared. To this accusation, Rav Landau responded with an offer to buy the bread—provided that the bakers tasted it first. When the bakers showed a reluctance to do so, their evil plot was uncovered.

The Jews of the town were saved—thanks to *Hashem's* timely aid and Rav Yecheskel Landau's kindness to a gentile boy.

SILVER COINS

After *Hashem* revealed to Avrohom Avinu that his children would suffer greatly as slaves in Egypt, He promised that they would "go forth with great abundance" as free men.

Our Sages tell us that this "great abundance" refers to the Torah received at *Har Sinai*. But if this were so, why were the *Bnai Yisroel* commanded to ask the Egyptians for money and spoils before leaving Egypt?

The Rabbis tell us *(Shemos Rabbah,* Ch. 8) that the four cups of wine drunk at the *Seder* symbolize the four Divine promises of Redemption found in the Scripture in connection with Israel's liberation from Egypt: "... I will bring you out ... I will deliver you ... I will redeem you ... I will take you to Me ..." *(Shemos* 6:6-7)

Each of the four cups of wine must hold at least a *reviyis* of wine. The first time, the cup must hold at least 4.42 ozs. and the other three times at least 3.3 ozs. One should drink the entire *reviyis,* although one can fulfill the *Mitzvah* by drinking at least most of it. The drinking should be completed within 1 minute, but one should preferably drink everything at once. It is preferable to use red wine as a reminder of Jewish blood shed during the oppression in Egypt. There is a controversy as to the acceptability of grape juice (where wine poses no health problem).

5. One washes his hands by pouring water over each hand as is done before eating bread; however, no blessing is recited.

6. One dips a vegetable in salt water, recites the usual blessing, *Borei Pri Ho'Adomoh* and eats less than a *kezayis* (olive size) of the vegetable. When reciting the blessing, he should intend to include the blessing for *marror* that he will eat later.

7. We eat *karpas* (greens) on *Pesach* because when its letters are read in the reverse order, we discover the "sixty myriads" of Israelites who were oppressed with heavy and arduous work. *(Mogen Avrohom* 473:4)

8. One breaks the middle *matzoh* into two uneven pieces, the larger of which is hidden and is to be used for the *afikomen.*

The Maggid of Dubno answered this with the following *Moshol:*

A young man had hired himself out to a wealthy merchant for six years. At the end of his service he would receive a bag of silver coins. When the six years were over, it occurred to the master that a bag of silver was too small a reward for the splendid services the boy had rendered him. He, therefore, put the silver aside and instead wrote out a check in an amount many times that of the total value of the silver coins. Instead of thanking his master for his generosity though, the servant sullenly stuffed the piece of paper into his pocket and went home.

The next day, his father called at the merchant's house and said to the wealthy man, "You have been most generous to my son, and I want to thank you. But the boy is still a child and doesn't understand the value of a check. He expected to receive a bag with shiny, new coins and instead got a plain sheet of paper. I would therefore be most grateful if you would let him have at least part of his wages in silver."

* * * * *

In the same manner Avrohom came to *Hashem* saying, "You have been

9. One raises the plate with the *matzohs* on it and recites *Ho Lachmo Anyo.* The plate is removed, and the second cup of wine is poured. *Mah Nishtana* is said, the plate is returned, the *matzohs* are uncovered and the narrative in the *Haggadah* is begun.

10. The reason we call the story of *Pesach* the *"Haggadah"* is because the word *"Haggadah"* connotes a "narration," as in *"Ve-higad'ta Levincha"*—"You should tell your son on that day." *(Shemos* 13:8) *(Abudraham)*

11. When one says *"V'Hi Sheomdoh"* and *"L'fichoch,"* the *matzos* are covered and one takes the wine cup in his hand. When mentioning the ten *makos,* we pour out wine with a finger. When one says *"Matzoh Zu"* and *"Maror Zu,"* one lifts up the *matzos* and the *maror* respectively.

12. After *Go'al Yisroel,* one recites the usual blessing, *Borei Pri Hagefen,* and drinks the second cup of wine. He then washes his hand for the *matzoh* as for bread. According to most authorities, two whole *matzohs* are required for *lechem mishne,* (besides the remaining piece of middle *matzoh)* and the *Hamotzee* blessings are recited. Then one should break off a piece from the top *matzoh* and another piece from the broken *matzoh* and eat an olive-size piece of *matzoh* from each one, preferably simultaneously. If one cannot eat both pieces simultaneously, he should first eat an olive-size piece of the whole *matzoh,* than an olive-size piece of the broken *matzoh* within a maximum of 4-9 minutes. At the very least, however, one olive-size piece of *matzoh* must be eaten by each participant in order to fulfill the biblical obligation. It's best that each olive-size piece of *matzoh* be completely consumed within two minutes.

generous indeed in promising the Torah to my descendants. But the nation will be young and not mature enough to understand the value of the Torah, and if they go forth from slavery with empty hands they will say, "Indeed, *Hashem* has fulfilled part of His promise. We did become slaves. But what about the great abundance which we were to receive at the hour of our deliverance?"

It is for this reason that *Bnai Yisroel* were commanded to take gold and silver from the Egyptians. This would be tangible wealth which they could appreciate at that time.

It was only as Israel grew in wisdom that it came to understand that its true wealth lay not in coins and trinkets gathered in Egypt, but rather in *Hashem's* gift of the Torah which has steadfastly kept the Jewish people alive throughout the years.

* * * * *

THE OVERNIGHT MIRACLE

About 2,500 years ago, there reigned in Judea a pious and wise king whose name was Chezekiah. For 13 years he ruled in peace and happiness

13. One must eat *matzoh* while reclining on the left side. If one forgot to recline, he should eat the *matzoh* once again, without reciting the blessing. We are commanded to recline at the *Seder* table to recall the position of free men at banquets in olden times. One should always recline on the left side for health reasons. (*Levush* 472:3)

14. One may use romaine lettuce, freshly ground horseradish, or endives (thoroughly inspected for leaf boarers or other insects), for *maror*. He should preferably use the stalks of these vegetables. (The endives commonly sold are really chicory and their use is questionable). We eat these bitter herbs to remind us of the bitter life our ancestors led in Egypt as slaves. Another reason why we eat romaine lettuce on *Pesach* is, just as the lettuce stalk is soft and pleasant on top but forms a hard lump on the bottom, so did the Egyptians use soothing words at the beginning, saying "Settle in the best part of the land." Finally however, they embittered our lives and made us miserable.

15. The *charoses* dip is made of apples, nuts and wine, preferably prepared before *Yom Tov* begins. If *Pesach* occurs on *Shabbos,* the wine must be added before *Shabbos.* The mixture should have a thick consistency to recall the mortar from which our forefathers were forced to make bricks in Egypt. One dips an olive-size of *maror* into *charoses,* then shakes off the *charoses,* recites the blessing *Al Achilas Moror,* and eats the olive-size piece of *Moror* without reclining.

16. An-olive-size piece of *matzoh* is taken from the bottom matzoh and broken into two pieces and an olive-size piece of *maror* is placed in between them. One dips this into *charoses* (for *korach* i.e. the sandwich)

and there was not one person from Dan to Beersheva who did not know the laws of purity. Then came Chezekiah's greatest test.

Across the Jordan River, not far from Judea, reigned a mighty king, Sannecheriv of Assyria. All neighboring kings and princes feared him, and even Chezekiah paid tribute to him, until his treasury was empty. Then he claimed bankruptcy. But this excuse was not good enough for Sannecheriv, who mobilized his army for an invasion of Judea. Never before had the world seen such a mighty army— 45,000 gold and silver chariots and over a half a million trained swordsmen. When they crossed the Jordan River, there was no water left, for the horses had drunk it all. With this large and mighty army, he easily captured all the fortified cities in Judea until he came to Jerusalem.

At this point, Sannecheriv boasted, "I could raze this city to the ground with even just a few of my legions." Although his men were eager to fight, Sannecheriv told them to rest from their weary journey. In the morning he commanded them, "Let every warrior bring me but one brick from the walls of the city."

shakes off the *charoses* and eats it while reclining. The dipping of *charoses* is done only if it is one's custom to do so. The reason we eat the *matzoh* and *maror* together is to fulfill Hillel's opinion that the *matzoh* and *maror* must be eaten together. After one has recited the blessing on the washing, one should not speak about matters unrelated to the meal until after he has eaten this combination.

17. At the *Seder*, no barbecued or roasted meats or poultry may be eaten. Meat should be cooked in water so one will not mistake it for the roasted meat eaten for the *Korbon Pesach* during the time of the Temple. The *zeroah* (the roasted wing) on the *Seder* plate symbolizes the *Korbon Pesach*. Another thing it symbolizes is the outstretched arm which *Hashem* displayed to the Jewish people in Egypt. If a *zeroah* is not available, another piece of meat—even without a bone may be used. The piece of *Matzoh* that was hidden for the *afikomen* is brought to the table and distributed at the conclusion of the meal. One must eat at least one olive-size piece of *matzoh*, and preferably two, while reclining. If one forgot to recline, there is doubt whether he must eat the *afikomen* again. The *afikomen* should be eaten before midnight, and nothing further may be eaten that night after the *afikomen*. This symbolizes the last thing eaten at the *Bais Hamikdosh* during the *Seder* night.

18. We hide the afikomen for educational purposes, so that the children should ask why we are hiding the *afikomen* even before eating our meal. This will give the parent the opportunity to tell the children the story of the Exodus from Egypt. *(Levush)*

The *Shelah* writes, "I saw people kissing the *matzohs* and *maror* for

Up stood Ravshakeh, his leading general, who called out to the defenders of the city to surrender. "Do not let Chezekiah deceive you into thinking that G-d will save you." On and on Ravshakeh ranted arrogantly, finally demanding that the defenders revolt against Chezekiah and surrender the city.

When news of this reached Chezekiah, he went to the *Bais Hamikdosh* (Holy Temple) to pray to G-d. He also ordered all his people to observe a day of solemn prayer, for victory lay only in G-d's hands.

Almost all remained loyal to the King, except for a traitor named Shevna the Scribe. He decided to make peace with the enemy at any cost. In the middle of the night, he led his men to the gates of the city and forced his way out. Suddenly the gates swung closed and he found himself alone. When he was brought before Sannecheriv, the king was furious. "Have you come to mock me? Where are your followers? I'll teach you, you deceitful traitor." Shevna was immediately put to a horrible death.

It was the first night of *Pesach* in Jerusalem, but the holiday spirit was gone. All the Jews prayed to G-d for love of the *mitzvah*. Happy is the person who serves G-d with joy".

19. The third cup of wine is poured before *Birchas Hamazon*. The cup should be washed out if it is not clean. After the completion of *Birchas Hamazon*, one recites the blessing and drinks the third cup while reclining. Then the cup of Eliyohu is poured, the door is opened, and *Shefoch Chomoscho* is recited.

20. At the *Seder* we recite "*Shefoch Chamoscho*" and open the door in order to remember that it is *Leil Shemurim* (the night of protection). We are told that in merit of this act, *Moshiach* will come and punish those who deny G-d's existence. The custom is to pour one extra cup called the cup of Eliyahu Hanovi, to symbolize that we believe, just as G-d redeemed us from Egypt, so, too will He redeem us again.

21. The fourth cup of wine is poured, and the *Hallel* is completed while one is sitting. The blessing on wine is recited, the fourth cup of wine is drunk while one is reclining, and the blessing of *Al Hagefen* is recited. It is a *mitzvah* to say *Hallel* with a *Zimun* (a company of three male adults) so that *Hodu* and *Onoh* can be recited responsively. The *Hallel* should preferably be completed before midnight. Nothing may be drunk after the fourth cup other than water or tea. Then we complete the reading of the *Haggadah*.

22. Before one goes to sleep on the first two nights, he need say only *Shema* and the *Hamapil* blessing.

deliverance. Soon after the prayers, the prophet Yeshaya appeared before the King and brought G-d's message to him. It was a message of comfort and hope, of victory and triumph.

"G-d has heard your prayers. No enemy shall come into this city. G-d Himself will defend and save this city ..."

When midnight came, the Angel of Death smote thousands upon thousands in the Assyrian camp. When Sannecheriv rose up early in the morning to storm the city of Jerusalem, he found dead corpses in the place of his mighty army.

In the Land of Israel, the Festival of *Pesach* was an occasion for double rejoicing for the people of Jerusalem

and their King Chezekiah. It was as though the miracles of G-d which had saved and delivered their forefathers from Egypt many years before had been repeated again.

* * * * *

The custom of having at the *Seder* a fifth cup of wine which we do not drink, which we call "Cup of Eliyohu," came about because of a debate in the Talmud. There was a question whether or not we should have a fifth cup of wine drunk at the Seder because of the additional promise of redemption. The sages decided to wait until the Prophet Eliyohu comes to let him decide whether we should drink a fifth cup of wine or not. (Gaon of Vilna)

MATZOH—GEBRUKT

When *matzoh* in any form (e.g. matzoh meal, cake meal) comes into contact with water, some communities have a minhag not to eat it on the first seven days of *Pesach*. What is the reason for this custom? The *Knesses Hagdolah* says that it was made as a *gezerah*, (Rabbinical decree) lest one might in error come to use flour instead of *matzoh* meal during *Pesach*. Another reason mentioned is that there is a possibility that some of the *matzoh* flour may not have been kneaded well and when it gets wet it might become *chometz*. Since the last day of *Pesach* is *Mid'rabbonon* (from our Sages) many of those who accepted this minhag did not accept it for the last day of *Pesach* because of *Simchas Yom Tov*. Thus, *Gebrukt* (matzoh and liquid) is not real *chometz* and therefore does not have to be sold through a *Rav* or burned.

CHOMETZ REMAINING IN STORES AFTER PESACH

One must be aware that he cannot buy any real *chometz* products (like bread, noodles, cake, etc.) in a store that is owned by a Jew who did not sell his *chometz*. He should wait until he can ascertain that the stock the merchant kept over *Pesach* has been sold and replaced by new stock. In large supermarkets, it is important to find out whether the owner is a Jew or not. If he is not, then there is no question about using his products; it is permissible. But if he is, then one must be careful not to buy his stock until it has been replaced.

TEFILLAH DURING PESACH

During the entire month of *Nissan*, we do not say *Tachnun* or *Tzidkoscho Tzedek,* nor do we fast or make eulogies. We do not say *Mizmor Lesodah* and *Lamnatzeach* on *Erev Pesach* nor during *Pesach* itself. Some congregations have the custom of reciting the whole *Hallel* on the first two nights of *Pesach* after *Ma'ariv*. Everyone recites the whole *Hallel* on the first two days of *Pesach* during *Shacharis*. During the rest of the holiday, half *Hallel* is recited. Beginning with *Chazoras Hashatz* of *Mussaf* on the first day of *Pesach*, one ceases to include *Mashiv Horuach Umorid Hageshem* in the blessing of *Mechaye Hameisim* in the *Shmoneh Esrei*. If one davens *Nusach Sefard*, one inserts *Morid Hatal*.

SEFIRAS HAOMER—INTRODUCTION

"You shall count to yourselves seven weeks; from the time the sickle is first put to the standing corn you shall begin to count seven weeks. You shall observe the feast of weeks unto the L-rd your G-d after the measure of the free will offering of your hand, which you shall give as the L-rd your G-d blesses you. You shall rejoice before the Lord your G d, you, your son and daughter, your man-servant, and maid-servant, and the Levite who is within the gates, and the stranger and the fatherless and the widow who are in your midst, in the place where the L-rd your G-d shall choose to cause His name to dwell there." (Devorim 16:9-11)

"It is a positive commandment to count seven complete weeks from the day the Jews brought the Omer. The whole reason for freeing Klal Yisroel from Egypt was to give us the Torah, an event which took place 50 days later. Just as a slave counts the days left until he is to be completely freed from his master, so too, do we count how many days have passed from Pesach until the giving of the Torah, which took place 50 days later." (Sifre, Parshas Emor).

HILCHOS SEFIRAS HAOMER

1. Each night from the second night of *Pesach* through the night preceding *Shavuos*, one must count the *Omer*. The blessing *'Al Sefiras Haomer'* is recited before the counting.

2. In counting the *Omer*, one counts the days and the weeks. For example, on the 32nd day, one says, "Today is 32 days, which is 4 weeks and 4 days to the *Omer*." One must understand what he is saying in order to fulfill the *Mitzvah* of counting the *Omer*. If one does not understand Hebrew, he must count the *Omer* in a language he does understand.

3. One should count the *Omer* while standing, as soon after nightfall as possible. If one counted at dusk, he should count again after nightfall without reciting the blessing.

4. If during the day, one realizes that he did not count the *Omer* the night before, or if one is not sure whether or not he counted, he should count it immediately without reciting the blessing. He may then continue to count with the blessing on the following evenings. If, however, one forgets to count for an entire night and day, he must omit the blessing for the duration of *Sefiras Haomer*. If one is in doubt if he missed one day's count, he may continue to recite the blessing. If one said only "Today is 32 days" and forgot to say "4 weeks and 4 days to the *Omer*," he has fulfilled the *Mitzvah*. However, it is still best for him to say the omitted part in a correct manner without repeating the *Brocho*. If one said only "4 weeks and 4 days" and did not say "the 32nd day," he has still fulfilled

the *Mitzvah*. However, mere mention of the number of weeks without any mention whatsoever of the days, is not sufficient. For example, if on the 21st or 28th day, he mentioned only "this is the 3rd or 4th week," without mentioning the exact day, he has not fulfilled the *Mitzvah* of counting.

5. If one is asked during dusk or after nightfall to tell the *Omer* count of that night and he has not yet counted for that night, he should respond by giving the count of the previous evening. If he answered with that night's count (i.e. the correct count), he may not recite the blessing that night.

6. It is preferable for one to know the proper day of the *Omer* before reciting the blessing. If one counted erroneously, but corrected himself immediately, he need not count again. If he did not correct himself immediately, he must repeat the blessing and count correctly.

7. For thirty-three days during the period of *Sefiras Haomer,* it is customary to observe certain aspects of mourning. This is to commemorate the tragic deaths of Rabbi Akiva's students during this time. Therefore, weddings, concerts, parties at which there is musical entertainment, and taking haircuts or shaving are prohibited during this period.

8. There are different customs concerning when this period of partial mourning is observed.

a) Some observe this period from the second day of *Pesach* until *Lag Ba'Omer* (the 33rd day of the *Omer*) and all mourning ceases at daybreak on *Lag Ba'Omer,* or the night before.

It was on this day that a plague that had killed thousands of students of Rabbi Akiva (about 130 C.E.) suddenly stopped. It has therefore been observed as a day of joy ever since. All festivities usually forbidden during the days after Passover are permitted on *Lag Ba'Omer.*

b) Some do not begin the mourning period until the first day of the month of *Iyar* and continue until 3 days before *Shavuos,* except for *Lag Ba'Omer* during the day.

c) Some begin the mourning period on the first day of *Rosh Chodesh Iyar* and observe the mourning period until after daybreak of the third day of *Sivan,* except for the day of *Lag Ba'Omer.*

d) Some observe mourning for the entire *Omer* period.

9. If *Lag Ba'Omer* occurs on Sunday, the custom is to permit haircuts on Friday in honor of *Shabbos.*

10. *Tachanun* is not said on *Lag Ba'Omer,* nor during the *Mincha* of the previous day.

11. Weddings are permitted on *Lag Ba'Omer.*

שבועות

Shavuos

SHAVUOS—INTRODUCTION

"And Moshe called unto all Israel and said unto them: Hear O Israel

SHAVUOS

WHY ISRAEL WAS CHOSEN TO RECEIVE THE TORAH:

We are told in the *Midrash* and in the *Gemara* that, before giving His Holy Law to Israel, G-d offered it to every other nation. However, each one in turn rejected the Torah, for none was willing to have its lifestyle restricted by G-d's regulations. It was only the people of Israel who accepted the Torah freely and unconditionally. *(Yalkut Shimoni)*

Asked the Maggid of Dubno: How did G-d go about presenting His Law to one nation after the other, offering it for unconditional acceptance? He proceeded to illustrate his answer with a *Moshol:*

A tradesman once went to a wholesale store to buy clothing on credit terms. The storekeeper was rather reserved and showed him some of the items for sale, but he did not bring out any special clothing and he quoted high prices for everything he had on display. In the end, the tradesman left the store without buying anything. A little later, another customer entered and said that he was willing to pay cash. This time, the storekeeper brought out the best and fanciest clothes in his stock and quoted reaso-

nable wholesale prices. The customer made several purchases and left, well satisfied. After the door of the shop had closed, an apprentice, who had been watching the proceedings, asked his employer why he had so obviously discriminated against the customer who had wanted to purchase on credit. The storekeeper answered, "Did you see that first man? I could tell at once that he wasn't dependable and would never pay his debts. I had to be courteous to him, but I wasn't anxious to have his trade, and I acted accordingly. Now, the other man, who always pays cash for what he buys, is an old customer, a trustworthy gentleman to whom I would have extended unlimited credit if he had requested it. Naturally, I am pleased to do business with a person like that, and I did my best to accommodate him."

The One Above, said the Maggid of Dubno, had the most precious merchandise of all to offer—the Holy Torah. He knew in advance what the attitude of the other nations would be. They were anxious to enjoy the pleasures of this world to the fullest, and, therefore, they could hardly have been relied upon to keep the Law. Hence, G-d was not anxious for them to acquire it. Nevertheless, He did not wish to be unfair and so He offered His

151

the statutes and the ordinances which I speak in your ears this day, that you may learn them, and observe to do them. The L-rd our G-d made a covenant with us in Horeb. The L-rd did not make this covenant with our fathers, but with us even us, who are all of us here alive this day. The L-rd spoke with you face to face in the mount and out of the midst of the fire." (Devorim 5:1-4)

It is a positive commandment to rest from work on Shavuos, as it says, 'You shall call this same day a holy convocation.' (Vayikra 23:21)

Shavuos *(Feast of Weeks) is celebrated on the sixth day of* Sivan. This

Torah to one nation after the other. However, in each case, He emphasized that aspect of the Torah which would be the most difficult for that particular nation to accept. Thus, for example, when He presented it to the Edomites, He told them first of the Sixth Commandment which prohibits murder, for the children of Esau had made murder a part of their way of life. The Ammonites and Moabites, who were notorious for their promiscuity were first told of the Seventh Commandment, which forbids adultery. All these nations had demonstrated throughout their previous histories that they would be unable to observe a Code of Law such as the Torah contained, and G-d preferred not to give it to them, for the laws of the Torah are meant to be kept, not violated. The Children of Israel, however, had proven from the very beginning their readiness to do whatever would be G-d's will. They, in their zeal, responded 'Na'ase V'Nishma' (We will do the Mitzvos. Now let us hear them.) Therefore, G-d, anxious that they should have His Torah, revealed to them all the profound wisdom that is contained in His Eternal Law.

"And Moses called unto all Israel, and said unto them: Hear O Israel

the statutes and the ordinances which I speak in your ears this day, that you may learn them and observe to do them." (Devorim 5:1)

And you shall teach them the laws diligently unto your children and you shall talk of them when you sit in your house, and when you walk by the way, and when you lie down and when you rise up. (Devorim 6:7)

"Oh, how I love Your law. It is my meditation all the day." (Tehillim 119:97)

The Holy One Blessed be He, the Torah and Israel are all one. (Zohar Parshas Acharei)

* * * * *

THE ROYAL VISIT

In our daily and holiday *Tefillos* we read the verse, *"Yismach Hashem Bema'asav"* (Let *Hashem* rejoice in His works). We can better understand the meaning of these words through the following Moshol:

A great king was once traveling on the road with his attendants. Toward evening, the skies became cloudy and it started to thunder. Lightning lit up the sky as a heavy rain fell. The travelers rushed to the nearest village and stopped at the very first house they reached. Since it looked as if the storm

two day festival is observed for two reasons: to commemorate the giving of the Torah on Har Sinai, *and to remind us of the* bikkurim *(first fruit's offerings) that were brought to the Temple as a thanksgiving offering of the early harvest. It is also called* Chag Habikurim.

During this festival, both the synagogue and the home are decorated with green branches as a symbol of the harvest season and to remind us of the greenery surrounding Har Sinai *when we received the Torah.*

Shavuos *thus is the culmination of the holiday of* Pesach. *The freedom the Jews had gained on* Pesach *would have been meaningless if it were*

would last all night, they decided to spend the night there. The next morning they continued on their journey.

For many days, the man who had been host to the king went about boasting to his neighbors that the king and his ministers had done him great honor by spending the night with him.

The townspeople laughed and said, "Did the king choose your house because he knew you? Not at all. He stopped in your home only because the heavy rain had driven him there. Your house just happened to be the first in the village."

Some time later, the king and his attendants once again passed this way. The weather was fine and everyone in the village was eager to play host to the king. Although there was time for the king to travel on to the next village before nightfall, he remembered the man who had been his host during the storm and so went out of his way to spend the night at this man's home. Now, of course, the man could truthfully say that the king had honored him with his presence.

The same is true of *Hashem*. It is no wonder that the *Ribono Shel Olam* "makes His home" with the Jews, for at the time that He wanted to give His Torah to the people on earth, it was only the Jews who accepted it unquestioningly.

* * * * *

A beloved princess was given in marriage to a distant prince. The wedding day was a great holiday in the city of the prince, but a day of sadness in the city where the princess had grown up.

So too, when the Torah was given, the earth rejoiced, but the heavens wept.

R' Nechunya son of Hakanah said: "Anyone who takes upon himself the yoke of Torah, will have removed from him the yoke of kingdom and the yoke of worldly cares. However, anyone who removes the yoke of the Torah from himself, will place upon him the yoke of kingdom and the yoke of worldly cares."

(Avos, Chapter 3, Mishnah 6).

Great is Torah, for it gives life unto those that practice it in this world and in the world to come. The splendor of men is their Torah.
(D'Be Eliyahu Zuta 5)

THE LOYAL CONVERT

Onkelos was the son of Emperor Titus' sister. He was a clever, handsome well-mannered young man with

not fashioned and guarded by the Torah, which they received on Shavuos. *It is called the Festival of Revelation.*

It is a positive commandment to learn Torah and to teach it, as it says (Devorim 6:7), *"You shall teach your children."* This Mitzvah *is obligatory until one's death. The father is commanded to teach his son before anyone else. He is also obligated to teach his grandchildren, as it says, "You should make known to your children and your children's children." When a child begins to speak, his father should teach him Torah and say with him the* Posuk, *"Torah Tziva Lonu Moshe . . ." (Devorim 33:4)*

a most promising future as a leader of the mighty Roman Empire.

By chance, Onkelos became acquainted with some of the Jewish nobility who had settled in Rome. Through them, he was introduced to the Jewish religion, and found himself very much attracted to it. He had to remember, however, that he was a member of the most eminent family in the Roman Empire. It was unwise for him to be observed associating with Jews. It would have been still more dangerous for him to openly state his intention of converting to the Jewish faith.

After long deliberation, he worked out a solution to his problem. During a visit with his uncle, the Emperor Titus, he casually mentioned an interest in the world of commerce. Titus, who was very fond of his nephew, was very pleased.

He gave him the following advice: "The best way to get rich is to find a way to deal in a highly marketable product which has yet to come before the public. This type of merchandise can provide you with the most profitable kind of business."

This was exactly what Onkelos wanted to hear. Now he had a chance to travel about and to associate with

merchants, many of whom were Jews, without attracting undue attention and giving cause for suspicion.

In the course of extensive trips, he visited the Holy Land and remained there to study Torah. Gifted with an exceptionally keen mind, he easily overcame the difficulties of learning the Hebrew language, laws and customs. After a while, he was ready to adopt the Jewish religion and to abide by the commands of the Torah, though still in secret.

In those days Rabbi Eliezer and Rabbi Yehoshua were the spiritual leaders of the Jewish people. Onkelos visited them and begged them to accept him as their disciple. The Sages saw the deep change in the attitude of the young Roman, since he had studied Torah and had then become a Jew.

He now showed humility and a readiness to study, like all true students of Torah. They finally agreed to accept this young *"Ger"* (convert) and spent much time and effort giving him a proper Jewish education.

Onkelos delayed his return to Rome as long as possible, until the confrontation with his uncle could no longer be avoided. Titus had already sent several delegations of soldiers to bring

HILCHOS SHAVUOS

1. In most communities *Ma'ariv* is delayed on the eve of *Shavuos* until after *tzais hakochavim* (the time when the stars appear) so that the *Omer* period has been completed.

2. On the first day of *Yom Tov*, after the *Kohein* is called to the Torah, the prayer *Akdomus* (praising Hashem) is recited. On the second day, after saying the first two sentences of the *Haftora*, some congregations have the custom to recite another prayer called '*Yetziv Pisgom.*'

3. It is customary to decorate the synagogue and home with greenery

his nephew back.

When he finally did appear before the Emperor, Titus noticed the deep change that had come over his nephew during his long absence. It was a more humble, yet wiser Onkelos who now stood before him.

"What has happened to you, my dear nephew? Did you meet failure in your business ventures or did anyone dare to harm you?"

"Who would harm the nephew of the mightiest man in the world?" replied Onkelos.

"Then why do I see such humility in your manners and appearance?"

Onkelos decided to be straightforward. "The reason for the change in me is the fact that I have spent much time and effort in the study of Torah, the Law of the Jewish people. What is more, I even went so far as to adopt the Jewish religion as my own."

One can imagine the fury of the Emperor Titus over his nephew's confession.

"You fool! You have ruined my high hopes and expectations of you. Your political career is over—finished" Then Titus paused a moment. "Yet, I am curious to know what caused someone as clever as you to seek such a foolish way of life."

"My dear uncle, what made me take such a serious step was none other than your own sound advice before I parted from you. You advised me to search for merchandise that had the promise of being a best-selling article.

"On my extensive trips I discovered no merchandise that was considered lowlier or cheaper by most people than the Jewish religion and the Jewish people. Yet, there is also no doubt in my mind that it will become the most valuable merchandise of all in the future. I should think no reasonable businessman would miss the chance of such great profit!"

Onkelos continued his life as a pious, observant Jew. He became a great Sage and wrote the Aramaic translation and commentary on the Torah, known as "*Targum Onkelos.*"

WHEREVER YOU GO

During the days of the *Shoftim* (Judges), the Jewish leader, Elimelech came to Moav to escape a famine in Israel. With him were his wife Naomi and his sons Machlon and Kilyon, who soon married Moavite women Orpoh and Ruth. Then Elimelech and his sons suddenly died, leaving the three women impoverished widows. Naomi decided to return back to Israel.

When she left Moav, Ruth insisted on following her. She told her mother-for *Shavuos*. Through this we are reminded that the fruits of the trees are being judged on *Shavuos* and that we should pray for them. *(Magen Avraham* 494:5). Also the greenery symbolizes the grass which grew around *Har Sinai* at the time of the giving of the *Torah. (Levush* Ch. 494)

4. There is a custom to remain awake all night and study Torah (on the first night of *Shavuos.)* For those who follow this practice, there are a number of points to bear in mind if one has not slept at all.

a) The blessings *'Al Netilas Yodayim'* and *'Asher Yotzar'* may be said only after going to the bathroom, and not in their normal place in the davening.

in-law, "Where you will go, I will. Nothing will separate us."

*   *   *   *   *

The stories of the two converts to Judaism, Ruth, the Moavite princess, and Onkelos, nephew of the Roman Emperor, seem to have many similarities.

Both gave up royalty, honor and wealth to become observant Jews. Both then had a major impact on Jewish history. Ruth was privileged to become the ancestress of the Royal House of David, and Onkelos' commentary has been studied for centuries together with the Holy Torah.

Both converts showed dedication, self-sacrifice and determination to be part of *Hashem's* Chosen People. Their reward was having a permanent influence on the lives and history of the Jewish People.

*   *   *   *   *

According to the Talmud, (*Bava Basra* 14b) the prophet Shmuel is the author of *Megillas Ruth.* In the conflict between King Shaul and Dovid, Shmuel did not side with either party. However, when he heard that Dovid's opponents wanted to undermine his authority completely by questioning the purity of his descent, Shmuel

wrote *Megillas Ruth* to testify to Dovid's unchallengeable ancestry. He clearly demonstrated why Dovid's ancestress, a Moavite princess, was legally permitted to enter the Jewish fold. The reason for this is that only a Moavite man can not enter in marriage with a Jewess, but a Moavite woman is allowed to marry a Jew.

*   *   *   *   *

The *Midrash* says that *Hashem* regards the *Ger Tzedek* (the genuine convert) as equal to an Israelite by descent, or even to a Levite. This is inferred from *Devorim* 14:29, where the Levite and the *Ger* are grouped together.

Moshe Rabbeinu, in astonishment, asked *Hashem,* "Is a Ger really to be regarded in the same category as a Levite?"

Hashem answered Moshe: "How much did I toil for *Bnai Yisroel?* I took them out of Mitzrayim and lit their path through the wilderness. I brought them down *Mahn* (manna) and fed them quails. I caused a well to come up for them and surrounded them with clouds of glory. Then they accepted My Torah. But, in contrast, this Ger came to Me of his own free will and accepted the commandments of the

b) The following blessings should not be said: *'Al Mitzvas Tzitzis'*; the blessings on Torah study; *'Elokai Neshomo'* and *'Hama'avir Sheino.'* If possible, one should hear someone else who has slept during the night say them and intend to fulfill his obligation by listening to the other's recitation. (The individual who is saying the blessings must also have in mind to allow the listeners to fulfill their obligation through his recitation.) If there is no one to recite these blessings, then the blessing for the *Tallis Gadol* can be used to cover the *Tallis Koton* as well. The blessing of *'Ahava Raba'* can cover the blessings for Torah study if one specifi-

Torah without having benefited from any miracles. Should he not be considered at least the equal of even a Levite?"

When the Jews said, "Na'aseh" ("We will do") before "Nishma" ("We will hear") 600,000 servants of G-d came to each one and tied on them two crowns: one crown for 'do' and the other for 'hear.' (Shabbos 88a)

"Write down these words" refers to the written scriptures; "For according to these words have I made with you a covenant" refers to the Mishnah and Talmud, which separate Israel from the nations of the world. It has been the Oral Law that has preserved the Jewish people and the integrity of its faith. (Gittin 60b)

*   *   *   *   *

HOW TO WIN A PRINCESS

A king once called together his advisors and announced, "My daughter has turned eighteen making her old enough to marry. She is beautiful, talented, and kind-hearted, and she would make a wonderful partner for the right man.

"But I don't want her to marry someone just because he is rich or handsome. I want someone who can prove that he is intelligent and willing to work hard to win my daughter's love and respect.

"Therefore, I have decided to keep my daughter in the castle tower. No one but her servants are allowed to see her. The door to the castle has been sealed off. And even if someone does manage to find it and enter, he will find the path to my daughter's room very difficult. It will take a very clever and determined young man to reach my daughter.

"The first man to reach her room will become her husband. If he is wise enough to discover the way to her room, he deserves to have her as a bride."

The word soon spread that the King's lovely daughter would marry the first man who could reach her castle room. That same day, a crowd of men surrounded the castle walls. Some searched for the doorway. Others played musical instruments outside, hoping to gain her attention and her aid. But the door was impossible to find, and there was no sign from the princess that she would help. Soon the men gave up and went home.

They were followed by other men, also eager to wed the princess and share her riches. They, too, tried to awaken her interest. Some even tried

cally has this purpose in mind and if immediately after the *Shmoneh Esrei* one recites some Torah passages.

5. It is customary to eat dairy foods on the first day of *Shavuos*.

YOM TOV

I. HILCHOS YOM TOV

1. The *Mitzvah* of *Kibbud* applies to *Yom Tov* as it does to *Shabbos*. Thus, one should honor the *Yom Tov* by bathing on *Erev Yom Tov*, by wearing better clothes on *Yom Tov*, and by participating in some of the preparations for *Yom Tov*.

---

climbing the castle walls, but they fell flat on their faces. Before long, everyone agreed that reaching her was a hopeless task.

Yet there was one young man who did not give up. He was neither rich nor famous, but he had intelligence and persistence. He set up camp outside the castle, and spent all his waking hours searching for its entrance. Finally, one morning, he noticed a small crack in the walls. "This must be it!" he shouted and pushed against the wall with all his might. Sure enough, the bricks near the crack soon gave way, the entrance was revealed, and the man was able to go inside.

Once there, he was faced with many hallways, each leading somewhere else. It was only after many false starts that he found a passageway that led him up a long flight of stairs. He thought his journey was over, but when he reached the top of the stairs, he was face-to-face with a long, long row of doors. Desperately, he tried one door after another, but they were all locked.

The man was extremely discouraged. After all his hard work, he had reached a dead end. He was about to give up like the others—but then he had an idea. "Princess," he called out,

as loudly as he could. "Can you hear me? I've spent many days trying to find you, and I've managed to come all the way to the top of the stairs, but now I'm lost. Please help!"

There was a moment of silence, but she had heard him. "This man has tried very hard to find me," she thought to herself. "He must really be eager to marry me. I think I owe him some help."

Suddenly there came a voice from one of the locked rooms. "This is the princess. The keys to the rooms are hidden right next to the staircase. Take them, and come all the way to the end of the hallway. There you will find my room."

The man smiled. She was on his side. He followed her instructions exactly, and within a few minutes he had opened her door. The King was overjoyed at finding someone who had been willing to spend so much time and thought in seeking his daughter's hand, and the man and the princess were wed a short time later.

Hashem Yisborach also searched for a suitable "mate" for His holy Torah. Of all the nations only the Jews showed that they were willing to work hard to observe and honor the Torah. But studying Torah is not always an

158

2. One should not eat a meal on *Erev Yom Tov* after most of the day has passed, in order to have an appetite for the *Yom Tov* meal at night.

3. The *Mitzvah* of *simcha* (enjoyment) also applies to *Yom Tov*, as it does to *Shabbos*. On each day of *Yom Tov*, one must eat two meals—one at night and one on the following day—and at each of the two meals there must be *lechem mishna* (two complete loaves of bread). Furthermore, one should partake of wine and meat in these meals according to his means.

easy task. Sometimes, like the man in the story, we must search for a long time before finding the right interpretations in the Torah or *Gemara*. Yet, if we work hard at it, our efforts will eventually succeed. Like the princess, the Torah itself will often provide the "key to the correct path" in learning. And, if we continue trying to observe the Torah, the marriage between the Torah and the Jewish nation that occurred at Mt. Sinai will last joyously forever.

* * * * *

A young man was asked by the Gerer Rebbe if he had learned Torah. "Just a little," replied the youth. "That is all any one ever has learned of the Torah," was the Rebbe's response.

* * * * *

There are three crowns with which the Jews were crowned: The crown of Torah, the crown of priesthood, and the crown of kingdom. The crown of Torah is greater than the other two. (Avos 4:17)

He who exerts himself in learning of the Torah, stands, as it were, all day on Mount Sinai and receives the Torah. (Zohar)

* * * * *

A man once came to Rabbi Yisroel Salanter to ask his advice on how to devote the mere fifteen minutes a day that he had available for Torah study, since he was completely occupied with his business.

"Study *Mussar* (a guide to self-improvement)," was the reply, "and you will see that you *can* arrange for more time for Torah study every day."

The learning of Torah is greater than all the Mitzvos, since the study of Torah leads to doing Mitzvos. (Baba Kama 17a)

THE JEW AND THE TORAH

An eternal covenant exists between the Jew and the Torah. Ever since Sinai, the two have been joined together, bound by a common fate. Yet, at no other time in the history of our people has this bond been more pronounced and more deeply felt than in our own, when the accursed Nazis plotted to wipe the Jews from the face of the earth.

Let us take two incidents from the annals of the Holocaust, and tell of some Jews, who fought for the honor of the Torah, and who, in that same act, fought as well for their own honor and for the honor of the entire nation.

SAVING TORAH SCROLLS FROM BURNING SYNAGOGUES

The first thing the Germans did when they entered a Jewish commun-

159

II. CANDLE LIGHTING

1. It is a rabbinical commandment to light candles before *Yom Tov*. The candles should be lit prior to the last eighteen minutes before sunset on *Erev Yom Tov*, just as on *Erev Shabbos*, although in the case of *Yom Tov*, one can light candles past the time of the *shkiah* (sunset). According to most customs, the blessing of *L'Hadlik Ner Shel Yom Tov* is recited before lighting the candles (unlike the candle lighting of *Shabbos* when the blessing must be recited after the lighting). According to most authorities, the *Shehecheyanu* is said during the lighting of the candles.

ity in Europe was to set fire to the local synagogue. The purpose of this act was to terrorize and demoralize the Jews. It was done openly, in broad daylight, sometimes to the accompaniment of a German army band. On occasion, the enemy would gather the local Jews and force them to watch the destruction. More than once, though, someone among the oppressed and persecuted Jews would defy death and rush forth into the Shul to rescue the scrolls of the Torah.

In the community of Pshevorsk, Poland, both the synagogue and *Beis Hamedrash* (House of Study) were engulfed in flames. Hordes of German soldiers and officers stood there enjoying the spectacle. Many Jews were gathered behind them, their heads bowed in pain and humiliation. The Rabbi of the community had been ordered to stand in the front row, himself the object of scorn and derision. But suddenly the Rabbi broke away and began to run. Two more Jews were seen running after him. The Germans stopped laughing and shouted after him to halt. But the Rabbi did not hear a thing. Nothing could stop him, not even the flames. He and the other two disappeared inside the burning building. The Germans were speechless with astonishment. A few moments

later the Rabbi reappeared. His clothes were singed, but his face shone with a triumphant smile, as his two hands held a scroll of the Torah.

"Jewish impudence!" the German commander grumbled, accompanied by the rest of his men. They pointed their rifles at the burning Synagogue, so that the two men who assisted the Rabbi would not be able to come out. They attacked the Rabbi with the butts of their rifles, but the Rabbi held on to the Torah as if he and the scroll were one and inseparable, as, in fact, they were . . .

WITH A TORAH IN HAND ON THE LAST ROAD

In the community of Tchernowitz, Rumania, the order of total evacuation astounded the Jewish population. Within a few days all the Jews in the city were forced to leave their houses and all their possessions, and assemble on the road. The confusion among them was great, and the fear of the unknown was even greater. Young and old, women and children, babies in arms, the sick and those near death, all huddled together. Behind them was their home town, the only home they had ever known and loved. Before them—a road shrouded in fear and desolation.

2. It is not permissible to do any activity on the first day of *Yom Tov* in preparation for the second day. Therefore one must not perform the candle lighting on the night of the second day of *Yom Tov* until after *Tzais Hakochavim* (the time of the appearance of the stars.)

III. PRAYER ON YOM TOV

1. At night, the special *Kiddush* for *Yom Tov* is recited. The blessing of *Shehecheyanu* is recited in *Kiddush* on every *Yom Tov*, with the exception of the last two nights of *Pesach*. On the second night of *Rosh*

Suddenly, the white bearded Rabbis appeared, holding the scrolls of the Torah with all the silver adornments. They proceeded calmly and peacefully, holding the scrolls on high, as if in a joyous celebration. This splendid sight calmed and soothed the multitude. There was neither cowardly nor hysterical behavior, and the armed guards who accompanied the crowd were denied their amusement. Imbued with a sense of dignity, the Jews set out on their last journey.

Reb Chaninah ben Tradyon was among the ten martyrs tortured by the Roman Emperor Hadrian for their continued faith in *Hashem*. All ten chose to remain faithful and died "*Al Kiddush Hashem.*" Though the Emperor had forbidden all forms of Torah study, Reb Chanina persisted in delving in G-d's Holy Books. He was caught with the Torah in his hands and was condemned to death by burning. To compound the torture, the Roman authorities put wool soaked in water on his heart to prolong the agony of his burning, and wrapped the parchment of the Torah around him. As he died, Reb Chanina was asked what he saw. He replied, "I see the parchment burning, but I see the letters on it ascending to heaven." The words of the Torah and the soul of Reb Chanina went on to everlasting life, but the Roman

Empire eventually crumbled. (*Avodah Zarah* 18a)

* * * * *

When G-d gave the Torah, the birds and animals did not make any sound. People did not speak. The sea did not move and the angels of G-d did not say Kedusha. *The world kept quiet and the* Bas Kol *went out and said, "I am G-d your G-d."* (Medrash Rabbah, Shemos)

* * * * *

The stranger's watch had stopped and he wanted to know the correct time. He looked up at the clock in the tower of the City Hall building but had difficulty in seeing the time.

He remarked to a passerby, "Why is it necessary to have this clock so high up? Wouldn't it be better to have this clock placed within reach so that it could be seen more readily?"

"You don't understand, my friend. If the clock were within reach, everyone would seek to adjust it according to the time of his watch, and no one would ever know the correct time."

The same is true about the Torah. It must be kept high and aloft; it cannot be tampered with and adjusted to suit the whim of different people at different times. We are the ones who must adjust our watches, in other words,

Hashono, it is customary for the one reciting the *Kiddush* to wear a new garment or to have a fresh new fruit on the table, because of the question whether the second day is an extension of the first.

2. When *Yom Tov* occurs on Saturday night, *Havdalah* must be recited both in the *Ma'ariv* prayer *(Vatodienu)* and with the *Kiddush* (with the reciting of a special *Hamavdil).* The blessing on *Besomim* (fragrant spices) is omitted in the *Havdalah,* but the blessing on fire is said.

our lives, to the "Divine" clock, the Torah, that *Hashem* gave us for eternity.

"Give me understanding that I may keep Your Law, and observe it with my whole heart."

(Tehillim 119:34)

"Ben Bag-Bag said: 'Turn it over (the Torah) and turn it over, for everything is there. And look into it, and become gray and old therein; do not budge from it, for you have no better standard of conduct.' (Avos 5:25) *"The Jews had light . . ."* (Esther 8:16)—Light is Torah (Megillah 16b)

The Torah is compared to water: Just as water is found everywhere, so is Torah; just as water ensures the life of the world, so does Torah; just as the water is free for everyone, so is Torah; just as the waters (rain) descended from Heaven, similarly the Torah came down from Heaven; just as the waters come down to the accompaniment of thunder, so the Torah was accompanied by thunder and lightning when it was received at Har Sinai; just as water revives and refreshes, so do the words of Torah bring new life to a person.

* * * * *

In our own days, every Jew can share the experience of our ancestors at *Har Sinai.* The Talmud states that he who leads a child to study Torah is regarded as if he, himself, had accepted the Torah at Sinai. It is Torah study which continues the unbroken chain of our heritage directly from Sinai. It is Torah study which guarantees the future of our people.

The father or mother who leads the child to the *Yeshiva* to study *Aleph-Bais,* the *Siddur, Chumash* and finally *Gemara,* creates another link in the strong chain leading from the past to the present, and into the future of Am Yisroel. *(Kiddushin 30a)*

* * * * *

The mother of Rabbi Yehoshua brought his crib to shul so that he could listen to Torah. *(Yerushalmi Yevamos, Perek 1)* In *Avos* (2:11) it says of Rabbi Yehoshua, "Happy is the one that gave birth to him." Because of his mother, he became a *Talmid Chochom,* for every day that his mother was pregnant she went to all the *Batei Medrashim* in the city and said to them, "Please, I ask you to daven for this child, so that he should become a *Talmid Chochom."*

"The one that teaches his neighbor's child the Torah is considered as if he had himself begotten him."

(Sanhedrin 19b)

3. On each day of *Yom Tov*, one must eat two meals with bread, and *Yaale Ve'yovo* is inserted in the *Birchas Hamazon*. If one forgot *Yaaleh Ve'yovo* and remembers after completing the blessing '*Boneh Yerusholayim*' but before beginning the next blessing, he should say the following: '*Boruch Atoh Hashem . . . Asher Nosan Yomim Tovim l'Amo Yisroel, L'Soson Ul'Simcha Es Yom Chag Hazeh, Boruch Atoh Hashem Mekadesh Yisroel V'Hazmanim.*' If he already began the next blessing, he must repeat the *Birchas Hamazon* from the beginning.

4. Each morning of *Yom Tov* after the *Shacharis* service, the *Hallel* is

Every Jew, after his life in this world is ended, will be brought before the Heavenly Tribunal.

He will be asked, "Why did you neglect Torah-study which is the primary occupation of every Jew?"

The pauper will defend himself, saying, "What should I have done? I had to support my family. How would we have lived, had I studied Torah?"

"Who was poorer, you or Hillel?" will be the reply. "Hillel earned next to nothing, a trepika (small coin) a day. Yet half of it he spent to pay the guard at the door of the *Bais Hamedrash* and thus gain entrance, while the remainder had to provide for the needs of his family. One day, when he had no money and was not admitted, he climbed up to the roof of the building to hear the words of Torah from the mouths of Shmaya and Avtalyon. It was a cold winter day and the snow began to fall. The next morning which was on *Shabbos*, Shmaya and Avtalyon noticed that the *Bais Hamedrash* was dark. Looking up the roof, they saw the frozen figure of a man in the skylight. They took him down, washed him, put oil on him, and revived him by the fire. 'This man is truly worthy of having the *Shabbos* profaned for his sake!' they proclaimed.

"If Hillel could do it, why not you?"

When questioned about his lack of Torah learning, the well-to-do businessman will come forward and excuse himself, saying, "What could I do? I had to keep my business going. I was unable to study any more Torah than I actually did."

The reply to this seemingly simple answer will be, "Are you wealthier than Rabbi Elazar ben Charsum was? Rabbi Elazar possessed a thousand villages and a thousand ships, but he never knew what they looked like. He did not want to take out time to inspect his various properties because he preferred to spend day and night studying Torah. His own servants did not know their master. When they once saw him pass by, they thought he was a laborer and they forced him to go to work. He begged them, 'Please let me go! I must learn.' It was only when they found out who he was that they freed him.

"If he could do it, why not you?"

A sensuous person will be asked, "What stopped you from learning Torah?"

"What should I have done?" he will excuse himself. "I am handsome and was unable to control my passions. Life is full of pleasures! How could I pass them up to study Torah?"

163

recited (except for *Rosh Hashono* and *Yom Kippur*). On *Pesach* the entire *Hallel* is recited only on the first two days; on the remaining days only "half" *Hallel* is said. On *Succos* and *Shavuos*, the entire *Hallel* is recited each day.

5. After the close of *Yom Tov* (both at the beginning of *Chol Hamoed* and at the very end of *Yom Tov* at the start of the regular weekdays), the *Havdalah* is recited, consisting of two blessings: *Hagefen*, and *Hamavdil Bein Kodesh L'chol*.

"Your excuse is not acceptable," he will be told. "Are you more handsome than Yosef? Potifar's wife tempted him daily, changing her clothes three times a day, but nevertheless he overcame his *Yetzer Hora*. Why couldn't you take an example from Yosef?"

(*Yoma* 35b)

A well known idea is told in the name of many great Chassidic Rebbes, including Reb Zusha. He often said that after a person dies and ascends to the heavens for judgment, he will be required to defend his past actions and behavior. But a person will never be asked why he was not as great as Moshe, or as learned as Rabbi Akiva or a Torah giant like Rabbi Akiva Eiger. Hashem gave to each individual different capabilities. Not everyone was given the intelligence to be a *Rosh Yeshiva*, and therefore not all can be expected to be a *Rosh Yeshiva*. He should, however, live up to his full potential in Torah learning, whatever that may be.

Chazal say: "Read it (the Torah) all the days of your life." If a king who is working for the needs of Klal Yisroel *must read it always, of course a regular person must do so too."* (Yerushalmi Sanhedrin)

"Shamai used to say: 'Make your study of Torah a permanent practice.' " (Avos 1:15)

An intellectual was once crossing a river on a small ferryboat. During the passage, he struck up a conversation with the ferryman.

"Tell me, my good man. Do you appreciate classical music?"

"No, not really."

"I'm sorry for you," said the intellectual, "for a quarter of your life is lost."

A while later he asked the ferryman, "Do you have any knowledge of math and science?"

"No, I have no need for it."

"Too bad, for a second quarter of your life is lost."

After a short pause, he asked the ferryman whether he ever had time to enjoy a good game of chess or to view a soccer match.

"In my spare time I'd rather sleep."

"I really feel sorry for you, for a third quarter of your life is lost."

Just then, the boat struck a rock in the water. "Can you swim?" asked the ferryman.

"No, I can't!"

"Well, I'm very sorry for you, for your whole life is lost, as the boat is sinking."

One may be highly cultured and achieve intellectual greatness. But there comes a time when secular knowledge can offer little. Only by means of the "life-saving" powers of the Torah and its teachings can one

IV. MELACHA (WORK)

1. Two types of *Melachos* that are prohibited on *Shabbos* are nevertheless permitted on *Yom Tov:*

a) *Melachos* involving *ochel nefesh* (food), e.g. cooking or baking food which is needed for the day.

b) Certain *Melachos* involving *tzorech hayom k'tzas* (that which is needed by all people somewhat for the day), e.g. heating water to wash one's face; burning logs to keep warm; carrying a *Tallis, Machzor* or *Lulov* to the synagogue; wheeling a baby carriage in the street, etc.

---

successfully meet the challenge of life. *"Ki Hem Chayenu V'orech Yomeinu Uvohem Neheqeh Yomom Volayloh"* (For they are our life and lengthen our days, and in them—Torah and its teachings—I will study day and night).

Rabbi Yose ben Kisma said: "If you should give me all the silver and gold, precious stones and pearls that are in the world, I would not dwell anywhere except in a place of Torah; for in the hour of departure of a man from the world there accompanies him neither gold nor silver nor precious stones nor pearls, but Torah and good deeds alone." (Avos 6:9)

Rabbi Nehorai said, "I disregard all occupations in the world and I teach my son only Torah." A person who learns Torah has his reward in this world and the next. In the case of other occupations, when a person gets sick or old and can no longer work, he may die from loneliness and despair. However, Torah keeps him from all evil when he is young and gives him hope in his old age. *(Kiddushin 82a)*

＊　＊　＊　＊　＊

"**They have all** the luck!" sighed the *meshuloch* (fund-raiser) of the Volozhiner Yeshiva.

He had just finished telling the founder and head of the Yeshiva, the famed Gaon Rabbi Chaim Volozhiner, the news that a local university had received a contribution of half a million rubles.

"Why it would take me a lifetime of collecting to accumulate such a large sum of money," he cried.

Reb Chaim Volozhiner smiled and asked him to explain his method of raising funds.

"Well, I use the method of all *meshulochim.* When I arrive in a town I post announcements that I will speak in the *Shul* on *Shabbos* afternoon. The townspeople come to hear my speech about the importance of Torah study at the *Yeshiva*, and pledge a few rubles in response to my appeal for funds."

"Now," said Reb Chaim, "you can see why our merciful G-d makes it possible for the university to get such big contributions, while you have to gather small sums in so many towns. While you are describing the glories of Torah study, a woman sitting in the *Ezras Noshim* (women's section) is so inspired by your words that she decides to send her son to a *Yeshiva* to study. In this manner, many new Torah students are gained.

"Imagine, however, if the university

2. Any *Melacha* of *ochel nefesh* which can be done before *Yom Tov* with the same effect (e.g., the food would taste the same whether cooked before or on *Yom Tov)* should not be postponed until *Yom Tov.*

3. Although it is permissible to light candles and kindle logs (for *ochel nefesh* or for that which is needed somewhat for the day) from an already existing flame, it is not permissible to strike a match to start a new flame.

4. Although some *Melachos* are permitted for the purpose of *ochel nefesh,* not all *melachos* are permitted. For example, on *Yom Tov* it is not permissible to pick fruits from trees or vegetables from the ground, to squeeze juice from fruits, or to catch animals. When in doubt, consult a *Rav.*

---

fundraisers would have to go from town to town describing the advantages of attending college. So many fine young men might be tempted to abandon their Torah study in favor of a university education.

"Therefore," concluded the Volozhiner Rosh HaYeshiva, *"Hashem* grants the university all of their money at once."

"Remember Yehoshua ben Gamlah for good, because he instituted schools in every country and city and brought the children in when they were six or seven years old" (Baba Basra *21a).*

He who cannot learn Torah because he was not taught, or because he has no spare time, should support others so that they can learn. This will be counted as if he learned. (Tur Yora Deah *246)*

A Rebbe in a yeshiva once asked the Chazon Ish his advice about changing professions. He wanted to become a diamond polisher. "Aren't you already a diamond polisher?" asked the Chazon Ish of the teacher. (Biog. of Chazon Ish, pg. 229)

The daughter of an Emperor once approached a Torah Sage who had a

rather homely appearance and asked, "Why did G-d insert so much wisdom into such an ugly vessel?"

The Torah Sage replied by asking, "Where do you keep your wine?"

"In earthen vessels," was the response.

"But why not keep the wine in precious gold containers which would be more fitting for the delicious wine?"

The princess thought this over and decided it was a proper suggestion. She immediately went home and transferred all the wine in the royal household from earthen to gold containers. Two weeks later, she held a party and she ordered that the butlers carry in the wine in their new, glistening containers. However, at their very first taste, all the guests came to the same conclusion: the wine had turned sour. The golden vessels had looked magnificent but they had provided poor protection for the wine.

The princess went directly to the Sage the next day and asked what had happened. "What you have just learned," replied the Sage, "is how unimportant outward appearances are. The earthen container may have appeared drab, but it kept the wine tasting sweet, something that the shiny gold

166

V. SECOND DAY OF YOM TOV

1. The Torah calls for each *Yom Tov* to be celebrated for one day only, adding up to a total of seven days of *Yom Tov* each year: the first day of *Pesach*, the seventh day of *Pesach*, *Shavuos*, the first day of *Succos*, *Shemini Atzeres*, *Rosh Hashono* and *Yom Kippur*. Today, outside of Israel, each *Yom Tov* (with the exception of *Yom Kippur*) is celebrated for two days. However, *Rosh Hashono* is celebrated for two days even in Israel.

2. All of the prohibitions which apply on the first day of *Yom Tov* apply on the second day as well.

3. Permanent residents of Israel who happen to be visiting abroad on the second day of *Yom Tov* in a town where there is a Jewish community should consult a Rabbi as to whether they must observe the second day or not. The same is true of foreigners visiting Israel.

---

vessels could not do, for all their splendor. The same is true of the appearance of humans. Some individuals might look fair of form and face. Yet, this does not mean that their inner spirit is just as beautiful. In fact, their interest in their own appearance may cause them to become preoccupied with themselves. On the other hand, one who is ugly may appear repulsive, but he might also be kind and wise, and inwardly beautiful. Appearances can be deceiving. Therefore, do not always assume that if something looks unimpressive, it must be inferior. Sometimes it is the humble-looking item or individual that is the greater treasure." (*Nedarim 50b*)

* * * * *

Words of Torah are compared to water. Just as water goes from high places to low ones, so Torah is exemplified not by an arrogant person, but by a humble one who is always attached to *Talmidei Chachomim*. Torah is found with someone who removes the desires of this world from his heart and does a little work every

day in order to eat, while the rest of the day and night he learns Torah. (*Rambam, Hilchos Talmud Torah 3:9*)

Why are the words of the Torah compared to the three liquids: water, wine and milk? To teach us that just as these three liquids can only be preserved in the most inferior earthen vessels and not vessels made of gold and silver, so too, the words of the Torah endure only with one who is humble.

Be careful with the sons of the poor, for the Torah shall come from them. (Nedarim 81a)

* * * * *

A woman once appeared before the Taz crying bitterly that her only son was at death's door. Doctors had abandoned all hope for his survival. As a final desperate gesture, she had come to the Taz for help.

The Taz suggested that the woman pray to *Hashem* for her son's recovery. "But I have prayed already and will continue to do so," she responded. "Can't you offer your own prayers on my son's behalf?"

VI. EIRUV TAVSHILLIN

1. It is not permissible to do any *Melacha* or *hachono* (preparation—such as defrosting foods, etc.) on *Yom Tov* for after *Yom Tov,* or even on the first day of *Yom Tov* for the second day of *Yom Tov.*

2. When *Yom Tov* occurs on Friday, it is permissible to do the *hachono for Shabbos* on *Yom Tov.* Regarding *Melachos* (such as cooking food) done on *Yom Tov* for *Shabbos,* they are permitted by the Torah but forbidden by Rabbinical injunction, unless one sets aside an *Eiruv Tavshilin* on *Erev Yom Tov.* Even with the *Eiruv Tavshilin,* only such *Melachos* may be done for *Shabbos* which could serve some purpose or be utilized on *Yom Tov* itself. For example, if one prepares *cholent* on *Yom Tov* for *Shabbos,* the cooking should be sufficiently completed before *Shabbos* so that it would be edible on *Yom Tov.*

Overcome with compassion, the Taz became lost in deep thought. Suddenly, he lifted his face and said, "For two agonizing weeks I have been racking my brains to discover the answer to a complex Torah question. I pray to *Hashem* that the merit of my torment should serve as a blessing for your sick son."

The prayer was fulfilled and the son recovered due to the benefit of the Torah.

In addition to being a source of light, the Torah is also a source of life.

He who teaches Torah to his friend's child will merit to sit in the Yeshiva in Heaven. If one teaches Torah to an ignorant person's son, then even if G-d had decreed punishment for him, it will be annulled. (Baba Metzia 85a)

* * * * *

The reason why the Torah did not say "Today the Sixth of Sivan is the giving of the Torah" is because we should feel that we receive the Torah every day, not only on *Shavuos.* That

is also why the Torah does not say clearly that *Rosh Hashono* is the day of judgment. If it had, it would have seemed as if only on that day we should not sin, but the other days we would not have to be careful about sins. (*Kli Yakar* on the Torah)

* * * * *

When the Jews came back from Mt. Sinai, they were very hungry and wanted to eat something immediately. If they had proceeded to eat meat, they would have had to follow the laws that had just been handed down on Mt. Sinai. This would have meant (a) Sharpening a knife, and slaughtering the animal; (b) Examining the lung and other parts of the animal; (c) Removing the veins and the non-kosher fats; (d) Soaking the meat for half an hour; (e) Keeping the meat in salt for a full hour; (f) Rinsing off the salt, and finally, cooking the meat.

All this would have taken several hours. The Jews were very hungry, and it would have caused a tremendous delay to start this whole process from the beginning. Therefore, the

3. Each household must set aside its own *Eiruv Tavshilin*. The *Eiruv* is made as follows: At least an egg-size of a complete bread, roll or *matzoh*, and an olive-size of cooked food, such as an egg or piece of meat, are put aside for *Shabbos*. The blessing *"Al Mitzvas Eiruv"* is recited. Then the formula of the *Eiruv* (found in the *Siddur)* is recited.

4. The *Eiruv* one has prepared on *Erev Yom Tov* must still be intact on *Yom Tov* at the time that one is doing the *Melachos* for *Shabbos*. The custom is to eat the prepared *Eiruv* on *Shabbos*. If one forgot to make an *Eiruv*, he should consult a Rabbi.

Jews limited themselves to dairy foods. Since that day, the custom has remained to eat dairy on *Shavuos*.

Why do we not find the best fruits in Jerusalem or the waters of Tiberias in Jerusalem? So that the people who go to visit the Temple in Jerusalem on Yom Tov should not say, "If I came to Jerusalem for the hot baths or the good fruit, I would be satisfied." It would then be as if they were not visiting the Temple for G-d's sake. (Pesochim 8b)

Three times a year we visit G-d to give thanks to Him for watching the heavens and bringing food to the earth to satisfy the soul of man. *Therefore, the Torah says of visiting the Temple on* Yom Tov, *"Go in front of* Hashem." *He is the Master who supports His slaves and we give Him part of the share He gave us, to show our gratitude to Him (three times a year.)* (Ramban, on Chumash.)

"You shall count." The counting is for one to become pure before receiving the Torah. If not for this, G-d would have given the Torah immediately after the exodus from Egypt." (Abudraham)

TAANIS—INTRODUCTION

"And the L-rd shall scatter you among the peoples, and you shall be left few in number among the nations where the L-rd shall lead you away." (Devorim 4:27)

"Then My anger shall be kindled against them in that day; and I will forsake them and I will hide my face from them, and they shall be devoured and many evils and troubles shall come upon them; and they will say on that day: Have not these evils come upon us because our G-d is not among us? And I will surely hide My face on that day for all the evil which they have wrought, in that they turned to other gods." (Devorim 31: 17, 18)

There are four 'fast' days which remind us of the sins of our ancestors that led to the destruction of the Bais HaMikdosh *and the loss of the Land of Israel.*

TAANIS

The reason why we fast is not merely to inflict hardships upon ourselves, but rather to awaken our thoughts to *Teshuvah* (repentance). Those who have no intention of improving themselves are not accomplishing much with their *Taanis*. The *Mishna* states that the reason for a fast is to confess our sins, analyze our deeds, and improve our ways.

. . . And (you) shall return unto the L-rd your G-d and hearken to His voice according to all that I command you this day, you and your children, with all your heart and all your soul; that then the L-rd, your G-d, will return your captivity, and have compassion upon you, and will return and gather you from all

the peoples where the L-rd, your G-d, has scattered you; if any of you that are dispersed in the uttermost parts of heaven, from there will the L-rd, your G-d, gather you and from there will He fetch you." (Devorim 30:2-4)

* * * * *

Hostility among the Jews resulted in the destruction of the *Bais HaMikdosh*. The Romans controlled Yerushalayim, but the *Bais HaMikdosh* still stood.

In Yerushalayim, there lived a wealthy man who decided to celebrate a *simcha* with a party. His invitations were highly coveted, and he sent a messenger to deliver an invitation to his good friend, Kamtzoh. The mes-

Zecharia Hanavi refers to these fasts as: "Tzom Har'vee-ee, Tzom Hachameeshee, Tzom Hashvee'ee, Tzom Ha'aseeree."

The first of these, Shiva Asar B'Tamuz, *marks the introduction of the "3 weeks", which the Jews mourn as the inception of the downfall of the Jewish Temple and the exiling of them from their homeland.*

I. TZOM HAR'VEE-EE (Fast of the fourth month)—SHIVA ASAR B'TAMUZ (17th Day of Tamuz):

This day commemorates five sorrowful events in the history of the Jewish People.

1. On this day, Moshe descended from *Har Sinai,* saw the Golden Calf and then broke the *"Luchos"* (Tablets of the Law).

2. The *"Korban Tomid"* (daily sacrifice in the *Bais HaMikdosh)* was abolished on this day.

3. Apostomus the Wicked burned the Torah on this day.

4. Apostomus the Wicked placed an idol in the Temple.

5. The walls of the city of Yerusholayim were breached on this day by the Romans, which led to the destruction of the second *Bais HaMikdosh* by Titus *HaRosho* (Titus the Wicked).

II. TZOM HACHAMEESHEE (Fast of the fifth month)—TISHA B'AV (9th Day of Av):

a) Tisha B'Av is the saddest day of the Jewish year for it commemorates the destruction of both the first and the second *Botei Mikdashos.* (First and Second Temples)

senger did not know his employer well, and he mistakenly delivered the invitation to an individual named Bar Kamtzoh. This might not have proved calamitous but for the fact that the two were bitter enemies. Bar Kamtzoh was surprised to receive the invitation, but assumed that the other wanted to end their rivalry, and he decided to attend.

The moment he made his entrance at the party, though, Bar Kamtzoh realized that his coming had been an error. The wealthy man took one look at him, walked over, and snarled angrily.

"What are you doing in my house? What nerve you have to come here!

Pick yourself up and leave immediately!"

The host's outburst had captured the attention of the guests. Bar Kamtzoh looked around to see everyone staring at him. He turned to the wealthy man and said to him in a low, pleading voice, "It must have been my mistake to think you invited me. But please don't shout at me; everyone is watching."

"Let them watch," the host replied. "Let them see that I do not allow persons like you in my house."

"Not so loud, please," begged Bar Kamtzoh. "Don't worry, I'll leave and never set foot here again. But please, just this once, let me stay—just to

171

b) On *Tisha B'Av* it was decreed that *Bnai Yisroel* would not go directly into *Eretz Yisroel* but would travel for forty years in the *Midbar* (wilderness). That was the night that the *Meraglim* (spies) returned to give Moshe a highly critical report of *Eretz Yisroel* and the *Bnai Yisroel* cried without good cause. *Hashem* then decreed that years later they *would* have reason to cry on that night.

c) The *Har HaBayis* was plowed under.

d) On this day, Betar, the last stronghold in Israel after the destruction of the second *Bais HaMikdosh,* was captured and destroyed by the Romans. The sadness at this time was nearly comparable to that when the *Bais HaMikdosh* was destroyed, because so many thousands of Jews were killed.

III. TZOM HASHVEE-EE (Fast of the seventh month)—TZOM GEDALIAH (on the 3rd day of Tishrei):

Following the destruction of the first *Bais HaMikdosh* by Nevuchadnezzar, the King of Babylon, the remaining Jewish community was governed by Gedaliah ben Achikom. He had been appointed by Nevuchadnezzar after the majority of the Jews had gone into exile in Babylon. Under his leadership, the community was given new strength and there were thoughts of perhaps rebuilding the Bais HaMikdosh. Gedaliah's murder by an assassin who was sent by the Ammonite king, for certain military reasons, meant disaster for the remaining Jews. Many Jews were killed, and the rest were exiled to Egypt.

avoid a scene. I ask your help; I'll even pay for the whole meal. Only save me the embarrassment of having to make an exit this way."

"I make no deals with you," said the host. "Words won't help you. You'll leave now, and that's final!"

By now, everyone was watching closely. Bar Kamtzoh had no choice but to make his departure, under the contemptuous gaze of the assembled persons. "They may shame me now," he muttered as he was leaving. "But the day will come when they will suffer."

Bar Kamtzoh was as good as his word. Still stung by this display of intolerance, he concocted a plan to

punish those who had embarrassed him. He came before the Roman Emperor and accused his fellow Jews of conspiring against .the Romans. As proof of his claims, he cited the fact that the Jews would not allow a sacrifice selected by the Emperor to be offered in the *Bais HaMikdosh.* The Emperor decided to investigate this charge. He sent to the *Bais HaMikdosh* a sacrifice, but Bar Kamtzoh had made sure to render the offering unfit beforehand, and the Emperor's offering was refused. The Emperor was outraged, and he set in motion the intensified oppression that eventually resulted in the destruction of the *Bais HaMikdosh,* a tragedy that came

IV. TZOM HA'ASEEREE (Fast of the tenth month)—ASARA B'TEVES (10th day of Teves):

This fast day commemorates the beginning of the siege of Yerusholayim by Nevuchadnezzar when the city was completely surrounded. This siege eventually led to the destruction of the first *Bais HaMikdosh*

V. HILCHOS TAANIS:

The following *Halachos* are pertinent to the fast days, excluding *Yom Kippur* and *Tisha B'Av.*

1. All males over thirteen and females over twelve are obligated to fast on a *Taanis*, with the exception of a woman who is pregnant, nursing, or has just given birth, as well as any person who is sick or extremely weak. Even if it's not a *sakonoh* (where one's life is in jeopardy), a sick man does *not* have to fast.

2. On a *Taanis* washing one's hands and face is permitted.

3. Except for *Yom Kippur* and *Tisha B'Av*, fast days start from when the morning star appears rather than from the night before and one is allowed to wear leather shoes.

4. If the *Taanis* falls out on *Shabbos*, it is postponed to Sunday (except for *Taanis Esther,* which is moved to the preceding Thursday.)

5. The *only* time that a *Taanis* can occur on *Erev Shabbos* is *Asara B'Teves*, and the fast takes place as scheduled.

6. There are times when the *Rabbonim* decreed a *Taanis* on the

---

about because of one Jew's hostility towards another. (*Gitten* 55b)

Oh that my head were waters
And my eyes a fountain of tears,
That I might weep day and night,
For the slain of the daughter of my
    people (Yirmiyahu 8:23)
But from there you will seek the
L-rd, your G-d; and you shall find
Him, if you search after Him with
all your heart and all your soul.
(Devorim 4:29)

IS IT TOO LATE

The Jewish people have fast days during the year to remind them of the destruction of the *Bais HaMikdosh;* but these days also serve as a constant reminder that the Jews are in exile and subject to the whim of the surrounding

gentile world.

This was certainly true for the Jews of the Middle Ages. Pogroms, Jew-baiting and anti-Semitic acts of all kinds were part of the life of a ghetto Jew. The most insignificant and innocent act could cause non-Jewish mobs to wreak havoc upon an entire Jewish community. Of course, there were some communities that were blessed with peace and quiet for a number of years, but no Jew could or would delude himself into thinking that this was a permanent arrangement.

Things had been quiet for a long time in the little town of Heidensfeld, Germany. The Jews were loyal subjects of their Emperor; they paid their taxes on time and prayed that they

"Tzeebur" (congregation) because certain tragic conditions occurred. For instance:

a) A *severe* drought; b) A plague c) War, or an enemy attack.

The purpose of such a *Taanis Tzeebur* (public fast) is to make the community aware of the need to do *Teshuvah* and to cry out to *Hashem.*

One finds in *T'nach* and all through Jewish history that a *'Taanis Tzeebur'* was called during critical times, For instance:

a) Dovid Hamelech called for a *"Taanis"* to halt a plague.

b) The *Megillah* mentions that Queen Esther called a *"Taanis Tzeebur."*

7. There are times when one is *not* allowed to declare a *Taanis,* such as on *Rosh Chodesh, Chanukah, Purim, Yom Tov, Tu B'Shvat, Shabbos,* and *Tu B'Av.*

8. *"Taanis Yochid"* (Personal Fast)—An individual may accept a *Taanis* upon himself for certain reasons:

a) If someone in his family is very sick, imprisoned or missing.

b) *"Taanis Cholom"*—A person fasts because he had a bad dream that something will happen to him or to someone close to him.

c) On the *"Yahrtzeit"* (anniversary of a death) of one's parents, one's Rebbe or someone else close to him.

A *Taanis Yochid* should not be made on one of those days when it is prohibited to have a *Taanis Tzeebur,* except in the case of a Taanis Cholom.

---

would be left in peace. Who would have imagined that Mayer Levi, a simple, pious peddler, could have innocently brought a threat of doom upon the entire Jewish community?

Mayer Levi had just recuperated from a serious illness, and he felt a sincere gratitude to the Almighty. It was with this thought in mind that he purchased a lovely piece of dark blue velvet material at the annual fair in Wurzburg. His wife, Chana, who embroidered beautifully, could make it into a *poroches* (curtain for the Holy Ark) for the shul.

On the way home from the fair, Mayer decided that he would save time if he dropped off some wares he had purchased for the Mayor before going home. The Mayor's wife, Frau Schultz, was delighted to finally receive the trimmings she had ordered. When the peddler opened his pack, her eyes fell on the beautiful piece of blue velvet.

"Oh, how lovely it is! This would make a beautiful gown for me to wear to the next carnival. How much do you want for it?"

Poor Mayer Levi cringed with horror, and in an apologetic voice he said, "I'm sorry, but this cloth isn't for sale, at any price . . . I have already donated it to the Synagogue for a holy purpose . . . I will bring you a nicer piece of cloth . . . Please understand . . ."

9. A *Taanis Tzeebur* and a *Taanis Yochid* are like the other fast days when one is allowed to eat until *Alos HaShachar* (the rise of the morning star).

If a person intends to eat in the early morning hours before *Alos HaShachar*, he should make a *"Tnai"* (condition) before going to sleep so that if he awakens before *Alos HaShachar* he should still be allowed to eat.

10. One has to accept a *Taanis Yochid* before nightfall of the previous day (preferably during the *Mincha Shmoneh Esrei*, before *Elokai Netzor*). (The *Taanis Tzeebur* that is occasionally declared by our Rabbonim nowadays is comparable to the *Taanis Yochid*. This means that the person must be *Mekabel Taanis* (accept the fast upon himself the day before).)

11. One is allowed to be *Mekabel Taanis* for a half-day.

12. Those who are permitted to eat on a *Taanis* because of health reasons should eat only foods of nutritional value. They should refrain, however, from overindulging. This also applies to children who are not of age to fast. They, too, should refrain from eating candy and snacks, in order to feel as if they are participating in the *Taanis* of the *Tzeebur*.

13. One should not impose a *"Taanis Yochid"* upon himself if he feels that the fasting will disrupt his learning or *Avodas Hashem*. In such a situation, it is best that one increase his learning or Avodas Hashem in lieu of fasting as a means of doing Teshuva.

Frau Schultz turned crimson with rage. "I want this cloth and no other. How dare you refuse me, Jew?!"

"I am very sorry," Mayer Levi pleaded with tears in his eyes. The thought of this cloth, which was to hang over the Holy Ark, being turned into a gown for a carnival, simply horrified the pious peddler. Finally, he said he would ask the opinion of his Rabbi, who was respected even by the gentile community.

Mayer Levi rushed to the Rabbi's house and related the entire episode. The latter scolded him severely for having endangered the well-being of the Jewish community. Rabbi Yonah Chariff, an old and wise man, under-

stood that Frau Schultz wanted more than just the velvet material. She wanted a pretext to cause trouble for the Jews, whom she was known to despise.

The Jewish community tried desperately to appease the Mayor's wife. They sent her gifts of the most expensive dark blue velvet obtainable and elegant trimmings to go with it. They even sent gifts for the whole family, but nothing served to placate her. She was a vain, foolish, and heartless woman. She told her husband, the Mayor, that she was terribly insulted, and urged him to teach the Jews a lesson that they would never forget.

The Jewish community sensed that

14. A *Taanis* should not be accepted by someone who is in trouble and will need all his strength. For instance, if one found himself the victim of a kidnapping or a hijacking, he should not fast, because it might weaken him and be harmful to his health. (He may, however, accept a *Taanis* for a future date.)

VI. HILCHOS TEFILLAH ON A TAANIS:

1. *"Aneinu"* is said both by the *yochid* (individual davening alone) and the *Tzeebur* during the *Shmoneh Esrei* of *Mincha.* In *Shacharis* only the *Shliach Tzeebur* says it.

2. If one forgot to say *"Aneinu,"* he does not have to repeat the *Shmoneh Esrei.* If, however, he remembered before completing the *Shmoneh Esrei,* then he inserts it in the final paragraph of *"Elokai Netzor"* before the second *"Yeheyu L'Ratzon."*

3. If a person does not intend to fast the entire day, he may still say *"Aneinu"* in the *Shmoneh Esrei* of *Mincha* before breaking his fast. But once he eats, he can no longer say *"Aneinu."*

4. *Selichos* and *Avinu Malkeinu* are recited on the fast day.

VII. THE THREE WEEKS

The 3 weeks between the fast of the 17th of *Tammuz* and *Tisha B'Av* are a period of gradually intensified mourning. This period can be subdivided into three smaller groupings: a) from the 17th of *Tammuz* until *Rosh Chodesh Av* b) from *Rosh Chodesh Av* until the week in which

trouble was brewing. They did not know how it would manifest itself, but they were soon to find out. Mayor Schultz sent a message to the Emperor that the Jews were not paying their taxes. This, he said, was a sure sign that they meant to rebel. He requested the immediate assistance of imperial troops; otherwise, he would make use of his own loyal supporters (in other words, the "mobs").

When Rabbi Chariff found out about this plot, he called a meeting of the prominent leaders of the community. He explained the dire threat that hung over them, both from the "mobs" and the troops. Either one was quite capable of causing unimaginable destruction in the ghetto.

Rabbi Chariff addressed the small gathering. "Our Sages taught that whenever Jews are faced with a terrible catastrophe, sincere prayer and fasting have the power to overturn a bad decree. Let us, therefore, do as Mordechai did long ago, and gather in our shul for a day of fasting and prayers. Perhaps the Almighty will find us worthy of His help."

Meanwhile, the mob prepared to attack the undefended ghetto, while the Jews were gathering in the synagogue. Looting it would be easy. Just as they were about to break down the gates, a troop of imperial soldiers, led by an officer, arrived on horseback.

"Who is the leader of this mob?" the officer called out. "I have orders to

Tisha B'Av occurs and c) the week during which *Tisha B'Av* occurs. The latter two periods together are referred to as "the nine days." During the three weeks, one should not:
a) shave or take a haircut.
b) hold weddings or any other social parties.
c) listen to or play music, or dance.
d) wear clothing that have not been worn before, and require the Brocho of Shehecheyanu. (On *Shabbos*, one is permitted to do so, however.)

VIII. THE NINE DAYS

1. All court cases with a gentile should be delayed till after *Tisha B'Av*.

2. During the nine days, one should not wash clothing, or give clothing to a dry cleaning store, even one operated by non-Jews. However, one may wash babies' and children's clothing.

3. It is permissible to give clothing to a non-Jewish launderer before *Rosh Chodesh Av*, even if the clothing will be washed during the nine days; however, one should tell the launderer in such an instance not to return the clothing until after *Tisha B'Av*.

4. From the beginning of *Av* till after *Tisha B'Av*, one should lessen one's enjoyment. Therefore, one should not remodel his house.

5. It is our custom not to wear freshly laundered clothing during the nine days with the exception of clothing worn for the sake of a *Mitzvah*, like a *Bris*, a *Siyum*, or *Shabbos*.

---

arrest the leaders of the community who are at this very moment conspiring in their synagogue against his Imperial Majesty."

The Jews were so intent in their prayer that they hardly noticed the door being flung open, and the officer and some troops entering. The others remained outside and held back the crowd.

All heads turned to the officer as he declared in a loud voice, "I have orders to arrest the Rabbi and the heads of this community on charges of high treason against . . ."

The words froze on his lips, as his eyes fell on the saintly face of the Rabbi. In an apologetic voice he cried,

"Forgive me, dear Rabbi, it's all a mistake. Secret word was received from the Mayor of this town that the Jews were conspiring against the Emperor. But I can see that it was only a wicked attempt to make trouble for you. By the way, do you recognize me, Rabbi?"

"Of course, I do, and G-d has sent you to save us in our time of need!"

"Just as you saved me in my hour of need," the officer said. "I will never forget the day when you picked up a wounded, apparently lifeless soldier, and nursed me back to good health. I am happy that I am now able to repay your kindness." The officer and his troops departed, taking with them the Mayor to answer some questions be-

6. During the nine days, it is our custom not to prepare any new clothing or shoes for use or to purchase such items, with the exception of clothing prepared for a bride or groom.

7. During the nine days, it is our custom not to bathe for pleasure, even in cold water. Therefore swimming is prohibited during this period. Washing one's face, hands and feet is permitted. If *Rosh Chodesh* occurs on Friday, one may wash in hot water in honor of *Shabbos*. On the Friday immediately preceding *Tisha B'Av* one may shower in cold water in honor of *Shabbos*. Some authorities hold one may even use hot water. A woman may wash for the sake of her ritual immersion during this entire time.

8. One may cut one's nails during the nine days. However one should try to avoid cutting one's nails during the week of *Tisha B'Av*, since one authority prohibits it.

9. One should not eat meat or drink wine during the nine days, except on *Shabbos*. Even if *Tisha B'Av* occurs on *Shabbos*, one may eat meat and drink wine on this *Shabbos*. One who is ill or weak, may eat meat if necessary. There is a custom that one should not drink the wine of *Havdalah* on Saturday night but should instead give the wine to a child to drink. However, if no child is present, he may drink the wine himself. Other authorities allow anyone to drink the wine. Meat may be eaten and wine may be drunk at a *Seudas Mitzvah* (feast in honor of the perfor-

---

fore the higher authorities. The Jews breathed more easily now. The fasting and prayer had had an immediate dramatic effect.

LEST I FORGET THEE

The Emperor Napoleon was once proudly riding through a town of one of the countries he had conquered, and he passed a Jewish synagogue. As he neared the shul, he became aware of much crying and wailing coming from within, and he sent one of his officers to investigate.

The officer came back with the Rabbi of the synagogue, who explained: "Your Highness, almost 2,000 years ago our Holy Land was conquered and our Temple burned, on this very day. Every year since, we spend this anniversary in deep mourning, and pray to *Hashem* that we may return very soon."

Napoleon was amazed. "Two thousand years, and still you remember and pray! What a strong-spirited people you are. You, who do not forget, will surely return to your land, for you have an unconquerable spirit!"

"Since the day the Temple was destroyed there has been no rejoicing before the Holy One, blessed be He, and no sky bright and clear." (Avodah Zora 3b; Brochos 59a)

"If I forget you, O Jerusalem, let my right hand forget her cunning." (Tehillim 137:5)

A Rav was once visiting a certain town. On *Tisha B'Av* (the fast of the

mance of a *Mitzvah)* such as a *Bris,* a *Pidyon Haben,* or the completion of a Talmudic tractate.

10. It is our custom not to say the *Shehecheyanu* blessing during the nine days, even on *Shabbos.*

11. It is our custom not to say *Kiddush Levono* for the month of Av until after *Tisha B'Av.*

IX. EREV TISHA B'AV

1. The accepted custom is to eat a large meal before *Mincha* so one may be able to fast without difficulty.

2. During *Mincha, Tachanun* is omitted.

3. At the approach of sunset one should sit on the floor and eat the *Seudah Hamafsekes* (the final meal before the fast). At this time one does not have to remove his shoes, and should not sit and eat in the company of three others so that there is no *Mezumon.* Even if they did sit together, they do not bentsch *B'Mezumon.*

4. One eats only a piece of bread and a cooked item. Customarily, the cooked item is a hard boiled egg, which is dipped in ashes is used to symbolize there is no end to the Nation of Israel. (Also, it is the food of mourners.) After the *Seuda Hamafsekes,* one can still sit on a chair until sunset. We do not add any other food to this meal, and upon the completion of this meal one may say, "I do not accept the fast upon myself until dusk."

ninth day of *Av,* which commemorates the destruction of the *Bais Ha-Mikdosh)* he was informed of a bitter feud between two groups, and was asked to mediate between them.

"We assume, however, that you will not want to hear the two sides until tomorrow, since it is a fast day," they told him.

"On the contrary," responded the *Rav.* "The destruction of the *Bais Ha-Mikdosh* was caused by *sinas chinom* (unwarranted hatred). What is more appropriate than trying to promote peace and brotherhood on this very day?"

* * * * *

The Ari Hakadosh commented

that when the two *"yud's"* signifying the name of *Hashem* are written together, then the letters cannot be erased. However, if one *"yud"* is higher than the other, then it is not the name of *Hashem* and can be erased. The reason for this is that the two *"yud's"* must not be rivals but must consider themselves equal, and only then do they symbolize *Hashem.*

Similarly, two *Yiddin* (Jews) can evoke *Hashem's* spirit only when they work together harmoniously (and not when one considers himself above the other) towards the same goal.

Rivalry and hatred can only cause the downfall of the *Bnai Yisroel.* It is when the Jews are united and accept each other as equals that the *Bnai Yis-*

5. At sunset, all the laws of *Tisha B'Av* take effect. Therefore, one must remove his shoes before sunset and he must stop eating before sunset. On *Shabbos* one wears shoes till *Ma'ariv*.

X. PROHIBITIONS OF TISHA B'AV

1. The five things one must abstain from on *Tisha B'Av* are a) eating and drinking; b) washing in either hot or cold water (However, in the morning one should wash till the knuckles only. After wiping his hands, but while they are still damp, one is permitted to wipe his eyes. One may wash his hands during the day if they become soiled.) c) anointing one's body with any kind of ointment, lotion, etc. except for medicinal purposes. d) wearing shoes made partially or wholly of leather. e) having marital relations.

2. One is not permitted to study most of the Torah on Tisha B'Av. Instead one should study or teach the book of *Iyov*; the prophecies of evil in *Jeremiah, Eicha,* and *Medrash Eicha;* the account of the destruction of the Temple in *Gittin* and in *Sanhedrin,* the third chapter of *Moed Katan,* and the laws of mourning and *Tisha B'Av*. The Torah reader may review the Torah sections to be read on *Tisha B'Av*.

3. One does not greet another on *Tisha b'Av* but if he is greeted, he should return the greeting in a low tone of voice. One should not walk for enjoyment and should not jest and be carefree. One should deprive himself of some comfort when he sleeps, like using one pillow instead of two.

---

roel will thrive and flourish, and bring credit to *Hashem* and His Torah.

* * * * *

The Prophet Yeshaya said (*Yeshaya* 66:10): "Rejoice with Jerusalem and be glad with her, all of you who love her; rejoice with her with great rejoicing, all of you who mourn for her." This means, those who truly mourn our Temple, especially during the three weeks, and forego all pleasure and entertainment in memory of Jerusalem, will be privileged in due time to rejoice in the rebuilding of Yerushalayim and the *Bais HaMikdosh*. But why does the Novi say "Rejoice with *great* rejoicing"?

The Dubno Maggid explained this in the form of a parable:

A man embarked on a long sea voyage. After a few months, reports reached his home town that his ship had met with an accident and that he had drowned. His wife and children grieved deeply for him; his friends and acquaintances were sorrowful. As time went one, however, the memory of the man dimmed in their hearts. But though the months passed, his immediate family never stopped mourning for him.

Then, one day, the door of the man's house opened. There stood the man whom they had thought was dead, very much alive! The good news

4. One should refrain from any kind of work or business during the whole day and if not, then at least until midday. One should not prepare food or sit on a chair until after midday.

5. Until midday of the day following *Tisha B'Av*, one is prohibited from eating meat and drinking wine. Also, all of the prohibitions of the nine days apply until the midday of the tenth of Av, except when *Tisha B'Av* is on Thursday in which case bathing, washing, and shaving are permitted after the fast because of *Erev Shabbos*. If *Tisha B'Av* falls on *Shabbos* and is therefore postponed till Sunday night, one may shave and bathe then but meat should not be eaten till the following day.

6. *Kiddush Levono* should be said the night following *Tisha B'Av*.

XI. PRAYER ON TISHA B'AV

1. At night, the curtain of the ark is removed and the congregation recites *Ma'ariv* slowly and in a weeping voice while sitting on the floor or on low stools (approx. 11 inches high). After *Kaddish* with *Tiskabal*, the congregation sits on the floor and *Eicha* is read slowly in a wailing voice, followed by *Kinos*, *V'Atoh Kodosh*, and *Oleinu*.

2. In the morning neither the *Tefillin* nor the *Tallis Gadol* is worn. The *Tallis Katan* is donned without reciting the usual blessing. *Kinos* are recited in the morning after the Torah reading, and if possible should be read until midday. The following prayers are omitted from the *Shacharis* prayers: a) in some congregations, *Birchas Kohanim*. b) *Tachanun* c) *Kel Erech Apayim* d) *Lamnatzeach Mizmor L'Dovid* e) From *Uvo Letzion*, the posuk "Va'ani Zos". f) From full *Kaddish*, *Tiskabal* g) *Shir Shel Yom* h) *Pitom Haktoras*.

---

quickly spread through the town. Soon the house was crowded with friends who were happy to hear that he had returned safely. Those who were only acquainted with him were pleased for him and his family. But his intimate friends, who had felt genuine sorrow when he had been presumed dead, were more than pleased; they were overjoyed that their friend was still alive. His family, of course, were beside themselves with happiness. Those who had mourned the most for him were the happiest now that he had returned.

The same is true of our own mourning for Yerushalayim and the *Bais HaMikdosh*, and the happiness that will be ours when they will be rebuilt. The degree of our rejoicing will be directly proportionate to the degree of our mourning. Those who genuinely mourned for Jerusalem will indeed rejoice with "great rejoicing" at its rebuilding.

R' Yochanan said: Great is the day of ingathering of the exiles as the day of the Creation of Heaven and Earth. (Pesachim 88a)

3. For *Mincha, Tefillin* and *Tallis Gadol* are worn. One who doesn't wear a *Tallis Gadol* should now touch the *Tzitzis* of the *Tallis Katan* and recite the blessing. However, one who makes the *Brocho* on the *Tallis Godol* includes the *Tallis Katan* instead. Also the *Shir Shel Yom* is said at *Mincha*. The Torah reading for *Mincha* and the saying of *Aneinu* are the same as on other fast days. At *Mincha, Nachem* is inserted in the *Brocho* of *Bonei Yerusholayim*. One concludes the *Brocho* with *"Menachem Tzion U'Voneh Yerusholayim."* If one forgot to say *"Nachem,"* he may insert it immediately before *"V'sechezeno"* without this ending. If one forgot to say *"Nachem"* and remembers only after *"V'sechezeno,"* he does not go back.

XII. TISHA B'AV ON SUNDAY

1. When *Shabbos* is Erev *Tisha B'Av,* some say learning is permitted all day. The *Seuda Hamefsekes* is a regular *Shabbos* meal, and *Birchas Hamazon* may be said together *B'mezumon*. One must be careful to stop eating while it is still day.

2. One does not remove his shoes until after *Borchu,* and he should be careful not to touch his shoes when removing them so that he should not have to wash his hands. The *chazan* says *"Hamavdil Bein Kodesh L'Chol"* and removes his shoes before *"Borchu."* One does not recite the *"Vehee Noam"* and *"Vayeeten L'Cho."*

3. On Saturday night only *"Borei Me'Orei HaEish"* is said. *Havdalah* is postponed till Sunday night, before eating, when the *Brochos* on *Besomim* and fire are not said.

Glossary

Afikomen—last piece of matzoh eaten at the conclusion of the Passover seder meal

Agadah—homiletical portions of Talmud

Adar Rishon—first Adar

Adar Sheini—second Adar, occuring only in Hebrew leap years

Aliya—"going up" to recite blessing on Torah

Aleph Bais—Hebrew alphabet

Alos Hashachar—time when first rays of light appear in the east each morning

Am Ha'oretz—an unlearned man

Amidah—prayer of the 18 benedictions

Amos—cubits (each one approximately 22 inches)

Amud—lectern

Anshei Knesses Hagdolah—men of the great assembly

Aravos—willow branch

Aron Hakodesh—holy ark

Asseres Yemei Teshuva—10 days of penitence

Ashkenazim—Jews originating from North or Central Europe

Baal Agolah—wagon driver

Baal Habayis—head of the house

Baal Kriah—man who reads the Torah

Baal Midos Tovos—a person of good character

Baal Tokea—person who blows the Shofar

Bar Mitzvah—Jewish boy who turns 13

B'dee'eved—if already done, after the fact: see Mutar L'chatcheela

B'chor—first born son

Bedikas Chometz—search for chometz

Beis Din—rabbinical court of law

Beis Hamikdosh—Holy Temple

Beis Medrash—Torah study hall

Beitza—egg

Bein Hashmoshos—evening twilight

Ben—son

Bentch—bless, specifically saying the Birchos Hamozon

Ben Torah—a person who studies the Torah

Besomim—spices

Bimah—platform in synagogue used for reading of the Torah.

Birchas Hagomel—blessing of thanks to G-d

Birchos Hamazon—grace after meal

Birchos Hashachar—morning blessings

Birchos Hatorah—blessing of the Torah

Birchos Kohanim—blessing of the priests

Bishul Akum—food cooked by non-Jew

Bitul Chometz—nullifying chometz in one's possession before Pesach

Biy'mos Hamoshiach—in the days of the Messiah

Biyur Chometz—burning of chometz

Bnei Bayis—members of the household

Bnei Chorin—free men

Bosor B'cholov—meat and milk together

Briah Chadosho—new creation

Brocho—blessing

Brocho Acharono—blessing said after eating

Brocho L'Vatoloh—blessing said in vain

B'sesser—hidden

B'sever Ponim Yofos—with a pleasant face

Challah—braided bread made especially for the Sabbath

Chalom—dream

Chamar Hamedina—common beverage of the country

Charoses—mixture of wine, nuts and apples used on Pesach

Chatzee—half

Chassid—righteous one; adherent of a Chassidic sect

Chatzos—mid-point (noon or midnight)

Chazal—Talmudic Sages

Chazan—cantor

Chazoras Hashatz—repetition of the Shmoneh Esrei by the Shliach Tzeebur

Cheder—room (yeshiva)
Chessed—deeds of kindness
Chet—sin
Chidushim—original Torah commentaries
Chiyuv—necessity
Cholent—certain hot food cooked for Shabbos
Chol Hamoed—intermediate days of Pesach and Sukkos
Chollol—child born of a Kohein who married a divorcee
Cholov Akum—milk produced without Jewish supervision
Choson—groom
Chukim—unfathomable Mitzvos
Chumash—five books of the Pentateuch
Chutz La'oretz—lands outside of Eretz Yisroel
Chutzpah—audacity
Daven—pray
Derech Eretz—respect
Dinim—laws
D'Rabbonon—according to Rabbinic law
Duchan—the blessing of the Kohanim
D'var Torah—Torah thought
Echod—one
Egoz—nut
Ehrliche Yid—earnest Jew
Eiruv Tavshilin—symbolic dish making it permissible to cook on Yom Tov for Shabbos
Eliyahu Hanovi—Elijah the Prophet
Erev—day preceding
Esrog—citron
Ezras Noshim—women's section in Shul
Fleishig—meat product
Gabbai—1) synagogue attendant 2) collector of charity
Gam Zu Letova—it's all for the best
Gaon—Talmudic leader of post Talmudic era
Gartel—belt
Gebrukt—food containing matzo and water

Gedilim—strings prepared in the manner of Tzitzis
Gedolah—great
Gehenom—hell
Ger Tzedek—genuine convert
Geyores—convert to Judaism (female)
Gezeira—Rabbinic decree
Golus—exile
Hachnasass Kallah—mitzvah of supporting a bride
Hachnossas Orchim—receiving guests
Hachono—preparation
Hadassim—myrtle branches
Hafsokos—interruptions
Haftoro—passage from the Prophets read in the synagogue after the Pentateuchal reading
Hakodosh Boruch Hu—The Holy One Blessed Be He
Hakofos—dancing on Simchas Torah around the Bimah
Halacha—law
Hallel—prayer of praise to G-d
Hanetz Hachama—sunrise
Har Habayis—Temple Mount
Hashem—G-d
Hashem Yisboroach—G-d, Blessed be He
Hashgacha—supervision
Hashkomas Haboker—awakening in the morning
Hatofas Dom Bris—drawing of blood of circumcision
Havdalah—separation; Sabbath evening service to separate the Sabbath from the weekday
Hekdesh—sanctified for Temple use
Hashonnah Rabbah—7th day of Sukkos
Hiddur—enhancement, beautification
Hoshano—willow branches bound together
Ikur—basic principle
Im Yirtzah Hashem—if G-d is willing
Issur—prohibition
Kaddish—prayer recited by the chazon, or by mourners at various intervals during the service
Kaporo—forgiveness

184

Kashered—made kosher
Kedusha—holiness
Kehunah—priesthood
Kessel—kettle
Kezayis—amount the size of an olive
Kibbud Av'V'Em—respect for father and mother
Kiddush Levana—blessing made over the new moon each month
Kipah—skullcap
Kisei Shel Eliyahu—chair of Elijah
Kitniyos—beans
Kittel—long white coat worn at Seder and on Yom Kippur
K'laf—parchment
Klal Yisroel—nation of Israel
Kneidlach—matzoh balls
Koach Gavrah—by human power
Kochi V'otzem Yodi—done by own personal power (i.e. without Hashem's help)
Korach—sandwich of matzoh and morror
Kohein Godol—high priest
Korban Todoh—sacrificial offering of thanks
Kosel—wall, specifically wailing wall (Western Wall)
Kosher—ritually fit for use
Kovea Seuda—sit down formally to a meal
Kovod—respect
Krias Shema—reading of the Shema
Kugel—a pudding of baked noodles or potatoes made for Shabbos
Lag Baomer—33rd day of the Omer
L'Chayim—to life (used as a toast)
Lechem Mishneh—double portion of bread, used for Shabbos meals
Lechem Oni—poor man's bread (matzoh)
Laining—reading of the Torah
Lev—heart
Lishmah—purity of motivation (for its own sake)
Lo Saamod Al Dam Reyacho—exhortation not to stand by idly if another Jew is in danger

L'sheim Mitzvah—done for the purpose of performing a Mitzvah
L'Tzorech—for a necessity
Luach—calendar
Luchos—tablets of the Decalogue
Lulov—palm branch
L'vatoloh—in vain
Ma'ariv—evening prayer
Maaseh Bereishis—creation of the world and its inhabitants
Maaser—tithe
Machatzis Hashekel—half a shekel (coin)
Mafsik—interrupt by (talking)
Maftir—the last section of the Torah chapter read each week
Makom—place
Makom Kavuah—fixed place
Mamzer—illegitimate child
Matan Torah—giving of the Torah
Matonos Lo'evyonim—presents to the poor
Mayim Acharonim—water used to clean fingers before Birchos Hamazon
Mayim Rishonim—water for the washing of hands before the meal.
Mazal—luck
Med'orysoh—commanded in the Torah
Mechalel Shabbos—transgressor of the Shabbos
Mechila—forgiveness
Medrash—biblical exegesis
Midos—character traits
Melech—king
Mekabel—receive
Mekadesh—sanctify
Melava Malka—(post-Shabbos) Saturday evening meal
Melocho—work forbidden on Shabbos
Menorah—1) 8 branched candelabra used for the holiday of Chanukah 2) candelabra used in the Temple
Meoras Hamachpala—Cave of the Patriarchs
Meraglim—spies
Meshebeirach—a public blessing given for someone
Meshulach—fund raiser

Metzitza—extraction of blood by suction (circumcision)

Mevoreich—the one who recites the blessing

Mezuman—quorum of 3 adult males needed to say the Grace

Mezuzah—parchment inscribed with scriptural passages and attached to the doorpost

Midbar—desert

Mikveh—ritualarium

Milchig—milk product

Mincha—afternoon prayer

Minhag Hamakom—custom of the place

Minyan—quorum of 10 adult males needed for prayers

Misnagdim—opponents of the teachings of Chassidism

Mitzrayim—Egypt

Mitzvah Assei—positive commandment

Mitzvas Assei Shehazman Grommoh—ritual commandment performed only at specific times

Mitzvas Lo'Sa'aseh—Prohibitive Commandment

Mizbeiach—altar

Modeh Ani—morning prayer meaning "I thank you"

Mohel—circumcisor

Mohn—manna

Moled—monthly allignment of sun, moon and earth

Morror—bitter herbs

Moshol—parable

Motzee—1) to include others in the blessing 2) blessing over bread

Muktzeh—forbidden to be moved on Shabbos

Murkov—hybrid

"Mutar L'chatcheelah"—permissible before the fact

Naase V'Nishma—we will do and we will hear

Nedarim—promises, made in a ritually binding manner

Ner—candle

Neshama—soul

Neshama Yeseira—additional soul

Netilas Yodayim—ritual washing of the hands

Niftar—passed away

Nossi—civil and religious head of community

Novi—Prophet

Nusach Sefard—prayer arrangement according to the custom of Sefardim

Olam Habbah—the world to come

Oleh Al Shulchan Melochim—a dish worthy of being served to a King

Oleh Regel—pilgrimage to Jerusalem during the three holidays of Pesach, Shavuous and Succos

Olim—1) those called to the Torah 2) new immigrants to Eretz Yisroel

Omein—Amen

Oneg—pleasure

Ossur—forbidden

Orlah—1) foreskin removed during circumcision 2) fruits not eaten during the first three years of a tree's growth

Os—a sign

Ovel—mourner

Parsha—section of the Chumash read weekly

Pas Akum—bread baked by a gentile

Peleg Hamincha—final 1¼ hour period before nightfall

Perek—chapter

Periah—part of act of circumcision, peeling back of the lower foreskin

Pesach—Passover

Pesukei D'zimra—verses of praise taken from Psalms incorporated into daily Morning service

Pidyon Ha'Ben—redemption of the newborn

Pidyon Shevuyim—redemption of the captured

Pirsumei Neesah—publicizing the miracle

Pitum—protuberance opposite that of the stem

Podeh—redeem

Poroches—curtain for the Holy Ark

Possuk—biblical verse

186

Possul—invalid
P'sak—ruling
Purim—1) lots 2) holiday celebrating the victory of the Jews after Haman's evil plans to destroy them
Rabbosai Nevoreich—Gentlemen, let us say the Grace
Rav—rabbi
Rebbe—rabbi, teacher
Rekida—dance
Sakana—danger
Sandek—godfather at circumcision
Sanhedrin—supreme Rabbinical court of old
S'chach—covering of the Sukkah
Schnapps—whiskey
Seder—Passover meal
Sedra—weekly portion of the Torah
Sefardim—Jews originating in North Africa or Eastern countries
Sefer Torah—book of the Torah
Selichos—penitential prayers
Seudah—feast
Seudah Hamafsekes—last meal eaten before a fast (Yom Kippur and Tisha B'Av)
Sh'liach Tzeebur—messenger of the congregation, prayer leader
Shalach Monos—sending of gifts on Purim
Shalosh Seudos—third meal of the Sabbath
Shamas—sexton or beadle of a synagogue
Shamor—observe
Shavuous—festival commemorating the revelation at Sinai
Shechina—manifestation of the Divine Presence
Shechita—ritual slaughtering of animals
Shedra—spine
Sheebud Malchus—being enslaved by a foreign government
Shiur—required amount
Shekel—Hebrew coin
Shmoneh Esrei—silent prayer of 18 Benedictions
Shfichas Domim—spilling of blood

Shir Shel Yom—song of the day
Shiva—seven days of mourning
Shiva Minim—seven products which grow in Israel
Shkias Hachama—setting of the sun
Shlita—may he live long!
Shlug Kaporos—the ritual before Day of Atonement, performed with a live chicken
Shofar—ram's horn
Shoichet—ritual slaughterer
Sholeim—complete
Sholom Aleichim—peace be unto you
Sholom Zachor—welcome for a newborn boy
Shomrei Shabbos—Sabbath observers
Shtetel—small town
Shtiyos Hakos—drinking of the cup of wine
Shulchan Aruch—compilation of practical Torah law
Shul—synagogue
Shushan Purim—the day after Purim
Siddur—book of prayers
Simcha—happiness
Simchas Beis Hashoeivah—joyful drawing of the water performed in Beis Hamikdosh on Succos
Simchas Torah—holiday of rejoicing of the Torah
Siman Brocho—sign of blessing
Sinas Chinum—unwarranted hatred
Sippurei—stories
Sofer—scribe
So'oh—measure of volume: app. 3-4 gallons
Succas Ohr Shel Livyoson—Tabernacles made of Leviathan's skin to be erected after the coming of Messiah
Sukkos—Feast of Tabernacle
Stam Yayin—wine that came into contact with a gentile
Taanis—fast day
Tachanun—supplication
Tai'avon—appetite
Tallis Godol—prayer shawl
Tanach—scripture

Teenokos Shel Beis Rabban—small children who study Torah at school
Tefach—one sixth of a cubit: app. 3½ inches
Tefillah—prayers
Tefillas Haderech—traveler's prayer
Tefillin—phylacteries
Tefillin Shel Rosh—phylacteries placed on head
Tefillin Shel Yad—phylacteries placed on arm
Tehillim—Psalms
Tekios—blowings of the Shofar
Terumah—priestly portion
Teshuva—repentance
Teshuvos—responsa
Tish—table
Tisha B'Av—Fast of the ninth day of Av
Tnai—condition
Toch K'dei Dibbur—Halachic time measure—the time it takes to say "Sholom Aleichim Rabbi Umori"
Toluy—depends
Torah She'B'Al Peh—Oral law
Trief—not kosher
Tumah—ritual impurity
Tzaddikim—righteous men
Tzedakah—charity
Tzais Hakochavim—when the stars come out
Tzitzis—fringes worn at the corner of Tallis

Tzom—fast
Veeduy—confession
Yayin Pagum—wine from which people already drank
Yeshiva—Talmudic Academy
Yetzer Rah—the inclination to do evil
Yetzer Tov—the inclination to do good
Yirah—fear
Yiras Shomayim—fear of heaven
Yochid—single
Yahrtzeit—anniversary of death
Yom—day
Yomim Noroim—High Holy Days
Yom Kippur—Day of Atonement
Yom Tov—Holiday
Yotzai—to fulfill a Mitzvah or Brocho through another person's act
Yotzer Hameoros—Creater of the lights
Zachor—remember
Z'chus—merit
Zechuyos—merits
Zemiros—songs of Shabbos
Zeroah—roasted wing by the Passover table
Zimun—the joining of three males for Birchas Hamozon
Zman—time
Zman Kdei Achilas Pras—time span within which Kezayis must be eaten: app. 4-5 minutes
Zohar—the principle work of Kaballah